Experience

Experience

New Foundations for the Human Sciences

Scott Lash

Polity

First published in 2018 by Polity Press

Polity Press
65 Bridge Street
Cambridge CB2 1UR, UK

Polity Press
101 Station Landing
Suite 300
Medford, MA 02155, USA

ISBN-13: 978-0-7456-9514-3
ISBN-13: 978-0-7456-9515-0(pb)

A catalogue record for this book is available from the British Library.

Library of Congress Cataloging-in-Publication Data
Names: Lash, Scott, author.
Title: Experience : new foundations for the human sciences / Scott Lash.
Description: 1 | Cambridge, UK ; Medford, MA : Polity, 2018. | Includes
    bibliographical references and index.
Identifiers: LCCN 2017052173 (print) | LCCN 2018007921 (ebook) | ISBN
    9780745695181 (Epub) | ISBN 9780745695143 (hardback) | ISBN 9780745695150
    (paperback)
Subjects: LCSH: Experience. | Social sciences. | BISAC: SOCIAL SCIENCE /
    Sociology / General.
Classification: LCC B105.E9 (ebook) | LCC B105.E9 .L37 2018 (print) | DDC
    001.2--dc23
LC record available at https://lccn.loc.gov/2017052173

Typeset in 10.5 on 12 pt Sabon by
Fakenham Prepress Solutions, Fakenham, Norfolk NR21 8NN
Printed and bound in Great Britain by CPI Group (UK) Ltd, Croydon

For further information on Polity, visit our website: politybooks.com

CONTENTS

ACKNOWLEDGEMENTS

I want to thank Mike Featherstone and Yuk Hui for conversations about 'experience'. I want to thank John Thompson of Polity for helping me get this book off the tracks and keeping an eye on it until completion. I want to thank the two Polity readers for comments and criticisms that led to substantial changes, especially in the linkages between chapters and clarifications between Greek and Christian, between ancient, modern, technological and 'Chinese' experience. I want to dedicate this book to the memory of John Urry and Ulrich Beck.

INTRODUCTION: FOUR TYPES OF
EXPERIENCE

We speak of 'experience' in everyday life in a myriad of contexts. We speak of sexual experience or urban experience. We speak of tourist experience in, say, Venice or Macau. We speak of immigrant experience or gendered experience or how we experienced art and music, of museum experience in the Tate Modern Turbine Hall or the Museum of Modern Art (MoMA) or the Venice Biennale. Each of these types of experience involves perception or feeling. It also implies a particular point of view: say black female sexual experience, or transgender experience in the armed forces. But the notion of experience in the human sciences, to start with in philosophy and then later throughout the social sciences, presumes no particular point of view at all. Experience makes its most emphatic and influential, indeed foundational, impact with the phenomenon of *objective* experience. This is found neither in Greek antiquity nor in ancient China or India, but this type of experience from a general, human point of view, is a modern and Western phenomenon. It emerges in the wake of Galileo's and Newton's physics. We had always and everywhere encountered, perceived, registered and acknowledged things and phenomena. But only now with this modern, Western objective experience is there the emergence of a *subject*. That is, a subject that is independent of any particular individual. Only then do we have an object that is different to any of the myriad of particular things.

This objective experience, and associated subject–object thinking is the basis of modern knowledge whose benchmark formulation was Immanuel Kant's *Critique of Pure Reason* (1929 [1781]). Kant's subject was 'transcendental' to any particular individual; his object was located in a space and time that was the time-space of Newtonian physics. It, too, was no particular place or any historical time. Kant's trinity of

1

subject, object and time-space was joined by a fourth element: and this was cause or causation. On the paradigm of Newton's mechanics, the general and objective subject obtained knowledge through the causative action of objects upon one another in this time-space. These four elements – subject, object, time-space and causation – of Kantian experience became the foundation for now more than two centuries of thought across the human sciences, including philosophy, as well as politics, sociology, economics and even often history. It took and takes its inspiration and assumptions from Newtonian mechanics, hence from natural physical science. This objective experience is still, perhaps more than ever, dominant in the social sciences: it is neo-Kantian and is most often described as positivism. This objectivist experience is pervasive in economics, and through economics' *homo economicus* world view pervades not just the social sciences, but the assumptions of perhaps the majority of us in everyday life, even everyday life has often assumed away our particular experience, in the assumption that each and every one of us is *homo economicus*.

Not much later at all, and again in Germany, this time associated with Romanticism, a contrasting, rather opposite notion of experience began to raise it head. It is visible in Hegel and the young Karl Marx, and before in the thought of the poets, of Goethe and Hölderlin. It opposed the mechanistic assumptions of physics. Through this critique of mechanism, this contrasting mode of *subjective experience* began to enter the human sciences. This idea of subjective experience was given a name by Wilhelm Dilthey (1883), who called it *Erlebnis* (Caygill 1997; Jay 2005). This was opposed to *Erfahrung*, the word Kant had given to objective experience. The *leben* in *Erlebnis* means to live, or life, and *Erlebnis* is normally translated as 'lived experience'. So, the new mode of experience is subjective in that it is the way we as particular individuals encounter things. Moreover, it contrasts life, both human and biological life, to the mechanistic assumptions of objective experience. Thus, there is subjective and lived versus objective and mechanistic experience. There is desire, drive, energy and the body in this mode of subjective and lived experience that the human sciences encounter repeatedly, perhaps paradigmatically in Nietzsche and Freud. After all, your psychologist or psychoanalyst or counsellor is not interested in objective experience but in your subjective experience.

This book addresses this tension, this dialectic between objective experience and subjective experience in some detail and depth. This conflict and opposition between subjective and objective experience runs through the length of this not very long book. It is a social and cultural theory book, but one of its main pivots is methodological. Objective experience became a main methodological paradigm in the social sciences, while subjective experience became the preferred method in the humanities, in literature, art criticism and history. If there was one debate that encapsulated this objective-versus-subjective tension that is as much as ever with us, it took place again in Germany, its essence captured in Max Weber's famous methodological essay on objectivity in the social sciences (Weber 1949), that is addressed in some depth in Chapter 4 of this book. Here, Weber makes his benchmark methodological distinction between *erklären* or explanation, on the one hand, and *verstehen*, or interpretation, on the other. Weber argues that studies in the social sciences – and I think the human sciences – need to draw on both in order to be fully fruitful. In this context, objectivity is about *erklären* (explanation) and works primarily through causation, and subjective experience is about *verstehen*: about interpretation and, not so much cause as instead meaning (*Sinn*). Hence, for Weber, method in a given social science study needed to be *Kausaladäquat* – that is, valid on the level of objectivity or cause – as well as *Sinnadäquat*, or suitable or valid on the level of meaning.

What is less well known, and for this book as important, is the context of Weber's intervention. Again, this is about method and was known as the *Methodenstreit*, the methods dispute, which was about positivism versus interpretivism – that is, it pitted objective against subjective experience – but it did so in the context of economics. Though Weber saw both sides, in the dispute, he was on the side of the economics' objectivists. This debate was at the origins of neoclassical economics and its paradigm of utility maximization. If there is a dominant ideology today, if there is a dominant ideology in today's capitalism, it is that we are *homo economicus*; that is, that we are utility-maximizing animals. These assumptions are so pervasive that we take them as natural and do not even bother to formulate them. The domination in our societies of objective experience plays itself out in our *homo economicus* assumptions. Hence, we are calculating, strategic, self-interested, instrumental animals. And it goes without saying. This is taking on the assumptions of objective experience fully. The point for Weber's methodological thinking – and for most thinking today in regard to objective experience in the social sciences – is that not just the social-scientific observer, but also the individuals he or she studies, are objective, are engaged in objective experience. Weber was allied in this methods dispute with Gustav Menger, one of the founders of neoclassical economics. Thus, Weber and a very important dimension of positivism in sociology and political science

3

and media studies understands not just the social-scientific observer as undergoing objective experience, but also those s/he studies as being engaged in objective experience. This *homo economicus* involving objective experience of both actor and observer was at the heart of J.S. Mill's positivism, and Weber was very much influenced by Mill. Weber was only partly positivist in method, but to the extent he was, he understood humans as Mill's utility-maximizing *homo economicus*, which Weber called *zweckrational* action that is, mean-ends, instrumental or best utility-maximizing action.

If Chapter 4 – on methods and economics – addresses objective experience, this book deals with subjective experience most fully in Chapters 3 on William James and 5 on Hannah Arendt. Objective experience, as we mentioned, is based in a Newtonian temporality: a temporality of mechanical causality. William James gives us a polar-opposite temporality of, instead, the stream of consciousness. We see such a stream-of-consciousness temporality in the novels of James Joyce and Marcel Proust's *A la recherche du temps perdu* (*In Search of Lost Time*). Interpretive human science, from sociology to anthropology to philosophy and psychology, gives us such a stream-of-consciousness temporality. So will the Freudian unconscious, and in philosophy both Edmund Husserl and Henri Bergson. The operative term for this kind of experience, in the interpretive as distinct from objectivist, human sciences is indeed *consciousness*. If objective experience gives us subjects that encounter objects, then in subjective experience, subjects are replaced by consciousness and objects by appearances. If the subject is universal and general and is indeed no particular subject, then consciousness is particular and very different from one individual to another. This is how Heidegger on death and time can be understood. Heidegger is writing, despite disclaimers, in this subjectivist phenomenological time. In generalized Newtonian time of objective experience, death is general and abstract and the death of no particular person. In Heidegger's temporality, my death is 'mine and only mine'. In phenomenology in the broadest sense, there are equivalents of such a consciousness–appearances juxtaposition. For Freud, these appearances are in dreams. Thus, we have James's stream-of-consciousness psychology of subjective experience, in which events – in what he calls his 'radical empiricism' – are joined not by the causes of Newtonian mechanics but instead by conjunctions, by 'ands' and by disjunctions.

James was, along with John Dewey, a central figure of pragmatism. And pragmatism is such an empiricist challenge to rationalism's and positivism's a priori thinking. Positivism always starts with an a

4

priori, such as assuming we are utility-maximizing actors, or say with a notion of abstract justice that we see in a priori politics from Plato to John Rawls. Pragmatism starts from not such a universal, but an empirical and particular fact, a particular event. It starts from a particular experience, from a particular event, and works towards a universal, say in John Dewey (2012) in the constitution of public opinion, or of *public spheres*. We address such public spheres with Hannah Arendt in Chapter 5. Public spheres in Rawls and Habermas start not from experience but from an a priori, for Rawls (1971) the 'original position', in which people choose a social contract from the position of total lack of information regarding, for example, their class, status, gender, ethnicity and income. The society that would be chosen from this position – in which the strategy would be a game-theory type 'maximin', which would maximize the benefits of the least advantage, and would also include primary social goods of both basic rights and equity – would yield a just society. Rawls (and Habermas) do not proffer a mathematical a priori based on an axiomatic, but a normative a priori harking back to natural right and natural law theory in Hobbes and Rousseau. Habermas wrote on public spheres very early in his career in *The Structural Transformation of the Public Sphere* (1989 [1962]). Roughly some 20 years later he wrote *The Theory of Communicative Action* (1986 [1981]). Combining these, we see that a just public sphere has its foundations in reaching an agreement through reasoned communication and public justification. This starting point is an a priori universal of what Habermas calls discursive will formation and communicative action. Rawls and Habermas give us normative a prioris. Aristotle divided human reasoning into episteme, praxis (*phronēsis*) and technics. Episteme is about cognition, on the model of geometry and pure a priori thinking of axioms generating theorems. Praxis addresses ethics and politics and hence can involve normativity. Technics is about making.

Classically, the a priori comes not from the normative and praxis but instead from episteme; that is, mathematical thinking in Euclid's *Elements* and implicitly in Pythagoras. At stake in public spheres and politics is instead a normative a priori. This was for Rawls and others a revival of social contract thinking, in which this new a priori of original positions or reasoned communication displaced the state of nature in Hobbes and Rousseau.

Dewey and especially Arendt start not from a normative or other a priori but from political experience itself, from a particular event or experience. Working from the universal to the particular is a priori thinking, while starting from the particular and working towards the general is an a posteriori method of research. Arendt does this not once but twice. In the *Human Condition*, she gives us a politics based largely in the virtues of Aristotle's polis. Her idea of politics and political action is on the lines of Aristotle's praxis. If episteme works a priori, then Aristotle's and Arendt's politics or praxis instead starts not from universal principle but from experience of a posteriori events. It is thus grounded in experience. But Arendt has also given us a modern public sphere. If antiquity was Greek, modernity for Arendt is also fundamentally Christian, as inscribed in Augustine's free will. Humans – like any other beings – in ancient Greek philosophy were understood as caused – in Aristotle's four (material, formal, efficient and formal) causes. Only from Christianity and Augustine were they understood as free. The Abrahamic God was the uncaused cause and He created man in his image as also given free will. The Augustinian free will in Arendt is the basis of modern experience and modern politics. Arendt's modern public sphere combines the virtues of the Greek polis with Augustine's free will. This free will is a necessary condition of both objective and subjective experience. For both objective and subjective experience, it is Kant who is the translator of Augustine's free will. For objective experience, this is Kant's First Critique, *The Critique of Pure Reason*. Arendt's modern public sphere is not based on this but instead in the subjective reason of Kant's Third Critique, *The Critique of Judgment*. It is based thus in Kant's aesthetic critique.

Chapters 2–5 juxtapose classical and modern experience, addressing the classical in Chapter 2 in Aristotle's technics and in Chapter 5 in Arendt's polis. Chapters 3 and 4 address subjective and objective experience, Chapter 4 foregrounding economic thinking, capitalism and *homo economicus*. And Chapter 5 with Arendt puts together the ancient and the modern in an experienced-based reconstruction of the public sphere. So thus far there are three modes of experience: classical, objective and subjective. Chapters 6 and 7 change registers sharply to give us a fourth type of experience. This is *technological* experience. And it, too, could have implications for method. If both the observer and the observed are now either technologically mediated or technologically constituted, often as objects themselves, the implications can be vast. If subjective and objective experience in the human sciences are with us since about 1800, technological experience is very much a twenty-first-century phenomenon. A phenomenon of digital media, user-generated content and social media, of the internet of things. The domination of the experiencing subject is

6

also challenged by the rise of the global South and especially China in world geopolitics and of the Western Greco-Christian individual. This sort of technological experience is addressed in 'object ontology' and the new materialisms.

I address this first in Chapter 6 through thinking about what might be 'technological forms of life'. Twenty-first-century capitalism is technological; as such, it is algorithmic. If power and ideology previously worked through language and were semiotic, now they work more through not letter but number in both debt and especially algorithms. Algorithm in Chinese is *suanfa* (算法), literally method of calculation. Correspondingly, perhaps contemporary method needs to be more mathematical, more about number, about the ordinal and the interval, about the discrete and the continuous. Perhaps so, but not exclusively. Technology may work in the register of number, but forms life work instead through language and meaning. The new materialism and object ontology, it seems to me, tend to forget this. Technological forms of life see us humans as two-sided, as about the fusion and sometimes even the implosion of forms of life into technology. But forms of life – even though technological – still persist. Here forms of life are like Wittgenstein's language games that are not themselves speech acts but form a background for our various modes of peformativity. We are thus not so much objects, or even technical beings, as this fusion. We are thus more like, though I do not like the term, cyborgs. These are fusions of number and letter, of matter and meaning, that operate through a sort of technological phenomenology.

This book and its theoretical and methodological implications are interdisciplinary, and, I think, may have implications for anthropology and literature studies. It ends with a turn towards sinology and China where I have been engaged in research for nearly fifteen years. Chapter 7 addresses aesthetic experience, not through Kant but through a quite eccentric prism. Experience has always been a question of viewing, and Chapter 7 is about the view, starting with Orhan Pamuk's enigmatic observations in *My Name Is Red*. The setting is with miniaturists in the Ottoman Empire at the turn of the seventeenth-century and the juxtaposition with 'Venetian' culture in the West. In this context, we find in Islam and Islamic art a 'view from above', in Renaissance and Western art a 'view from below', while in China the view is 'trapped in an infinity'. With Francois Jullien, we conceive this infinity as the unboundedness of the Dao: with the formless energy of *qi*, and its subsequent forming in *li*, and most of all in the resultant of the myriad of things, the *wan wu* (*Zhuangzi*) or

7

the ten thousand things. The ten thousand things are in an important sense 10,000 objects, and if we look at classical Chinese landscape painting, we see that the things – the mountains and streams and trees and clouds – are not only to be viewed but are themselves doing a considerable portion of the viewing. The ten thousand things are a myriad of objects who themselves are viewing. They are not only in the space of what is experienced, but themselves are experiencing. This takes us back to Walter Benjamin's fascination with Chinese mimetic culture, and Benjamin's own 'object ontology' in his essay 'On Language', in which there was not only the language of man, but also the language of things, of things that are in effect experiencing us. Benjamin's essay is also about communication, which is rendered in German as *mitteilen*, or sharing with. Communications technologies are at the heart of our technological forms of life, of our technological experience. Let us hope that they can escape the logic of command and control, of friend and enemy, and enter instead this register of *mitteilen*, of sharing with.

Coda

How to Read This Book

Some readers may want to skip straight ahead to Chapter 4 and objective experience, the *Methodenstreit* (methods dispute) before proceeding on to Arendt on politics and the final two chapters on technological and object experience. They can then go back and read Chapters 2 and 3. Chapter 1 is a more detailed laying out of the book and addresses experience in general. Chapters 2 and 3 in a sense lay foundations for the rest of the book. Chapter 2 is about Aristotle and technics, and more broadly about the background in classical thought against which experience, which is a modern phenomenon, can be understood. Modern experience and modern politics, we see in Arendt, are dependent on Christianity and Augustine's free will. With the Greeks, freedom was not a question of the 'I will' but instead the 'I can', in the sense that not being a slave was a condition of freedom. In antiquity, there is no free will in the sense that man himself was caused. Man was a substantial form, a substance. Hence man has material and formal, among other, causes. For Christianity, God is the prime mover, the uncaused cause. Man, made in God's image, is also uncaused as the free will. In modernity, formal and final cause disappear into the freedom of man's will, in which also man's cognitive faculties put an ordering onto the world. Material and efficient cause are absorbed by the mechanism of Cartesian extended substance and Newton's physics. This is the modernity of objective experience. This, however, is only one side of the modern. In subjective experience causality disappears and is reconstituted as meaning. As objective observers (Kant), we put causal order onto the objective world. Causes are connectors between events. As subjectively immersed these causes transform into conjunctions, much more ephemeral connectors of our stream of experience. The cause and effect of the subject becomes the and ... and ... and of consciousness: of (un)conscious experience.

Two Pairs of Keywords: A Posteriori and A Priori; Substance and Form

In Plato's Academy, only geometers were allowed enter, and geometry par excellence sets the paradigm for a priori thinking. A priori thinking starts not from experience or sense data but from a set of axioms. These axioms are taken as self-evidently true, as self-evident truths. The notions of a priori and a posteriori came to Western modernity through Latin translations of Euclid's *Elements*. A priori knowledge is deductive knowledge, in the sense that Aristotle could understand Plato's geometers. *Anamnesis* or unforgetting, mentioned in Plato's *Phaedrus*, presumes that humans have innate ideas and knowledge that they have somehow forgotten. It is through Socratic dialectic that they can 'unforget'. Aristotle, on the other hand, in his scientific work in both biology and political science, worked from the experience of a great number of cases, very much a posteriori.

Kant is the watershed for these usages in modern knowledge. Kant, whose break with pure metaphysics was occasioned by Newton and Hume, insisted on experience-based knowledge. Euclid's and Plato's geometry was fully independent of experience and prior to experience. Kant made a further, though parallel, distinction between analytic and synthetic propositions. Kant made the distinction between analytic propositions, which were independent of experience, and synthetic propositions, which 'synthesized' with experience to produce knowledge. Kant set the mould for modern, objective experience. Experience – on the lines of the objective observer in Newtonian physics – was so central to Kant that the Kantian and modern a priori was not a set of axioms à la Euclid, but instead the a priori conditions of possibility of experience itself. This starts as the

9

subject, as the possibility of cognitive experience in physics, and then generalizes to very much what we understand and live as the modern subject. Thus, Euclid's ancient axioms of non-experience become in modernity the very conditions of experience itself.

But what is the a priori in this, what are the elements of this modern a priori? They are not axioms such as 'a = a' of the classical a priori. They are instead an apparatus of faculties that make it possible for us to put order into the world: these are time, space, causality and the unity of the subject. We order the world temporally and spatially, enabled by (the faculty of) perception and causally through reasoning (Baehr 2006). Unifying this apparatus – these formal conditions of knowledge of empirical content – were the constancy and unity of the subject (the unity of apperception) itself. The Kantian a priori subject, with its unity and also with its axioms, has been a basis for positivism in the social sciences and neoclassical (neoliberal) economics. Thus social science and economics are not just analytic like Euclid's geometry, but synthesize with experience in the social world. They do not start from experience – they start instead with axioms like utility-maximizing social and economic actors – but then synthesize with the empirical and experience.

A lot of this book looks to deconstruct this Kantian and positivist subject through a posteriori thinking. Thus I want, together with, for example, Foucault, to rehabilitate the empiricism in Hume (Deleuze) and Adam Smith. This radical empiricism refuses the causality and even the unity of Kant's subject. It features not the understanding but instead the imagination, and works less with positivist *homo economicus* than the empirical economy. This – and subjective experience – is of a piece with phenomenology in its very broadest sense – one that stretches from Hegel to Husserl, Bergson, William James, Heidegger, Proust, Joyce and Freud and in Polanyi and substantivist economics. In each, Kant's (and positivism's) subject is disrupted. Objective time becomes the stream of consciousness, space is challenged by embedded place, the unity of the subject comes under pressure from disintegration and multiplicity, and cause becomes only one of many conjunctive connectors.

To recapitulate on the a priori:

1. The a priori of Euclid's axiom-theorem thinking is an a priori of axioms that is not directed to experience at all. This sort of a priori stays with us in logic and mathematics, not only in the social and human sciences. But it is important in this book because the notion of technological experience (Chapter 6),

10

or computer-mediated experience, is a question of algorithms, whose origin is in large part in Gödel's mathematics, in which algorithms mediate between the 'input' of (a priori) axioms and the 'output' of theorems, whereby theorems are proven from axioms. What Turing does is convert Gödel's mathematics and incompleteness theorem from the register of logic and episteme to that of technics and technology. It combines, indeed couples, with ongoing forms of life in contemporary technological experience.

2. Most important, the just-mentioned a priori of Kant's First Critique, the *Critique of Pure Reason*.

3. There is a less noticed a priori in the Second Critique, the *Critique of Practical Reason* (2017 [1788]), in the context of the moral imperative, which is 'categorical' in the sense that it has no conditions but is a condition of moral action. This recalls the notion of the good in Plato, which is a de facto a priori of justice in *The Republic*. Arendt rejects this for a politics of Aristotle's a posteriori praxis, which instead of starting from the universal of the Platonic good, starts from particular cases and events that we encounter.

4. Again less noticed is what Kant called the a priori of (aesthetic) judgment in the Third Critique, the *Critique of Judgment*. If Rawls and Habermas on the public sphere start from an ethical or normative a priori, whose roots have a lot in common with Kantian moral action, then Arendt rejects this, and her modern (and not ancient) public sphere is based on Kant's third, aesthetic-critique reasoning. In this sense, the Arendtian public sphere is at the same time classical and modern. But what Kant sees as a priori – that is, the condition of possibility of judgment – Arendt sees it as a posteriori and empirical. In Arendt, both the judger and what she judges are empirical and in that sense also fragile. While Rawls and Habermas speak of the condition of possibility of a just public life, Arendt looks at this public sphere – the rule of law, equity – as empirical and thus fragile.

This book develops a frame, a method for a largely a posteriori social and human science that starts from particular cases, events, works of art, issues, and works towards, and reasons towards, the general.

Substance and Form

These terms overlap a priori and a posteriori, with form running parallel to the a priori, and substance to the a posteriori. Kant himself

11

spoke of the transcendental (to experience) apparatus as form, in regard to which the stuff of experience was content. We may think of this content as substance. All the classical sociologists – Marx, Weber, Durkheim, Simmel – spoke of form and substance. The closest to what Kant was proposing in regard to form and objective experience was Weber's idea of formal rationality. Indeed, Weberian rationalization of society is formal rationalization. Formal rationalization is a process of disembedding economic and social relations (Giddens 1984). Karl Polanyi countered this with his advocacy of a re-embedding of economic activity in religion, in culture and in politics. Polanyi is in this context the founder, as it were, of substantivist economics, which so much of anthropology has engaged in. It is for Polanyi a method and a normative position. What I am suggesting is that form versus substance is about this disembedding (form) and re-embedding (substance). Polanyi opposed pure disembedded market relations. Substantivism is linked to Marcel Mauss's gift economy and the tradition of anthropology that descends from Malinowski's (2013 [1922]) gift, embracing Fei Xiaotong, Evans Pritchard, Marshall Sahlins, David Graeber and many others.

In the *Methodenstreit*, which, though Weber was involved, was primarily a debate among economists, the Historical School – notably Karl Knies, G.W.F. Roscher, Werner Sombart and arguably Simmel – proposed a substantivist economics in contrast to the formalism of both neoclassicism and classical political economy of Quesnay, Smith and Ricardo. Marx's *Capital* was a critique of such classical-political-economy formalism. Marx's notions of *Wertsubstanz* (value-substance) and use value (which was substantive and not utilitarian) made his materialism not formal and thus mechanical, but instead dialectical. The main point for us (Chapter 4) is that formal economics abstracts from experience while substantivist economics starts from the particulars of experience, in a given village, a given factory, a given McDonalds. The formalist a priori in economics is neither Euclid's nor Kant's a priori. It is, instead, an axiomatic that concerns valuing: a prism for how we value. For classical political economy, this was to do with factor-input, for Quesnay agriculture, for Smith and Ricardo (and Marx) it was labour. For Marx, the labour theory of value could give us an understanding of exploitation, but this was quantitative and abstract. It is not yet dialectical: it remains part of a formal and mechanical materialism. But the value-form of abstract, homogeneous labour and of exchange is about just one way of valuing. And this is objective value: value from objective experience. We also value subjectively.

12

Use values are valued subjectively. If the units of exchange value are – like atoms – interchangeable, every use-value good is different from every other: use-values are singular, and they are valued as singular. Much of this was recapitulated in the *Methodenstreit* (Gane 2012). But in the *Methodenstreit*, which was in important respects coterminous with the birth of sociology, perhaps more was at stake. In the *Methodenstreit* it was not classical political economy that was in debate with the Historical School. It was Gustav Menger and the Austrian School's emergent *neo*classical economics. Here Weber was Menger's ally against the Historicals. At the root of this is that the birth of the neoclassicals saw an important shift in the locus of value: from abstract labour input to utility maximization. This was also a shift from Adam Smith's Humean empiricism to the positivism of John Stuart Mill and the Panopticon's Jeremy Bentham. This birth of positivism – and not Smith's empiricism – was the birth also of *homo economicus*. The a priori axiomatic of *homo economicus* – and never of labour-value – has, unforeseen, spread as a mode of valuation and indeed general belief system among the lay population in the world today.

— 1 —

HAVE WE FORGOTTEN EXPERIENCE?

1.1 In Praise of the A Posteriori

Have we forgotten experience? If there is a dominant ideology today, it is more likely than not to have roots in neoclassical economics (Harvey 2007). Neoclassicism, which is the source of most neoliberal thinking, though it emerged as a force in the 1890s, has its roots in utilitarianism. Not the empiricist Adam Smith, but the utilitarian John Stuart Mill is the author of the idea of *homo economicus* (Gane 2014). There is a major difference. Smith, like his mentor David Hume, starts from sense data. He starts from experience. Mill, for his part, starts from the assumption, the axiom, that we, we human beings, are utility-maximizing animals. This is unlike Smith, for whom, with Hume, we are open to sensory impressions, for whom these impressions become for us 'facts' (Deleuze 1991). For Mill as utility-maximizing animals – or what have become known as social actors – we are already closed. We already filter out impressions and what might become other facts, through a sort of mechanism that gives priority to utility maximization. Mathematical thinking starts from a cluster of axioms. It is with a set of operations from these axioms that we get proofs and theorems. Mill and utilitarianism, and indeed capitalist ideology, start from one axiom, that of utility maximization, from us as *homo economicus*. Unlike Smith's inductive thinking, Mill's *homo economicus* starts from an axiom and is thus in large part deductive. Such deductive thinking is in major part a priori. It is a closing of ourselves off from experience. It is in this sense a forgetting of experience.

If David Hume was arguably the founder of empiricism, Mill was self-consciously influenced by Auguste Comte, and with Auguste

Comte, the founding figure of *positivism*. Unlike empiricism's openness of the senses, openness indeed to sensation, to sensory experience, positivism as a mode of a priori thinking starts from axioms, in Mill's case, the axiom of *homo economicus*. Max Weber's (1949) famous essay on 'Objectivity in the Social Sciences' was of course not just about objectivity but also about value. Weber himself was a sometimes contradictory amalgam of positivist and 'objectivist' *erklären* and interpretive or 'subjectivist' *verstehen*. The methodological essay gave us both sides and promoted a social science of both *erklären* and *verstehen*, both positivism and interpretation. To the extent that method was positivist and objectivist, its inspiration was pure John Stuart Mill. Its positivism was of *homo economicus*. This is not a surprise. It fully maps onto Weber's encounter with neoclassical economics. Weber's first main methodological intervention was in the *Methodenstreit* from the late 1880s. The *Methodenstreit*, or methods dispute, was between the German Historical School of Economics and the Austrian School, featuring Carl Menger (1883), perhaps the most important founder of neoclassical economics. Weber at that point in time sided very much with Menger. The Historical School, led by its second-generation advocate Gustav von Schmoller, was no match for Menger's analytic intelligence. But it is telling that Schmoller's attack argued that Menger was treating humans as if they were atoms in mechanistic physics. Weber's pivotal ideal type in his action theory was of instrumentally rational action (*zweckrational*), which was based on *homo economicus*.[1] The point for us here is that positivism and neoclassical *homo economicus* came from very much the same mould. It is that they share similar a priori assumptions: how both negate or at least drastically reduce experience.

If there is a dominant paradigm in the *critical* social sciences and humanities today, it may be the 'new materialism'. If the old materialism of Newton and Galileo was mechanistic, then the new materialism is vibrant. It is not a mechanistic but a vitalist materialism. For it, all matter, including inorganic matter, is vital. For the new materialism, humans and nonhumans congeal together on *assemblages*: actor networks in which subjects are more often understood as one kind of many different kinds of objects (Bennett 2009). This new materialism has produced some distinguished work: assemblage thinking, looking at assemblages of humans and nonhumans has become a fertile method (Lash and Lury 2007;

---

[1] This does not mean that Weber approved of this action type. See Chapter 6.

Marres 2012). Yet in this new materialism – this school, as it were, of assemblages of vital objects – there is most often little space for meaning or experience.

This new materialism is also an anti- or post-humanism. It wants to break with notions of human finitude. Hence, for example, Quentin Meillassoux (2008) cites approvingly David Hume and argues for an ontology of events that proceed outside of experience. Or in the words of Alain Badiou (2013), the founder of this speculative materialism, events 'subtract' from experience. But this is a rather odd reading of Hume. For Deleuze as well as almost all much less critical readings, without sense impressions there is no David Hume. Badiou's thought, for its part, has roots in Louis Althusser's core idea of scientific revolutions preceding philosophic revolutions: that Galileo thus preceded Descartes and Marxist science (historical materialism) preceded Marxist philosophy. Badiou is acute in his focus on Georg Cantor's set-theoretical mathematics as a pivotal scientific revolution with fundamental reverberations in philosophy, and we might add less directly today's computer-mediated technological experience. He is right also about the new importance and metamorphoses of infinity in Cantor. Cantor's set theory featured infinite sets, in which for example the set of natural numbers was infinite, and the set of rational and then real numbers were ever-greater infinites. There were then a number of infinities: an infinity of infinities. Cantor's indeed was quite a formidable scientific revolution. Logic, after Aristotle, had been for 2,300 years forged in a linguistic paradigm. Now, with Frege and Russell, logic had become mathematical. Predication becomes not about sentences and their subjects and qualities but about the predications of a set in its members. With, largely, Cantor, infinity enters scientific discourse and becomes effectively 'secularized'. But just because there is infinity does not mean that our finite experience is not important.

The subtext in this for Badiou is an a priori deductivism, a priori thinking. Frege, but especially Russell and Hilbert and Hilbert's disciples, not only put set theory at the heart of mathematical and philosophical thinking, but they consider this and their attached propositions to be descriptive of reality, at the basis of the real. This was an effective Platonism, in which the real was not so much the good and the true among the forms but instead the mathematical and mathematically informed predications themselves. Russell, Hilbert and indeed Badiou were in different ways frank about this. In this sense, and an important one, the new materialism can also be understood as 'speculative realism', in which the mathematical structures both material and real. But what if we take this thinking, as Alan Turing and technological experience do, one step further into the just as important scientific revolutions in Heisenberg and especially in Gödel? Gödel's incompleteness was an equally fundamental break with Cantor's set-theoretical assumptions in Frege, Russell and Hilbert. Gödel proved that no consistent set of axioms could account for all of the true theorems it generated: that the only way a set of axioms could account for all these true theorems was if the original group of axioms was inconsistent. This put a void of indeterminacy into mathematical space. Gödel referred to the transformational rules, the operations by which the axioms generated the theorems, as 'algorithms'. Alan Turing, along with John von Neumann and Claude Shannon, shifted Gödel's paradigm from science into engineering, where algorithms became operations for handling data. This space of indeterminacy along with recently noticed phenomena of machine inductive learning from data again opens up the possibility of experience (Mirowski 2002).

So, in contrast to the a priori of both *homo economicus* positivism and so much of critical theory, this book is a bit of a manifesto for the 'a posteriori'. It advocates a social science and human science that is basically *a posteriori*. This book, while at odds with *The Republic*, has more than great respect for Plato's *Laws*, *Symposium* and *Phaedrus*, even with his, as it were, pure theory of number. In *The Elementary Forms of the Religious Life*, Durkheim (1961 [1912]) understands not the profane's categories of classification, but instead the rites and rituals of the sacred as real. Not the profane, but instead the sacred was Durkheim's real. And we know that the Pythagoreans were also a religious cult. In this sense we are sympathetic to Plato's unremitting a priori. This said, this book is fundamentally *Aristotelian*. Its a posteriori is Aristotelian. In Chapter 2 we feature a technics that with Aristotle starts from the particular and then moves to the general or universal. In the *Nicomachean Ethics*, Aristotle's (2002) three modes of knowledge are *technē*, praxis and episteme. Here *technē*, which is making, reasons from the particular to the universal. So, does praxis, which is a doing, comprising both ethics and politics. Episteme, or cognizing, for its part is a priori and deductive. Its method is axiomatic, its paradigm geometry. In Michel Foucault's work, all of the normalizing and governmentalizing discourses of modernity come under the heading of episteme. In modernity, this episteme of what have become Kant's categories synthesizes with matter in Newtonian physics. A century later the episteme's a priori synthesizes with 'social matter' to give us neo-Kantian social-science positivism (Foucault 1966). As a counter to such governmentality through episteme, Foucault counterposes, like Aristotle, a version of *technē*, in his technologies or technics of the self. Here Foucault (1988) gives us an a posteriori, an anti-positivist, basically empiricist critique of episteme. In this, Foucault is on the side of experience.

If Plato gives us the Good as an Idea, as a Form, then Aristotle brings these forms into juxtaposition with matter as the good life. Plato's good becomes instantiated in Aristotle's good life. Chapter 5 below on politics of experience moves with Hannah Arendt's (1958) Aristotelian a posteriori, starting from the particular case or event or experience and moving – through reasoned, rhetorical and pluralistic speech – to the universal or general. Arendt gives us a very particular reconstruction of the public spheres.

The shift of the a posteriori from empiricism to pragmatism is one also from knowledge to politics. In Chinese, empiricism is *jingyan-zhuyi* and pragmatism is *shiyongzhuyi*. *Jingyan* is experience and *shiyong* 'true use'. Arendt's public spheres begin in experience and end in pragmatism-like practice, always starting with Dewey and the particular issue and moving to the universal. In the technological age, mediating this move from the particular of political data to the universal of use and action is, with Noortje Marres's *Material Participation* (2012), a combinatory of people and things, of subjectivities and technologies to the constitution of a myriad of publics.

1.2 Substance

Experience has to do with substance. Experience is downgraded of course in Plato's *Republic*. What we experience is mere *doxa* or opinion whereas the true and especially the good are a question of forms, which – though we can arrive at them through dialectic – have their origin in the heavens. In Aristotle, we have less the good than the good life. And this good life is a matter of experience. It is a question of everyday practices, of associations (institutions), the family, tribe and especially the polis. It is through the concreteness of participation in these associations that we realize the good life. Already we have the beginnings of the juxtaposition of substance and form: the form of the good, the substance of the good life. In *The Philosophy of Right*, Hegel (1972) – drawing implicitly on Aristotle – contrasts the abstraction and formalism of Kantian morality with, again, 'ethical substance', itself a matter of the everyday, embedded experience in what Hegel saw as *Sitten* – that is folkways, habits, customs. Again, there is the juxtaposition of form and abstraction, on the one hand, and experience linked with substance, on the other.

In Aristotle's *Metaphysics*, substances are understood in terms of matter and form, of formed matter, and – alternatively and consistently – in terms of the four (material, formal, efficient and final) causes. For his part, in what many have seen as the pivotal passage in the Preface to *Phenomenology*, Hegel (1977: 26) saw the transition from antiquity to modernity in terms of a move from substance to subject. In antiquity, we understood substances in terms of their forms, which were their properties or predicates: in modernity, we have subjects with their predicates. Aristotle distinguished between substantial and accidental forms: a substance's substantial forms or properties are those without which the substance would not be what it is. Its accidental forms are properties that are not thus necessary. If ancient logic and 'grammar' were about substances and their predicates, then modern grammar is about subjects and their predicates, in particular their verbs and their objects. Kant, and later neo-Kantian positivism, says we experience things only in terms of their properties: that we cannot experience things-themselves. Phenomenology, or today's 'ontological turn', and implicitly interpretive human sciences, give us method in which we are meant to experience, for example, social processes extra-categorically and ontologically; that is, as things-themselves.

I want to write this book for the human sciences in general, even for the post-human sciences and humanities. But I am a sociologist and this book is also a sociology book. And all of the founding figures of sociology – Marx, Weber, Durkheim and Simmel – gave to us notions of substance. For Marx in the *Grundrisse* (1993), this was *Wertsubstanz* (value-substance). This was contrasted to the value-form or exchange value. But how are we to understand such value-substance? On the face of it, it seems to be just about the labour theory of value, which Marx shared with Ricardo and Smith. Here value is comprised of labour power; that is, abstract, homogeneous labour, the variable capital that goes into making a commodity, into the value of a commodity, which is then exchanged at a higher price, yielding for the capitalist 'profits of enterprise'. But by definition substance is neither abstract nor homogeneous. Further, the *Grundrisse* is still in the transition between the early and late Marx, still nearly as much philosophy as economics. So perhaps abstract homogeneous labour is not what Marx was addressing in *Wertsubstanz*. We do not experience the abstract and homogeneous.

19

We experience instead the heterogeneous and concrete, which is much closer, as Arnaud Berthoud (2002) has implied, to Marxian use-value. Use-value has to do with concrete exchanges – including gift exchange arguably – on the ground and communications with other workers: it has to do with mutual recognition. You do not recognize another in their abstraction and homogeneity; you recognize them in their difference, as concrete and singular. You recognize them through experience.

For Durkheim, we see substance and forms in religious life. Here the substance of the rites and rituals of the Australian aboriginal tribes constitute the sacred, which itself is a basis of the forms of the profane: of the knowledge categories of Durkheim's and Mauss's *Primitive Classifications*. Substance here is at the basis of George Bataille's *l'informe*. In *l'informe*, or the formless, Bataille was making a gesture to the substance of Durkheim's sacred. Bataille's 'restricted economy' (*économie restraint*) was that of form or the profane, his general economy of the scared. MAUSS (Mouvement anti-utilitariste dans les sciences sociales) in France are with Bataille, Durkheim and Mauss on this – rejecting utilitarian abstract formalism for the sacred of substance. Bataille's 'accursed share' was indeed substance. Simmel, for his part, gives us a juxtaposition of life substance to the normalizing and stultifying social forms. In Simmel's *The Philosophy of Money* (2001), we see moves towards a substantive economy and away from the formalism of neoclassical economics (whose origins were of course utilitarian).[2] Simmel, alongside Weber and Werner Sombart, was part of the third generation of Germany's Historical School, and also they were part of the critique of formalist neoclassicism.

In Max Weber himself we see the juxtaposition of formal and substantive rationality. Formal rationality is the structural counterpart of *zweck*-, or instrumentally, rational action. Weberian rationalization is primarily formal rationalization. Weber was a legal scholar and he contrasted formal rationalization with substantive rationality in, notably, law. Formally, rational law is very much procedural, in the sense that it gives space for interest groups to pursue their interests. Rule of law, in the sense of formally rational law, gives a certain predictability and stability, a space of security in which entrepreneurs can pursue their activities. Weber saw this as a precondition for capitalist development. Formally, rational law reached perhaps its most systematic articulation in Hans Kelsen – who wrote the

[2] I am grateful to Mark Fitzgerald for this point on Simmel.

document forming the basis of Austrian constitutional law – and his *Pure Theory of Law* (*Reine Rechtslehre*). 'Substantivists' like both Leo Strauss and Carl Schmitt saw Kelsen's formalism as a primary opponent and constitutive of their own political thinking. For Schmitt, Kelsen's formalism is 'political theology', with origins in Augustine's free will. Strauss as Platonist is equally scathing.

This book in major part is about experience as critique of neoliberalism and thus neoclassical economics. Perhaps the most cogent discussion of neoliberalism appears in Foucault's *The Birth of Biopolitics* (2008), in which he, over several chapters, understands neoliberalism as a mode of governmentality, whose paradigmatic expression is in German ordoliberalism (which he extends to include Hayek). Carl Schmitt's rejection of Kelsen's legal formalism was extended to a critique of such ordoliberalism. For Foucault, ordoliberalism entailed a retreat of state administration, and state industrial policy, for the legal regulation of economic exchanges to ensure a fair playing field that would counteract monopoly and support competition. If the above is formally rational, what then is substantively rational law? If formally rational law yields a procedural space for economic exchange, then substantively rational law is in contrast a support of the above-mentioned good life, of Aristotle's eudemonia: of the good life of the virtues – justice, courage, moderation and reason. If Plato's *Republic* was about the ideal state, his *Laws* are much more grounded, much closer to experience, much more a grounding of such eudemonia. They are a sort of ideal-typical instantiation of substantively rational law.

The idea of substance in connection again to experience is pervasive in the work of Karl Polanyi (1957). Polanyi is the founding figure of 'substantivism', which is on the one hand economic and on the other very much cultural. Substantivism is omnipresent in economic anthropology, with origins in Marcel Mauss's *Gift* – a major influence on Polanyi, and also as a basis for Marshall Sahlins's *Stone Age Economics*. If formalism is 'epistemological' and reduces or negates experience, then substantivism is very much ontological and a question of experience. This is what Polanyi in *The Great Transformation* understood as 'embeddedness', in terms of which anthropology's 'ontological turn' can be partly understood. Arguably, however, anthropology was always and is constitutively ontological. We see this juxtaposition of gift and commodity economy in Appadurai and David Graeber's early book on value. We are aware of Graeber's and other substantivist anthropologists' connection to Immanuel Wallerstein and World Systems theory. We will show below how substantivism and world-systemic capital flow entail one another. All of the above have as switching point Polanyi's substantivism.

Polanyi's substantivism is again aimed at the formalism and utilitarianism of neoclassical economics. For formalism, and indeed modern capitalism in the great transformation, the economy ceased to be one of many institutions. The economy – that is, markets and market-determined pricing – has become such a driver of society that it is no longer even regarded as an institution, but somehow as 'natural'. Polanyi's and substantivism's idea of embeddedness is defined first as against the disembeddedness of formalism. Formalism and neoclassicism dismbed us from everyday life, and disembed experience from the everyday life to reinstate us as utility-maximizing actors in markets. We remember Aristotle spoke of substance as the unity of form and matter. For Hegel in the *Phenomenology*, we move from substance to subject. This is also saying, via the mediation of Christianity, that form, once intertwined with matter in substance, in modernity separates and disembeds from matter. It separates and re-emerges as something much closer to pure form, via Augustine's free will; that is, into this disembedded subject. Thus, there is form as pure subject in Hobbes's war of all against all, in natural rights theories of Locke and Rousseau, and finally via J.S. Mill and *homo economicus* into the Jevons–Walras–Menger synthesis of neoclassical economics. Karl Polanyi's re-embedding substantivism in this context is also opening up an economics of experience.

Disembedding also means the disembedding of institutions. For Polanyi, markets are only one of many institutions – including village, family, politics, lineage, religion and culture more generally. So in the great transformation, not only is our subjectivity disembedded from experience of everyday life, but also institutions are disembedded from one another to the total dominance of one institution, the market. In this quest Polanyi makes common cause with institutional economics. This is not to the new institutional economics – whose neoclassical assumptions we see in R.H. Coase and Oliver Williamson – but the original institutional economics of Thorstein Veblen and John R. Commons. For Commons, who subscribed to the theories of Henry George, property must not be allowed to lie unused while speculators wait for its right market valuation, but if allowed to stay unused it must be taxed, in order for it to contribute to the substantive public good. Veblen would not separate consumer experience from embedding in culture and fashion. Veblen and Polanyi were influenced by the institutionalism and de facto substantivism of the German Historical School. In fact, Veblen made a limited foray into the *Methodenstreit* in writing about the Historical School's Gustav von Schmoller. W.G.F. Roscher and Karl Knies were first-generation Historical School figures that Max Weber wrote about. The second-generation leader was the less talented Schmoller. Weber, himself, alongside Simmel but especially Sombart, has been seen as third-generation Historical School (Tribe 2008).

Weber's famous methodological 'objectivity' essay sets up against one another the *erklären*, objectivity and *homo economicus* of Gustav Menger and the Austrian School, and indeed the substantivism, along with interpretivism and *verstehen*, of the Historical School. The Austrians here are anti-institutionalist and the Historicals institutionalist. The Historical School's interpretivism and displacing the utilitarian objectivity with embedded subjectivity comes to rescue experience. Objectivity and formal *homo economicus* see only the smallest portion of what we encounter, unlike everyday economic subjectivity. Thus, economic life is embedded in institutions: like religious institutions, as Weber turned to the economic ethics of world religions (Whimster 2007).

This is a combination of *erklären* and *verstehen* as the economy is embedded in institutions. Here, if the institution at stake is a this-worldly religion as in China and India, you will not get capitalist development. If it is embedded in an other-worldly religion like Protestantism, there will be capitalism. But embedding in other-worldly religious institutions is a simultaneous disembedding. It entails a transcendental relation with a personal God, as in Protestantism. For his part, Polanyi was only marginally influenced by Weber. He was more influenced by Werner Sombart and also Sombart's contemporary Henri Pirenne. Pirenne is the inspiration for Braudel, and both are the inspiration for Wallerstein, Arrighi and World Systems theory. Max Weber's paradigmatic capitalist was Ben Franklin's shopkeeper, which was on the lines of Adam Smith's local trader or even Marx on manufacture in small workshops before the domination of *die große Industrie*. In each case, these are small-business and, for Marx, productionist notions of the origins of capitalism. For Sombart and Pirenne as for Polanyi and Braudel, these small shopkeepers and workshops were not capitalist at all. Capitalism for them was equivalent to formalism, and these small entrepreneurs were instead part of the *substantive* economy. For the substantivists, the origins of both capitalism and formalism did not start there. In modernity they started exterior to substance in the huge concentrations of capital and long-distance trade and banking in fourteenth- to sixteenth-century Venice. A lot of backslid Catholics, and the odd Jew (the Merchant of Venice), but not a lot of Protestants. We remember Weber wrote *The Protestant Ethic* in responses to – a review of – Sombart's *Der moderne Kapitalismus*. With Polanyi, we might decide that Sombart might have been right.

Pirenne's work on the origins of capitalism foregrounded the mediaeval city. We remember Polanyi gave special place to price setting. And in the mediaeval city, not markets but the guilds were largely the agents of price setting. If we rewind to Aristotle's polis, this time in the *Politics*, we see similar phenomena. And Marx was well aware of Aristotle's notion of 'chrematistics'. If economic activity in the polis is restrained by the virtues, then acquisition is limited. Here the virtue of justice and the idea of a just price are central. They are in accord with the substance of the polis: of the institutions (associations) of household, tribe and polis. Chrematistics, in contrast, involves unlimited economic acquisition. Such unlimited acquisition, for Aristotle, is unnatural and takes place outside the price-setting substance of the polis. This is again in long-distance trade. Normal economic activity was, for Aristotle, finite like the seasons and inscribed in a cyclical time. Chrematistics was instead infinite and inscribed in a rectilinear time. The connection with world systems is that the long-distance trade and rectilinear time are the unlimited acquisition of the capitalist world system.

This can relate quite closely to the work of the dear, departed Ulrich Beck. And this is important because substantivism is not just a question of embedded polises and tribes. It relates to modern individualism. In German language debates, Beck, before the work on cosmopolitanism, had two main theses, a risk thesis and an individualization thesis (Beck 1986). He also always and increasingly had a very strong sense of institutions. For Beck, individualization was a more or less institutional process. In this sense, there is a dovetailing with Polanyi and substantivism. There can be an individualization of substance and one of form. The possessive individual of utility maximization curves is both disembedded and atomized, homogeneous. As disembedded atoms, all are the same. Substantivism is surely more relational than formalism, but there is a distinction between the formal and the substantive individual. The substantive individual or substantive individualization is not equivalent to all others but is instead quite singular. He or she is embedded in a set of intertwined institutions, and encounters them not objectively like *homo economicus* but instead subjectively. At stake in this

HAVE WE FORGOTTEN EXPERIENCE?

substantive individualization process is the subjectivity of experience. What about risk? Frank Knight distinguished between risk and uncertainty on the grounds that risk was insurable while uncertainty was not. The financial crisis of 2008 was based on what was seen as insurable risk, in derivatives, futures and mortgage-based and other complex financial products. We all know what the unintended consequences of such insurable risk have been. Uncertainty, unlike risk, is uninsurable. It is a one-off. It is not a set of similar atoms in an insurance portfolio but an individual case. It is singular. What Beck meant in his substantive individualization, which is also that of experience, was not risk but uncertainty.

1.3 New Totalitarianisms and Technological Phenomenology: The Chapters

All this said, let us have another look at the book's chapters. Chapter 2, as we said, addresses technics, Aristotle's technics, which in the mould of experience, of empiricism, move from the particular to the general. Chapter 3 addresses William James's radical empiricism. There is a lot in common with David Hume's empiricism here. It is telling that Deleuze's very early book on Hume is entitled *Empiricism and Subjectivity*. Deleuze's Hume is cast as a rejection of the Kantian subject: Kant's disembedded and objectivist subject is displaced by an immediately perceiving subjectivism. This happens through a Humean rejection of Kantian causation as metaphysical. For Deleuze, following Hume, events are not connected by causes but by conjunctions, by 'ands' and 'buts', or even prepositions (adverbs), under and over or after and before. But never causes or adjectives: that is, neither qualities nor properties. You get these connectivities also in Deleuze and Guattari's *Anti-Oedipus*, and the rejection of extensive qualities (for quantitative intensities) in Deleuze's (2006b) *Nietzsche and Philosophy*. Here Hume would not accept the subsumption of the (metaphysical) categories of Kant's understanding, and built instead any possible knowledge from perception, the imagination and induction. James makes the same move in his radical empiricism. Only he gives us a different type of subjectivity. For Hume, experience is an openness to sense data, to sensation. For James, experience is prior to the separation of subjects and objects. It is in this sense very phenomenological. Husserl recognized this and appreciated James. But both of these notions of experience are central to this book.

Chapter 4 addresses economic experience, which we have already introduced at length above. Chapter 5 turns towards politics and the work of Hannah Arendt. John Milbank and Adrian Pabst (2016) have made an impactful intervention in post-Brexit debates with their book *The Politics of Virtue: Post-liberalism and the Human Future*. Their book is a categorical rejection of liberalism, one that uses Aristotelian virtue and the Christian Holy Spirit for a notion of substance that is again set up against liberal formalism. Milbank and Pabst dismiss not just neoliberalism but also liberalism. In Milbank and Pabst we see that not only the Polanyian left but also the post-liberal conservative right can use the language of substantivism. In the first instance, Hannah Arendt seems equally to be anti-liberal. Her *Human Condition* is, of course, situated in the juxtaposition of Aristotle's polis and its opposite in the *oikos*. *Oikos* is, of course, the root of economy and for Agamben and Foucault what is at stake in governmentality. But when we look more closely, we see Arendt has a strong notion of institutions: of, indeed, not so much substantive as formal institutions. Thus, for her, not the Greeks but the Romans were the political people par excellence, with their abstract property and contract law, their republican institutions of deliberative democracy, advanced bureaucracy, infrastructure, engineering.

A great number of cultural and social theorists – from Wendy Brown to Aihwa Ong to Maurizio Lazzarato to Latour – are these days drawing very much on Schmitt. Agamben counterposed favourably Benjamin to Schmitt in that Benjamin gave us pure justice, while Schmitt instead gave us too much law. With Arendt, it seems to me that Schmitt may have given us not enough law. Not enough *rule* of law. For Schmitt (1985), modern politics was a political theology and this was the problem. In political theology there is too much a *nomos* (or normativity) of the referee, of the arbiter, whether this is the law courts or God, against which Schmitt (2003) contrasts the *nomos* of the earth: the norms of the soil, of blood, in the political as war of friend versus enemy. Here the political enemy is defined as not being the same as the friend, even if at points the friend engages in commerce with the enemy. As opposed to this, Arendt recognizes the above sorts of institutions of the Romans, which are to do with a much more universal, and indeed not substantivist but formalist, *nomos*. This does not mean that Arendt rejects the substantivism of the polis, but only that these formal institutions of Rome are a sort of necessary frame – a frame that makes world-building possible. For Arendt it is Augustine who is at centre stage: Augustine who straddles the fall of the Roman Empire and the consolidation of Christianity. Augustine's free will as the basis of the modern subject is fundamental to Arendt's plural political world building as ever starting anew. Arendt valued the stability of (formal) institutions: Greek democracy lasted 50-odd years, Rome a thousand years, the Third Reich (thankfully) twelve years.

For Schmitt, we are of necessity living in a frame of political theology, in which his *nomos* of the earth can play out. An ever-delayed 'End Times' and redemption mark this: the space of this forever-delayed is the *katechon*, which is the frame of politics and why the state of exception is also a legal order. In this context, for Schmitt modernity as political theology is fundamentally illegitimate. In opposing this, Arendt is very much on side with Hans Blumenberg, whose *Legitimität der Neuzeit* (*The Legitimacy of the Modern Age*) is about not legitimation but legitimacy. Blumenberg's again Augustinian and Christian-constituted modern secular institutional world is a frame for the justice and reason the West has inherited from Greek antiquity. Blumenberg's Christianity is very different to Milbank's substantivist understanding of the Holy Spirit. Trump, Brexit and Russian and East European plebiscitary authoritarianisms are at home with Milbank's post-liberal substantivism. Plebiscite here is arrayed against formal institutions and the rule of law, as of course was Article 48 of the Hugo Preuss-drafted constitution of the Weimar Republic. Chapter 5 underscores Arendt's marriage of the substantivist ethos of Aristotle's polis with their necessary grounding in Roman and Christian-inherited institutional forms. Yet Arendt's world building, her ever starting anew through public plurality, always starts from particular to universal. Her worlds are never Heidegger's a priori worlds: that is, as condition of possibility of authentic *Dasein*. Arendt's worlds are always empirical, always a posteriori.

Chapter 6 addresses forms of life. It starts off in a linguistic dimension, via Aristotle's rhetoric, through the early Wittgenstein's *Tractatus Logico-Philosophicus*. In the *Tractatus*, language is a matter of predication. The axioms of the *Tractatus*, the elementary propositions, very much can tell us all that can be 'said'. These are less like classical logic than like the mathematical logic of Frege, Russell and Hilbert. They indicate a Platonic-like notion of the real shared with Russell. The real is these elementary propositions. We then switch to late Wittgenstein in the register of speech acts and performativity. We consider who does and who does not get the chance to speak. But we understand performatives less as disembedded speech acts à la Austin and Searle; instead, we see them as contiguous with the integument of forms of life themselves. Meaning here is much less predication, or representation or rules, than practices of experience. Then we fast-forward and ask what happens when forms of life become technological. I addressed this nearly two decades ago (Lash 2002) also on considerations of technological forms of life. But this is a lot different. Because technological forms of life themselves have changed. We mentioned above the new materialism: its assemblages and vibrant matter presume a ubiquity of matter with very little, if any, space left for meaning. But this is not the case in, for example, the work of Karen Barad, for whom meaning and matter meet halfway. Barad, herself a quantum physicist, focuses not so much on Heisenberg's uncertainty as on Nils Bohr's use of the double slit apparatus in order to enable registering matter as both waves and particles. The wave and particle nature of physics has been around for centuries, but Newtonian mechanics and arguably Einstein's photoelectric effect gave priority to particles (photons). Bohr and Barad insist also on waves. In Barad, this gives us a rather different idea of the material as being comprised not just of objects or things or particles, but also of phenomena. Waves are not objects, not even vibrant objects: they are phenomena. Thus notions of matter are extended in Barad.

What Barad (2007) gives us, indeed quite explicitly, is an emergent phenomenology. Phenomenology constitutively displaces the encounter of subjects and objects for that of consciousness and phenomena. Consciousness and phenomena are much more closely intertwined than is subject–object dualism. Barad is thus giving us a phenomenology. Which already entails a displacement of experience. Her book is the entanglement of matter and meaning. Here meaning meets matter (or 'the universe') halfway. What is it that mediates between meaning and matter? It is the device, the two-slit measuring device. We see already that this mediating between meaning and matter is about measuring. And in this sense the technological is about mathematics as much or more than about language. We human beings are symbol-using animals, and in technological forms of life these symbols are as likely to be mathematical as semiotic (Lazzarato 2015; Lury and Wakeford 2013). We can extend these ideas of meaning and matter to computing (technology) and media, of not propositional description, but instead of performativity. First, we should note that Barad's technological phenomenology is the most recent and perhaps best conceived of a series of efforts in this direction, from, for example, Stiegler, Luhmann, Sloterdijk and

28

Maturana and Varela. The key is to put in the place of consciousness and meaning making, social forms of life like in Wittgenstein's *Philosophical Investigations* (2009). Here we are getting closer to what we mean by technological experience. What Barad does is cross-cut the new materialism's idea of assemblage with that of apparatus, and in doing so rescue both meaning and experience while keeping a radicality of matter.

Let us change registers quickly to cultural and media studies. The canonical and founding text in cultural studies is Stuart Hall's (1973) article on encoding and decoding of television discourse, which is clearly about different kinds of meaning, of hegemonic, oppositional and negotiated meanings. More recently, this sort of analysis is amplified in Norman Fairclough's (1995) *Critical Discourse Analysis*. The canonical text of media studies may well be Shannon and Weaver (1963), a very fully engineering notion of media with channels, signal, noise and the like. To understand media or technological experience more generally, we need both Hall and Shannon. Shannon was, of course, one of the originators, with Turing, von Neumann and others, of the computer. Whereas Wiener's cybernetics were negentropic, featuring steering mechanisms of control, command, communication and intelligence, not fully different from the Gaia hypothesis, Shannon and von Neumann were very much entropic, in this sense of a piece very much with Gödel's incompleteness. This opens up the very porosity of communication. If we again change from the register of science to that of engineering, it is *algorithms* that translate axioms into theorems, inputs into outputs for Gödel and Turing. Incompleteness is tied up with this very entropic porosity, much more a phenomenon less of Freud's sex or life drive than instead the death drive.

At stake again is not semiotics but number, but mathematics in algebra and topological geometry. Algorithms are instructions, but they have much more than only a linguistic dimension. In Gödel's incompleteness, if the axiomatic, the set of axioms that you start with as input, is consistent, then it cannot account for all the true theorems, i.e. the output that can be proved from it. And you can only prove all the true theorems if the axiomatic is made inconsistent. What mediates between input (axioms) and output (theorems), Gödel said, were algorithms. Here algorithms are operations or operators mediating between input and output. Thus, when we shift to the register of engineering and computation with Turing, we see again algorithms as mathematical operators. In Chinese, algorithms are *suanfa* (算法), or method of calculation. But in rankings like Google

PageRank, valuing which is also mathematical, measuring and the like are at the heart of this move from a semiotic to a technological culture in that number largely displaces language. Even Mark Zuckerberg's idea at the origins of Facebook, about students ranking one another on scales of their 'hotness', is about number. Thus, Lazzarato (2015) speaks of post-semiotic modes of power that we see in algorithmic control and control by debt of complex financial products. Lury is clear that this post-semiotic control is through number (Lury and Wakeford 2013). This brings us to second-order cybernetics and Katherine Hayles. She features Maturana and Varela. Autopoietic systems can be just as much entropic as negentropic. They work for Maturana and Varela also on the level of this sort of Wittgensteinian phenomenology. They can be more or less open. As open, they are constitutively indeterminate and more or less entropic. It is here that they can work through structural coupling with other systems.

What we are saying is that technological forms of life can take the form more or less of first-order cybernetics. This, with Wiener, works from C3I (command, control, communication and intelligence). It is negentropic, and features isolated, hierarchical, closed systems. Or, with Hayles's, they can take the form of second-order cybernetics – that is, with Humberto Maturana – entropic, relatively open and structurally coupling systems. Donna Haraway in *Staying with the Trouble* calls these second types of systems 'sympoetic'. She contrasts this with Bruno Latour's (equally new materialistic) Carl Schmitt-influenced view of the autopoietic Gaia as disembedded, hierarchical, negentropic and closed. This critique can be extended to the disembedded instrumentalist assumptions of actor-network theory more generally. Haraway, not Latour, is dealing in the register of experience. Central to this is the question of meaning. What I'm saying with Barad is that technological experience needs to have a very important dimension of meaning. You do not have to be a 'humanist' to have notions of meaning. But you must deal in the paradigm of experience. Maturana's cognitivism presumes cognitive experience by the animal or cellular system and its environment. It is perception rather than symbolic encounter, but it has to do with meaning and experience. Von Uexküll's (2010) *A Foray into the Worlds of Animals and Humans* is subtitled 'With a Theory of Meaning'. Animals clearly have perception; they also have imaginations, looking backwards with memory and forward in anticipation. They do not, however, symbolize. But this is not just matter but also meaning at stake.

Chapter 7 addresses aesthetic experience. It starts in the ambience of Kant's third, aesthetic critique. Here we see straightaway that there is a vastly different type of experience at stake. The *Critique of Pure Reason*, the First Critique, is the mould both for positivism and neoclassical economics in its foregrounding of objective knowledge and causation. First-Critique Kant makes *homo economicus* possible. The Third Critique, *Critique of Judgment* (2009 [1790]) is rather different. No longer is there the objectivity of the distanced observer, which for us is destructive of experience. Instead, there is immediate subjectivity; we are more or less in the world with what we are experiencing. The art object is vastly different from the First Critique's object of physics. Newtonian mechanism is replaced by a more or less vital organicism. In the Third Critique, nature and the work of art are no longer governed by causal laws. Neither is subjectivity, as it moves outside of the realm of necessity. Transposed to the realm of practice, the observer from the First Critique becomes the actor of instrumental reason, becomes *homo economicus*. Here we treat nature and others as means to our ends. In the Second Critique, morality and the realm of freedom, we treat others and things as pure ends (*Endzweck*). In the Third Critique, both judger and judged are instead pure means (*Zweckmäßigkeiten*). This is the aesthetic of pure means implied in Walter Benjamin's essay on language. It translates into a politics of pure means, an anarchist politics, in Benjamin's (1977b) 'Critique of Violence' (Agamben 2005). Things and humans become their own internal ends as on the lines of a self-organizing system. This is at the same time an anarchist politics. Negri and others among operaista thinkers have spoken about formal and real subsumption in economic and social life more generally. In the Third Critique, there is no such subsumption of particular by universal; instead, as in English Common Law, there is only the juxtaposition of particulars. Such a (quasi-anarchist) politics of means without ends, without subsumption of particular by universal, we see in Occupy and Hong Kong's Umbrella Movement.

We move on to the art of radical experience in Francis Bacon as described by Deleuze (2005). Here we see a radical openness to experience, in which the sense data of Hume's cognitive sense data becomes sensation, in which the logic of sense becomes the logic of sensation, like an electric charge, flows of desire, registered as sensation. This is not a question of flows in excess of form, not a sort of Bataille-type *informe*. The aesthetics of sensation in Bacon's, say, 'screaming popes' take on form, take on very unstable form, as particular slides into general, in a more or less topological formation and deformation that is always in process. This is not about the qualitative extensity of the Renaissance, but again an issue of quantitative intensity. This is a Humean not a Kantian radially empiricist subjectivity. One for which judgment is beside the point. We segue to Chinese art in the work of François Jullien (2016). Again, like Deleuze, this is art without the classical Western subject. Without the subject and the transcendental unity of apperception. Without even Augustinian free will. At stake is a situated intersubjectivity, where the view is neither from above nor below but from a sort of infinity, trapped in an infinity. At stake in the art – in say Song Dynasty paintings of Huang Shan (Yellow Mountain) – in these *shanshui* (山水) or landscapes is a great object without form or maybe also in a process again of formation and deformation, one that is going nowhere (Jullien 2009). If Western art in the mould of the Renaissance focuses on the object and the foreground, at stake in Chinese art, which is as much decorative as beautiful, is the background: a background that, like forms of life, is always in process.

— 2 —

EXPERIENCE IN ANTIQUITY: ARISTOTLE'S A POSTERIORI TECHNICS

To understand modern experience fully, it is necessary to understand it in the context of what it emerged in contrast to: that is, ancient experience in classical Greece.[1] This book argues that experience is a characteristically modern phenomenon and depends on the emergence of the free will. But it is of importance to see what it emerges from. This chapter looks at such a precursor of modern experience (in the human sciences) through considering the Aristotelian background. We do it specifically through an inquiry into what is technics in Aristotle. We look at his technics because (1) it is not a priori, but very much a posteriori; (2) technics is a basis of 'technological experience' – and of the 'making' in aesthetic experience – addressed in Chapters 6 and 7; and (3) Chapter 4 looks at economic experience, and technics gives us also a bit of a basis for this, as does our short discussion in this chapter of Aristotle's chrematistics. Chrematistics is very much a template for the unlimited accumulation of capital. Aristotle's most focused discussion of technics is in the *Nicomachean Ethics*, also the place of, together with the *Politics*, the most important source for his political thinking. To engage with the technics as we do below is also to engage with Aristotle on praxis; that is, with his politics: his equally a posteriori politics. This thus also is a basis for Chapter 5 on Arendt's a posteriori politics.

Let us have a systematic look at where technics or *technē* stands in the *Nicomachean Ethics*. It is, for the *Stanford Encyclopedia of Philosophy* the best place in the Greeks to look at this. But we need

---

[1] Parts of this chapter have previously appeared in German in J. Lamla, H. Laux, H. Rosa and D. Strecker (eds.) *Handbuch der Soziologie*, Frankfurt: UTB, 2014. This is substantially rewritten.

to remember that *Nicomachean Ethics* (NE) is not primarily about *technē*, but about wisdom or practical reason: it is an ethics. Through the NE, we see such wisdom as defined in contrast to both 'theoretical reason' and technical, or 'productive', 'expertise'. We want in what follows to ask what kind of politics is possible in today's technologically driven media cultures. We want to explore an idea of technics that is the other side of instrumental reason: a technics that offers a critical alternative to that prescribed in neoliberal and neoclassical economics. So, we are looking at technics to think about an ethics and a politics. There is a more or less explicit connection in Aristotle between technics and economic activity. We began to address this in Chapter 1 in starting to look at Aristotle's chrematistics (Alliez 1991; Vogl 2014). Thus, I also want to understand modes of economic activity in terms of technics.

Technics would be for Aristotle part of the substantive economy, in very much Polanyi's sense as discussed in Chapter 1. In this sense technics and economic activity in the polis would be rather opposite to the excesses of unlimited wealth accumulation in long-distance trade external to the polis, which is a question of chrematistics. In the polis, prices were set fairly with an eye to justice. The institution of the market would set prices in chrematistics, which stands in contrast to the institutions of household, tribe and polis setting prices in *technē*-related activities. *Technē* helps build – as we see in Arendt (Chapter 5) – the public worlds in which political praxis takes place. This for me is very much of a piece with Amartya Sen's (2009) *The Idea of Justice*, which develops a more or less, not positivist, but instead empiricist, notion of justice, based not on rights but on 'capabilities'. This non-juridical notion of justice is developed in contrast to John Rawls's more a priori rationalism. A central text for Sen's justice is Smith's *Moral Sentiments*. Sen contrasts Smith's reasoned empiricism with Hume's more radical sense-based empiricism. Similarly, the *Nicomachean Ethics* can give us a more or less reasoned 'empiricist' notion of technics.

2.1 Technics and Praxis: Aristotle

For Aristotle, all things have functions (*ergon*), and all species have their own goods. The second sentence of *Nicomachean Ethics* states, 'the good is that which all things seek' (2002: 95). This good is their end, their telos. This is a pluralism, not derivable from the one Platonic Good. It is a pluralism of function, in which both humans and things have capabilities (Sen) or functions.[2] Aristotle states that the specifically human good is happiness (*eudaimonia*), and that happiness comes not from good fortune but from the 'excellent activity of the soul'. These excellences are also the virtues – courage, justice, moderation, prudence (MacIntyre 1981). This is not an ethics based on an imperative or rules or even norms, but a question of character. These excellent activities or 'excellences' are a question of character excellence (*ēthikē aretē*), in which *ēthikē* (*ēthos*) refers to character. These excellences are not expertise or *technē*. The foremost of all the expertises for Aristotle is political expertise (2002: 96): this enables others to develop and practise their excellences, to practise the good. These excellences all operate through a paradigm of, not theoretical knowledge, but instead wisdom. The expertises, or *technē*, are not these excellences, are not these virtues. Sarah Broadie in her introduction (2002a: 19) to the *Nicomachean Ethics* is explicit that the excellences, i.e. practical reason or wisdom, work through practical preparedness, but that such preparedness is very different from an 'ability', or skilful expertise.

Again, for Aristotle 'the good is that which all things seek'. For humans both practical reason and expert knowledge seek some good. So, all things have *ergon* or function and all seek the good or goods. Goods are also ends. These ends are in some ways similar to the notion of final cause. And the discourse of cause is important in NE. Thus, happiness is not by chance but by 'genuine causes', and the best of these causes is the cultivation of excellence (Broadie 2002b: 289). In this, happiness is the principle (*archē*) and cause of the other goods (NE: 108).

Each thing has its own end, its own good. For productive or technical expertise, the good is *a good*. That is, among these ends, some are activities and some are products 'over and above those activities themselves'. The goods here, the products, are for Aristotle by their nature (NE: 95) 'better' than the activities themselves. What are these goods? For military expertise, they are military victory; for household management, it is wealth; for shipbuilding, ships; for medicine, the end is health (NE: 100). For technics, the good is goods 'with qualifications': for example, the good of the body in health is a qualifying expression in a given project. In contrast, for excellences the good is the activity, not separate from any product. For excellences this is the 'good without qualifications'. The good without

---

[2] I do not think this disagrees with Bernard Stiegler's (1998) views on technics and memory in *Technics and Time*; I think it complements his position.

qualifications is the topic of 'the practical philosophy of ethics' (NE: 101). Here the end is not necessarily better than the activity, though only with realization of this end is an activity of practical reason complete. To repeat, all things have functions and the human telos or *archē* is happiness. In this regard, the human function is 'activity of the soul in accordance with reason' (NE: 110).

The good in *technē* in all projects can be an activity itself or a product (process) that survives the activity (NE: 95). But even in a service the good is not the activity itself as it is in practical wisdom. Unlike in praxis where the good is *sui generis*, the good in technics is always 'subordinate to another'. Hence the bridle maker's bridle is subordinate to the general's horse riding. Even political expertise – as distinct from political wisdom – makes goods for others. Hence the idea of a public servant, i.e. subordinate to the desire (*orexis*) of another. The *Nicomachean Ethics* addresses the 'chief good' of happiness, or happiness through excellent activities. Political expertise will make this possible for others. Thus, political objectives are the *ergon* of government, which is to make excellent citizens who are doers (*praktikos*) of fine things (NE: 109). If the doctor needs to know about the body, the political expert should know about the soul.

If the good is a universal – as is the truth of Aristotle's theoretical reason – then both goods and products as goods are somehow *particulars*. Unlike for science or philosophy, for both technics and practical reason, at stake is the particular. The idea of happiness and the good as rational excellent activities is neither a prescription nor a concrete end. The ends of practical activities as well as their means are particulars. So are the ends of productive activity. Thus, for the doctor and much of technics the good that is sought is not health in general, but *this person's* health. The good of technical expertise as opposed to praxis is a question of completeness, not of universality, because we are mainly operating in the realm of the particular. The ends of technical expertise are less complete, thus more qualified.

Both excellences and expertise (though not theoretical reason) work through goods. But expertise is also always a question of production (*poetike*). Socrates and Plato understood the *value* of goods as derived from the form of the good. Aristotle rejects the Platonic good because it is not practicable. For Plato, the distinctive nature of each good is irrelevant as to its value. In Aristotle value does come from excellent activity of the soul, i.e. practical reason. This is the human good. This is not Plato's form of the good, but the human good as character excellence, as 'excellent rational activity' (Broadie 2002b: 266–72). All other types of value are derivative of this, including the value of products or goods. Value for Aristotle, then, is derivative of happiness or *eudaimonia*, via the practice of the various excellences – moderation, justice, courage, prudence. And the value of a good – produced through technical expertise – is derivative of these. 'Technical goods' (as distinct from ethical goods) can be a basis of another's excellence. This can happen through exchange, though this is not exchange-value. It is non-utilitarian, unlike value in neoclassical economics. It is also different than Mauss's symbolic or gift exchange, though it may be in some way derivative of gift exchange. For Aristotle, substance was not the basis of value. Instead, something like final cause or teleological cause is. Here value is an end: it is an ethical good as an excellent activity. Goods as well as theoretical reasoning can be means to these ends.

We must note that substances were particulars while their qualities are universals. Hence Aristotle in *The Categories* notes that substance is unlike the other categories. Substances are particulars that universals like quantity and quality and white and straight qualify. Aristotle makes the distinction of substance and accident, in which the qualities or predicates are accidents. Yet it is these 'accidents' that are the universals, that are the most important categories. Value for its part inheres in the particular, in the particular ethical good or practice, from which the value of, also not universal but particular, technical goods are derived.

To rephrase, expert knowledge and character excellence seek some good. Technical expertise makes goods: goods, which are separate from the activity. Ethical goods or excellences are not separable from the activities: they are the activities. Finally, both technical expertise and the excellences aim for a sort of mean, for moderation. Yet it is only the latter that are specifically about a *hexis*, an ethical disposition. Dispositions are qualities, such as just, courageous. They are dispositions for activities. In addition, whereas technical expertise pertains to a given sphere, character excellence (from firm and unchanging dispositions) is about the whole person. In Aristotle, the value of a technical good is a question of the desire of another.

2.2 Against Theoretical Reason: Praxis, Technics, Contingency

Let us consider Aristotle's method. It is in an important sense more inductive, a posteriori and empiricist than it is deductive, a priori and rationalist. Aristotle wants to identify the first principle (*archē*) of ethics in NE. To identify the first principle, which will then be a sort of a priori starting point, he must get there with effectively inductive (*epagōgē*) and a posteriori argument. Aristotle starts with experience of everyday well-brought-up people who can discriminate right from wrong and good from bad (Broadie 2002b: 266–7). He assumes that intuitions regarding these phenomena are obvious. He looks at how in this everyday experience the best decisions (*prohairesis*) are made. From this line of argument, he arrives at the starting point, the *archē* of ethics, of this eudaimonic ethics in which happiness is excellent rational activities. This starting point, for Aristotle, is grasped sometimes by induction, sometimes through perception, sometimes through habituation (2002: 103–4).

Perhaps the best material to reflect on technics comes in Book VI, where there is a rigorous analytic distinction of theoretical reason from practical reason and technical expertise. Thus, the carpenter and the geometer look at the right angle in a different way: the geometer for what sort of thing it *is*, i.e. the truth; the carpenter for how it is useful as a product. Whereas theoretical reason deals with universals and with necessity, both practical reason and technical expertise deal with 'things that could be otherwise'; that is, with contingent things (NE 2002: 177). Practical reason is a question of wisdom, of *phronēsis*. And wisdom (*phronēsis*) is a question of 'decision' (*prohairesis*). If theoretical knowledge requires a *demonstration*, then practical reason requires a *decision*. On this view, theoretical reason works mainly deductively, as episteme. Theoretical reason, or episteme, is systematic knowledge. Deduction here is syllogistic thinking, starting from (necessary and eternal) universals and reasoning towards the truth of a particular. In such knowledge, which may be propositional, theoretical claims are about the sort of universals that qualify a particular p. Thus, horses are fast and four-legged, and (to systematic theological knowledge) God is ubiquitous, great, good, intelligent and resides in the heavens. In contrast to episteme or systematic knowledge, *phronēsis* or practical reason is about, not demonstration, but decision. Unlike demonstration *phronēsis* is not about proof or even mainly about argument: it is about decision, about making decisions. *Sophia* or 'intellectual accomplishment' is a combination of *epistēmē* (systematic knowledge) and *nous* (intelligence). Whereas *epistēmē* reasons a priori from the starting point, *nous* works inductively from experience to grasp the starting point's first principles. *Phronēsis* for its part works from a combination of (1) 'disposition' (*hexes*), which is excellence of character; and (2) wisdom as cleverness (*denotēs*). We make a decision in accordance with a 'prescription' (*orthos logos*). But this decision is not a set of rules (NE: VI.1): the prescription is from the situation itself. This stands in contrast to the more abstract notions of justice in Rawls and Habermas, or Kant, contract theory and Plato. We remember here that *technē* too is rooted in the particular and contingent. If science deals in the episteme, the systematic knowledge of universals, then the technics of the engineer or Web designer or algorithm writer are working in the particular, the contingent: in the situation. This correct prescription (NE: VI.1) applies also to the specialized knowledge of the doctor. This is not *phronēsis* or wisdom: i.e. not a question of what is good for the human being as a whole. But the doctor is acting *as a doctor*: he is pursuing not what is good for his own eudemonia, but instead what is good for the health of another.

At stake are two types of reason: theoretical or demonstrative reason and practical or 'deliberative reason' (NE VI.1: 1139.5–15). Demonstrative reason deals with universals and their truth, deliberative reason with the contingent, with things that 'could be otherwise'.[3] Deliberative reason, unlike *sophia*, does not come from the highest (geometer-like) part of the soul. Theoretical reason is scientific or *epistemonikon*, dealing with necessary and universal truths, while deliberative reason is *logistikon* or calculative (NE: 188), dealing with the contingent and the particular. The scientific grasp of a fact works through demonstration, through argument showing the cause or explanation of how a fact follows syllogistically from first principles' premises. Theoretical truth is a question of what is. Practical truth is instead a matter of the *right* decision. The right decision (*prohairesis*) comes from a combination of desire (*orexis*) and thought (*dianoia, nous*): a combination of true thought and right desire, in which desire is right largely through pointing in the right direction (NE: 177; Broadie 2002b: 362).

So, we have a trinity of theoretical truth, practical thought and productive thought or productive reason. If theoretical reason is a question of true and false, and practical reason about right and not-right, then productive (technical) reason is about well and badly (NE: 178; Broadie 2002b: 362). For Aristotle, as we see in VI.2, the main distinction is between theoretical reason on the one hand, and both practical and technical reason on the other. The distinction between practical and technical reason is only secondary and derivative. To reason theoretically is to work deductively, while to reason

---

[3] In this context, it would seem to me that deliberative democracy in contemporary critical theory operates too closely to the universals of theoretical reason. The kind of justice or ethics or politics advocated in this chapter is, with Aristotle and I think Sen, one that is contingent and situational, yet is reasoned: based on a kind of empirical reason.

practically or technically is to give an account. Aristotle distinguished between the effectively inductive reason of the master craftsman and the more or less pure empiricism of the journeyman. Unlike the journeyman, the master can teach. And to teach is to give an account (*Stanford Encyclopedia of Philosophy* 2010). Here even theoretical reason is not about 'semantic properties of propositions' (Broadie 2002b: 374), but like practical reason, a relationship of the mind to the domain it addresses. Theoretical reason, too, entails a disposition of mind and the soul, in which dispositions are the non-rational part of the soul. The dispositions are, however, 'derivatively rational' (Broadie 2002b: 363) in that they obey the higher parts of soul. Unlike theoretical reason, both practical and technical reason are modes of thought that 'set in motion'. Both bring about change in the world. Compared to the theorist, the builder is like an efficient cause but with only contingent effect.[4] The difference is that practical thought does this autonomously while technical thought is heteronomous. The technical is derivative of the practical: for example, the technical process of building the wall is dependent on another's practical decision to expand their house or expand the city.

For Plato's Academy, *epistēmē* is systematic knowledge of what is: what is by necessity, without qualification and eternal. Plato is less interested in what 'could be otherwise'. Platonic justice and his philosopher-kings are a priori and categorical, while Aristotelian justice and politics are instead situational and deal with contingency. Contingency on this view is what is 'hypothetically necessary'; that is, hypothetically necessary for some end or necessary under some condition. This end is never demonstration, but instead world-changing. This is also involved in technical reason. For example, for the contingent end of building a house, foundations are necessary, are hypothetically necessary. Again, against Plato, before *epistēmē* can engage in deduction (*sullogismos*), *nous* is involved in thinking through particulars in order to arrive at the universal principles that serve as a starting point. Here deduction is literally syllogistic thinking in subject–predicate propositions in which both terms are logical universals. Aristotle contrasts the excellence of practical reason to the production of *technē*: to *technē*'s productive *hexis* (*hexis meta logou poētikē*). Technical expertise is driven, not by *eudaimonia* but by empirical ends. These are contingent principles and contingent things. Aristotle identifies two types of cause of contingent things – first nature

---

[4] Indeed, all the causes are related to the contingent in that the thing explained in causation is particular and contingent.

or the *physis* of a natural substance, and second technical expertise, where the source is other than the material at stake (NE: VI.3 and 4)

In VI.5 and VI.6, Aristotle distinguishes between processes of deliberation and production. In decisions, the wise are 'those who can deliberate well regarding their own good from the viewpoint of life in general. Life in general is a very different focus from the concern of *technē* with the empirical thing. Praxis is about deliberation on your own projects while *technē* considers what customers expect from you. In *technē* there are more established sets of rules or techniques, which themselves rule out very much deliberation. Wisdom is in regard to a whole life, while technical expertise is in regard to departments of life. The producer asks, 'what is the best I can do to achieve the special end T?', while the question for conduct is, 'what is the best I can do?' (Broadie 2002b: 359).

Happiness is an honourable and godlike thing. In God there is no distinction between disposition and activity. The divine is thus pure activity and God is a (not universal but singular) substance such that to be it is *eo ipso* to be good. Only for God does efficient cause have necessary effect. The highest thought for humans is, like for God, discursive thought or intellectual accomplishment (*sophia*). In a sense God is the great geometer. Only God's geometry has unmediated effect in changing the world. For man, theoretical wisdom plays a subsidiary part in praxis or conduct. It is desire that identifies the ends, and only then does theoretical reason devise means for such ends. Even technical activities are more rule-bound than *phronēsis*. Technical activities in some, but not most, cases are deliberative, where one can talk of a wise doctor or a wise architect. Technical activities are in contrast calculative and not epistemic: thus, the engineer focuses on the contingent and particular. Conduct is mainly driven by character excellence (*ethikē aretē*) or virtues (MacIntyre 1981). This disposition can filter out unacceptable means to achieve ends. Both praxis and *technē* are about man. The heavens, God or the gods, the universe and mathematical reason and not man are among the highest things. The 'objects of intellectual accomplishment' (of *nous* and *epistēmē*) are not accidental but 'sublime'. Thus, *sophia* deals with what is always the same: a same which is never for others, but always in-itself. In contrast, wisdom considers things in relation to the reasoning individual, and decisions are based on the relations of things to the self. Wisdom depends on the nature of its adherent in a way that neither theory nor *technē* does.

Sections VI.7 and VI.8 of NE address perception. The target is Plato's dismissal of perception: his radical dualism of sense-perception

41

and reason. Aristotle seems to be proposing a sort of perception-based reason or a way that reason, instead of deducing, perceives. He starts with a distinction between the architectonic of the master builder and the ground-level view. Thus, he distinguishes political expertise from political wisdom. Here it is political expertise that more closely resembles theoretical reason. Political expertise provides an architectonic of legislation, and its institutional techniques. Wisdom, by way of contrast, is about not legislation but decrees, which are to do with the ground level of the particular. Wisdom has for its object (not the empirical thing of *technē*) but 'what comes last' (*eschaton*) in the process of deliberation. Only with the completion of the *eschaton* is wisdom fully practical. This needs to be a practicable end. So while *technē* can be close to *phronēsis's* particular, it can approach also the universality of theoretical reason. It does not take a lot here to see in germ Carl Schmitt's (1996) notion of the political, in its promulgation of decrees of *das Politische* versus the institutional formalism of *die Politik*. Here, too, there is a notion – like in the late Heidegger – of technology linked to theoretical reason rather than a more *phronēsis*-like, open-ended idea of technology in, say, Simondon and Stiegler. The practical ends of *das Politische* or other human ends are identified partly through perception. Here, perception, unlike in Plato, is not divorced from reason. If you are concerned with your health, you will eat light meat and not red meat, for reasons of digestion. Reasoning in this is not sufficient; you must also be able to identify what is light meat in, say, chicken or fish. This is a question of perception. It is perception as informed by *nous*. Thus, the intellectual accomplishment of *nous* arrives at 'basic definitions (accounts) that make other things intelligible' while 'practical reason wisely reaches good decisions through which other things become practicable'. So, the object of deliberation may be less a question of *epistēmē* than of perception. This is not unmediated sense-perception, like taste or smell, but more like the geometer who approaches an unanalysed hexagon and sees two triangles. This is wisdom as a sort of, as it were, inductive analysis, or perception as inductive analysis.

Let us summarize:

1. *Technē* (and *phronēsis*) presumes that both humans and nonhumans have functions (*ergon*).
2. *Technē* produces goods, which are resources that are governed by the projects, the *phronēsis*, of others. This is the source of the value of technics-produced goods. There is a relation of this, as Berthoud (2002) notes, to Marxian use-value. In Aristotle, the

price of a good is set by other institutions than markets, and needs to be a just price. The value of a good lies in its institutional world building. From polis as mediated by tribe and household.
3. These goods are derivative of good as the end of ethical activities, of others.
4. Technics (and *phronēsis*) are driven – unlike episteme – by a logic of not the universal (necessary and eternal) but the particular (contingent and transient).
5. Neither *technē* (nor especially *phronēsis* – again unlike episteme) are primarily rule-determined. Both are non-juridical.
6. *Technē* is driven by *phronēsis* and not by episteme.
7. Technics is not irrational. It entails a mode of reasoning, just like *phronēsis* is a form of reasoning.
8. *Technē*, unlike episteme, does not work in an a priori mode. It is instead based on experience leading to a posteriori reasoning through giving an account.

2.3 Form and Substance: Ancients, Christians and Moderns

Let us situate this a bit more in Aristotle's thought. First, in Aristotle, technics and praxis do connect to ideas of form and substance. Aristotle's discussions of form and substance are most specifically in the *Physics*, the *Categories* and the *Metaphysics*. Aristotle, of course, gives us hylomorphism, in which a being or a substance (*ousia*) is the combination of matter and form. Matter is *hulē* and form is *morphē*. Hylomorphism is already different from antiquity's atomistic or mechanistic explanations. It also rejects Plato's notion of forms, which are radically separate from and transcendental to matter. In humans, for Aristotle, matter and form connect to substance in man as the soul, which is the basis of – which animates – life. For Aristotle, unlike the atomists, substances are singular: they are not particulars subsumed by universals. Each substance is thus different from every other substance. With Aquinas and Christianity, of course, these become Christian souls, all different from each other. Aquinas and the Church take on not just Aristotle's hylomorphism but also his opposition to chrematistics, substituting for it a notion of commutative justice. That is, for Aquinas as for Aristotle, it was not the supply and demand of markets that were to set prices.

This is important because by extension we can think of the polis itself as a substance: as a substantial form. Hence every polis would be different to every other polis and be comprised in some sense of formed matter. We see in Chapter 4, in the German Historical School, in Polanyi and in economic anthropology, that subjective experience, a posteriori thinking and substantivism (as opposed to formalism) are linked with one another. For Aristotle, a substantial form is different to an accidental form. Substantial forms contain only and all of necessary predicates (say colour, texture, shape, etc.) that make a substance what it is. Accidental form is to do with predicates without which a substance, a being, say Socrates, would still be what he, she or it is. Substances are caused by the four causes – material, formal, efficient (agential) and final (teleological, purpose) and qualified by the predicates without which they would not be what they are. Though substances are importantly driven by form, it is their matter that is the principle of their individuation, which makes each substance unique. Here again Aristotle differed from Plato and thought what made one human different to another were the material and efficient (agent) causes of their parents.

Aristotle distinguished economics from chrematistics. *Oikonomia* prescribed the acquisition of wealth in terms of what is necessary for the life and reproduction of the *oikos* or household, the household (*oikos*) being a natural and not political entity. But the household was driven by the principle of the polis, by the substance of associations from family to tribe to polis. Chrematistics took place, not at all in the agora, which is part and parcel of the polis, but in the more 'supply-and-demand' markets of trade and long-distance Mediterranean trade outside of the polis. Chrematistics thus followed not the logic of the cyclical and natural time of the seasons, the time of polis and household, but a rectilinear time, that will also be the temporality of capital accumulation. So outside of and excessive to the polis, whose substance is an amalgam of form and matter, is the substance-less and formlessness of chrematistics. It is interesting that the phenomenon of just price, as distinct from 'chrematistic' supply and demand, operated in mediaeval times. Here prices were largely set by producers' guilds in conversation with city councils. The guilds were also spaces of worship, and heavily Christian. Jewish merchants in Venice could not be admitted to the guild. Thus, a polis sort of principle combined with Aquinas-Christian anti-usury just price and with trade union-like power.

What then is the connection from substance and form in Aristotle to us moderns? How do we get from Aristotle to the juxtaposition of form and substance in classical sociology and the substantivist critique of form in today's neoclassical and neoliberal economy?

44

The transition from ancient to modern goes through Christianity. Thus Hegel in the *Phenomenology* saw the transition from ancient substance to modern subject as mediated by Christianity. Sociologists will have grown up with Weber's thesis about the Protestant ethic that also is implicitly about bases of not just capitalism but also modernity. We could say that Plato, with his a priori, is a formalist, while Aristotle, who gives lots of attention to matter and works largely a posteriori, is a substantialist. Plato's forms become substance as the forms become also material. Plato's formalist good becomes substantial as it 'embeds' in the good life of the polis. And the good life of individual human beings is indeed ensouled. Yet it is finite and every one is different from every other. This is clearly what is at stake in Carl Schmitt's rejection of political theology, and we see in Chapter 5 Hannah Arendt's acceptance of the theological in the political.

The mediator again from antiquity to modernity must be Christianity. And the specific difference, apart from the enhanced focus on the human soul in the Christians, was surely creation. Aquinas's starting point was Aristotle. Augustine, who for Arendt and us is the transition to modernity in the sense of the free will, was more influenced by Plato and Neoplatonism. He had read, as a young man, Aristotle's *Categories* and thought of the ensoulment of matter as a vivification, hence his view on abortion, questioning the moment at which the foetus was vivified by a soul. But 900 years later in Aquinas's Church, the Augustinians were arch anti-Aristotelians, almost fully other-worldly in orientation. Aquinas was a moderate Aristotelian, and the 'extreme' Aristotelians tended towards questioning creation and God as the final and uncondi-tioned cause. Aquinas's Christianized Aristotle is at the same time an Aristotelianized Christianity.

But once it is not matter, indeed material cause, that causes individ-uation, making each person different from every other, it becomes God who is formal, efficient and final cause rolled into one. God also becomes the principle of individuation, making all Christian souls different from one another. This is implicit in Aristotle's notion of God as the unmoved mover. In the *Physics* and *Metaphysics* Aristotle looks to explain change not in any particular being, which can be accounted for by the four causes, but to explain the basis of change itself. In this he refers to the pre-Socratics Anaxagoras and Parmenides for another notion of cause. In Parmenides nothing can come from nothing, so the cause of all motion must come from an uncaused cause, a prime mover. This unmoved mover is never completely central to Aristotle, whose focus is on natural and biological bodies. It is of course fully central to Christianity. Central, then, becomes where in Christianity do we get the transition from God, this unmoved mover, this prime mover, to human free will? This – that is, the free will in man who was created in God's image – was and is the subject of endless theological debates. Consider, for example, Leibniz and theodicy. But what if we look back from the point of view of the modern subject? The free will as the subject of modernity? Blumenberg (1985) looks to Augustine and his break with Manichaeism and Gnosticism. Arendt to looks to Augustine and the City of God.

There needs to be in both the movement from God as uncaused cause to man also as uncaused. In the Son of Man, Jesus Christ, we are halfway there. Also, of course, in the Old Testament, God created man in his image. God in this sense also gave man understanding and judgment. For Aristotle, these attributes are natural and come in man as biological strata in the great chain, with plants, which can sense and reproduce but not move, to animals who also have movement and also memory, to man who also has understanding and uses words as symbols (Benjamin 1977a).

Augustine is again very much the Neoplatonist and Aquinas the neo-Aristotelian. The Christians drew here heavily (Augustine) on Plato's *Timaeus*, with God as the great blacksmith, and Aquinas more on Aristotle's *De Anima*. In each case eudemonia is at stake. For Plato, his was the mutual harmony of the parts of the soul. Augustine found in Plato a way out from his previous Manichaeism, where there were two principles, but in Plato only one principle, as the forms fully were to govern the profane. So for Plato eudemonia is a question of the soul and not the body, but the soul is immortal. Augustine sees the eternal good as eternal life in the City of God. If for Plato eudemonia is a question of harmony of parts of the soul, and thus is other-worldly, for Aristotle it is a question of the virtues. The virtues are a mixture of the internal and external goods, of the other-worldly and this-worldly. The virtues are ends in themselves, they incorporate eudemonia, they are not just means to other super-natural ends, to other-worldly ends, literally the other world of the City of God, as they are for the Christians.

Both Augustine and Aquinas are closer to the Stoics than to Aristotle on eudemonia. Aristotle's this-worldliness proposes a balance of internal and external goods for eudemonia: indeed courage as a virtue and even moderation deal with external goods. The Stoics and Christians want to reject external goods for internal goods only. Even the Stoics are too this-worldly for Augustine. For them, pain in this life is a final good, a virtue. For Augustine the final

46

good (God) and eudemonia are only to be realized in the afterlife, in peace and harmony with God. We can detect here also the transition from the natural cyclical time of the Greeks to the rectilinear time of the Christians and the moderns. Rectilinearity is the time of both the individual in the City of God and chrematistics as accumulation of capital. The difference with Aquinas, who takes Aristotle much more seriously, is that he thinks the virtues of the *Nicomachean Ethics* are quite important. Only he wants to replace these natural virtues with theological virtues. What happens to substance? Well, God is a substance also for Aristotle, but is uncaused substance. Aristotle's man is fully caused. Man does not need to be uncaused cause, because the Greeks and Aristotle were not creationist. God did not create man.

Once man's eudemonia is separated from the polis – the just man and the just polis also in Plato – then it becomes much more just man and God. Man becomes that much closer himself to uncaused cause. The theological virtues change vastly from the classical ones. Justice, reason, courage and moderation are displaced by faith, hope and love (charity): faith in God, love of God, hope for the afterlife. The substance of God – and its ethos of moral obligation from man – displaces the ethical substance of the polis. Both Augustine and Aquinas see eudemonia in beatitude, which is unattainable by heathens because it is only attainable with God's (Aquinas) help as Divine Grace. Aristotle was a mortalist. Plato was not, so the soul that Augustine took from Plato could be immortal and immaterial. Aquinas saw Aristotle's prime mover as the perfect good, in comparison to which secular virtues could only be instruments to help attain this good. Finally, Aristotle's ethics in the polis were not primarily a question of moral obligation. Faith, hope, love, uprightness (righteousness) were all about moral obligations (Aquinas). The virtues become moral obligations, no longer embedded in ethical substance.

So we roll into modernity and here it is Hegel who gives us a view of both substance and subject, which influences us enormously. Hegel does talk about the move from ancient substance to modern subject in the introduction to the *Phenomenology*. And then he starts the *Phenomenology* not with substance, but instead with subject. That is, with subjective experience. That is why he calls this subject 'consciousness'. And it engages not with objects but with appearances; that is, with 'phenomena'. That is, not with objective reality but with what appears to consciousness. Dialectical movement and reasoning does not stop with this but moves through reflecting on

47

themselves and taking themselves as objects necessary to the subject of objective experience. If Aristotle married form and matter in substance, the Christian watershed drains matter from substance, and at the same time separates the very virtues from the material world. Substance for all purposes in Kant disappears, as we cannot know things themselves, and what is left is radically separated form and matter with form taking the position of the subject in the making of objective experience. So Kant's form becomes a transcendental condition (featuring time, space, cause and the unified subject), and fully separated from the 'content', the matter of experience. When Descartes gives us thinking substance (cogito) and extended substance (matter, motion and – efficient – causation), substance is already marginalized. The cogito takes the place of form, while extended substance is, for all practical purposes, matter.

Yet substance makes a comeback in the classical sociologists. Marx gives us value-form and value-substance, Weber, formal and substantive rationality; Simmel, social forms versus life substance; and Durkheim, the substance of the sacred, which constitutes the forms of the profane and its classifications. Substance raises its head very much in combination with modern subjective experience. If form is dominant in objective experience, then substance is in subjective experience. Substance does not recognize the radical opposition between form and matter: in substance, form is embedded in matter; transcendentals re-embed in the empirical. Substance always embeds form – say, economic forms – in matter. On this account, subjective experience is material, but only when it is dialectally material. All four of the classical sociologists were cognizant of the tension between form and substance. This is apparent when we look in Chapter 4 at the *Methodenstreit*, and Weber on objectivity: it is the tension between positivism and interpretive sociology. All four of the classics straddled this methodological divide: not that they were fence sitters, but they were aware of the tension. Durkheim might be of signal interest in this context. Durkheim's positivism is far different from Weberian. Weber, insofar as he is positivist, gives us an objective observer and an objective social actor, rationally choosing like *homo economicus*. Durkheim as positivist gives us surely an objectivist observer on Newtonian lines, but his social actors, which are also those of anthropology, are embedded in culture and in subjective experience. In Durkheim, positivist forms are constituted by anti-positivist and subjective experiential religious substance. You get the forms of classification in the profane that are constituted by the substance of religious life in the sacred. The sacred is always primary and is 'in excess' – as Durkheim's admirer Georges Bataille intoned, of the profane. The '*informe*' is always in excess of form, the *économie générale* always in excess of the restricted and formal economy. This excess is, on the one hand, chaos: it is thus *informe*. It is, on the other hand, substance: generalized substance.

Forms are disembedded, general and objective; substances are singular, subjectively experienced and embedded. Thus exchange-value is what Marx calls the 'value form'. It is comprised of inter-changeable units like atoms. In exchange value, universal subsumes particular just as capital subsumes labour. The singular – that is, difference, and which entails substance – disappears. In use-value in contrast, each use-value is different from every other. Use-values are singular: they are subjectively encountered, like *your* phone or *your* iPad. They are embedded in culture and in everyday life: they are embedded in forms of life. Thus economic anthropology needs to be substantive economics. Thus Marxism must be much more than just the formalism of classical political economy's mechanistic materi-alism. Marx was not a classical political economist. *Capital* was the critique of political economy. Mechanical materialism yields pure form. It becomes dialectical through the critique of form via form's own excess as substance: of value form by value substance.

— 3 —

SUBJECTIVE EXPERIENCE: WILLIAM JAMES'S RADICAL EMPIRICISM

Chapter 2 considered Aristotle on experience. We looked at Aristotle's technics, his praxis, his idea of substance, his chrematistics, and saw an important a posteriorism, and a notion of substance that connects importantly to experience more generally. We know that Aristotle undercuts and rejects Plato's geometric apriorism for this a posteriori thinking. But is it experience? Is there a notion of experience at all in Aristotle and the Greeks? Or is experience instead something that is modern? Is the Christian watershed necessary for experience? William James wrote *The Varieties of Religious Experience* (1983 [1902]). Would this have been possible without James's Christianity? Would it have been possible without a Christian, a Judaeo-Christian, an Abrahamic transcendental God? There is something radically Protestant about James's religious experience. It is not the book of a Roman Catholic any more than is Kierkegaard's *Fear and Trembling* (1985). James may have been thoroughly neurotic but he did not fear and tremble. His religious experience – as Durkheim noted – as well as his stream-of-consciousness radical empiricism was fundamentally a psychology. But a psychology that can perhaps be best grasped through the prism of the religious. Is the precondition of experience Judaic or Christian? The answer must be Christian. Greek philosophy was first necessary in order to think Augustine's free will. If you do not think of beings as caused – if you do not think of man to begin with as, in the Greek sense, caused – then it is very difficult to think of man or even God as the uncaused cause. Christianity arose with the notion of the city (of God) in an urban setting and not the rural setting of the Old Testament. It was, as David Graeber (2014) notes, the shepherds against Babylon. Judaism defines itself against Baal worship, against idols and polytheism. Christianity defines itself against man (and the Son of Man) as caused.

50

James and subjective experience are dependent on both Augustine's Adam and Kierkegaard's Abraham. With Adam we have original sin. But original sin presupposes God having created Adam in His image. It presumes Adam and Eve's living in the Garden of Eden, endowed with freedom of the will. Kierkegaard's Abraham has long before already fallen. It is he who is promised by God at the age of ninety not only a son, but centuries of fruitfulness as the patriarch of a people. God then says, take Isaac up to Mount Moriah. Abraham says, 'here I am'. But his loyalty is only possible because of his free will. No fear and trembling without the free will. This is the stuff of subjective experience for both Kierkegaard and James's religious experience. This free will is the basis of what Hans Blumenberg (1985) explicitly and Hannah Arendt implicitly – in both cases effectively contra Carl Schmitt – see as the legitimacy (despite its theological foundations) of modernity. Without this free will, there is no objective experience or modern subject of Kant's First Critique. Without this free will, there is no aesthetic judgment and subjective experience of Kant's Third Critique. Without it, there is no Kierkegaard, Heidegger or Sartre and existentialism.

Subjective experience entails a phenomenology – one stretching from Hegel and fellow young Romantics Schelling and Hölderlin; from Hegel's *Phenomenology* through the young Marx. This is a phenomenology of a stream-of-consciousness temporality that we meet in Proust and Joyce, in Husserl, Bergson and Freud. What is psychoanalysis if not the temporality of the stream of (un)consciousness? In subjective experience and phenomenology, subject does not meet object and nor does it meet objective experience. Instead, consciousness engages with appearances, including the appearances in the religious imagination and in dreams. James's radical empiricism is an a posteriori challenge to positivism. His notion of the conjunction is a challenge to objective experience and positivism's causality. His foregrounding of percepts, against concepts, is an underscoring of the centrality of the imaginary to subjective experience. It is thus that this chapter studies William James.

3.1 James's Radical Empiricism

3.1.1 James and Hume: Radical Empiricism and Classical Empiricism

It is not actually the idea of radical empiricism that is most exciting in James, but in fact the notion of *experience*. It is indeed what he sees as a 'monism' of experience. We need to keep in mind that this is a monism that is at the same time for James a 'pluralism', what we would today call a 'multiplicity'. We need to situate James in intellectual history. James is writing in the wake of, and as opposed to, Herbert Spencer's positivism. Spencer wrote *Principles of Psychology* in 1855; James wrote his *Principles of Psychology* in 1890. James's psychology and philosophy are one and the same thing. Unlike, say, Kant and Husserl, who were fastidious in separating psychology from epistemology and philosophy, James, like his contemporary Nietzsche, was not. Both wanted also to tie knowledge and cognition to practical interest, in Nietzsche's case, of course, to the will to power, in James's to the consequences of 'truth'; that is, to pragmatism.

James influenced both Bergson and Freud, who were some twenty years younger. He, like Nietzsche and Bergson, features a notion of 'life'. Indeed, James's core notion of experience is at the same time 'life'. 'We feel our thought flowing as a life within us' (2003: 19). His stream of consciousness – or better stream of experience – is not dissimilar to the temporalization in Bergson's *Matter and Memory* (2011b), and Freud's unconscious. Whereas physical reality is clear and distinct, James's (2003: 24) mental reality is what he describes as '*durcheinander*', suffusing and interpenetrating, recalling the displacement and condensation of the Freudian unconscious and often proceeding through 'association'. He was part of the intellectual ambience Freud drew on. James recognizes that positivism has broken with Descartes' and Kant's dualism. But he thinks they have done this only to reconstitute this dualism of thought and matter in what he sees as positivism's 'Spinozistic' monism. For James, Spinoza's God – whose attributes are simultaneously thought and extension – is only a replay of such dualism. What James is going to do instead is give us a veritable monism of neither thought nor matter – from which thought and matter are only derivative categories and do not indeed 'exist'. He will give us instead a monism of *experience*. Like positivism, empiricism (in both Hume and James) talks the language, not only of sense-impressions, but of 'facts'. Jamesian empiricism stands very much in contradistinction to, say, Durkheim's positivism. James's *Varieties of Religious Experience* was published in 1902 and Durkheim's *Elementary Forms of Religious Life* in 1912. Durkheim was, of course, very aware of James's work. Durkheim's social fact, his positivist social fact, is very different from James's facts, which are instead psychological facts. Durkheim was opposed to the psychologism and empiricism of early British anthropology and Spencer and James.

James's pragmatism defines itself primarily against Hegelian idealism, and its proponent F.R. Bradley. Pragmatism and radical empiricism are more a naturalism than idealism. This, however, is not a materialism, in that both matter and thought derive from experience. James and pragmatism go beyond the British associationism of Locke, Hume and J.S. Mill. And how it goes beyond associationism is what makes James's pragmatism, not a classical but a radical empiricism.[1] James investigates the associations not just of ideas but also of objects. James finds another way than Kant to move beyond Humean scepticism. Kant gives us a subsumption of Hume's particular by a universal (the 'transcendental unity of apperception') that makes knowledge possible. For James, in contrast, knowledge is made possible through the bridges or connectors between experiences. Focus is on the 'facts of consciousness'. And the bridge between these facts of consciousness is itself experienced.[2] So James radicalizes empiricism, so that the facts of consciousness – as distinct from external events – are primary. These facts of consciousness are what constitute experience. Knowledge is possible through the connections, the associations between these experiences. The bridges, the connectors, themselves are experienced.

There is a radicalization of contingency in James's notion of knowledge. His pragmatism takes this further in that its particulars or facts are also the facts of *practical* reason. Here, true beliefs are those proving useful to believers. James in 'What Pragmatism Means' insists that these 'facts' are themselves not true. Instead they simply 'are'. It is not in (deductive) demonstration but in *deliberation* that the facts of theory find their truth. It is their consequences in practice that make facts true. For James and pragmatism, truth is a function of beliefs that start in and terminate among fact. That is, knowledge starts in and ends in, not the universal, but the particular. James gives us a bridge between the facts that are themselves experiences and understood in terms of 'conjunction'. We experience the contiguous facts and their conjunctions. But even this conjunction does not become true until it bridges over again into practical activities. This truth, as a combination of fact and conjunction, makes up

---

[1] James's empiricism, in comparison to Hume's, is more a radicalization of experience than it is of the psychological fact. Hume's empiricism is much more one of the brute fact; James's of an originary experience.

[2] We will see below that Kant himself saw this as a kind of synthesis. But a synthesis linking two particulars is far different from one of subsumption. Hence Deleuze's desiring machines give you a synthesis of linkage, while Kant's subject gives us a priori synthetic judgments.

not a proposition but a judgment. Here we see the centrality of 'function'. There is clearly a bit of Darwinism in this, and surely positivism was Darwinist. It was Darwin more than Newton who sparked positivism. For James, we, like animals, live in a physical environment. For humans, this environment is a mosaic of diverse experiences. Through belief we put some order on this chaos.

Barton Perry (2003) compares rationalists as 'men of principles' with empiricists who are 'men of facts'. Whereas principles are universals, these facts are particulars. Aristotle in the *Nicomachean Ethics* makes the distinction between theoretical reason's universalism, necessity and eternity, on the one hand, and the particularity, contingency and transience of *phronēsis* or practical reason, on the other. The truths of radial empiricism are also like *phronēsis* in their transience. They are always 'hypothetical' truths that can be revised. Similarly, contingency is defined in the *Nicomachean Ethics* by its 'hypothetical' nature. Like in *Nicomachean Ethics* and indeed Daoism, James's focus is less on action and a completed action and more on ongoing activity. Experience is much more a question of activity than action, unlike the unit act of neoclassical economics, or Weber's and Parson's sociology. Radical empiricism and pragmatism also give a temporality that is much more than the Newtonian temporality of a succession of presents of positivism. This temporality resides in 'the meaning of a proposition' which is 'in some particular consequence of our future practical experience' (Barton Perry 2003: vi). As in Bergson and phenomenology, for James, every now contains a memory and a future in it, a retention and protention.

Hume gives three main principles of association, which, like in Locke, address the association of ideas. These are contiguity in time and place, cause and/or effect. Jamesian radical empiricism, and pragmatism more generally, are doctrines of perception. Here concepts can never supersede percepts, and only through 'perception can we find the deeper features of reality' (Barton Perry 2003: citing James's *Some Problems of Philosophy*). This seems to be something of a piece with Deleuze's transcendental empiricism, and looks to lead onto James on religious experience. Radical empiricism is post-Humean in that 'the parts of experience hold together from next to next by relations that are themselves parts of experience'. These are the 'conjunctions', the 'ands' that hold together the basic facts of experience. These 'ands' are relations. They are not verbs, they are not substantives or nouns, not adjectives (qualities, properties, attributes), nor adverbs like in Heidegger and Daoism/ Buddhism. They are, instead, relations that are either conjunctions or prepositions. They are before or after, on top of, inside, in front of, behind. There is one other such connective and it is the 'is', i.e. the copula. To be such a conjunction (and of course this includes disjunctions) is not to be 'connected by some trans-empirical support'. Neither substance, nor subject, nor transcendental unity of apperception (Kant), but very much what Deleuze and Guattari have understood as 'connective synthesis'. This is not Alain Badiou's subtraction from experience. It is an addition to experience: the relation as this addition to experience.

3.1.2 Experience and Its Functions

Radical Empiricism starts with the question 'does consciousness exist?' This is an important question because, in a similar way to society being the object of sociology, consciousness is the object of psychology. In Freud, too, the unconscious is largely a way of explaining what consciousness and the ego do. James's answer to whether consciousness exists is no and yes. It is that experience exists and that consciousness is derivative of experience. Consciousness exists for James only as a 'function'. Thus 'consciousness is a function in experience which thoughts perform' (2003: 2). Consciousness is necessary to explain that things are and get reported. Thus, facts of experiences only become facts of consciousness for James when there is reporting and explanation. What can be meant by 'function' here? In a Darwinian sense consciousness is a function that helps experience cope with its environment; it helps experience attain its interests. But consciousness only comes from a diremption of 'pure experience', of which everything (and James means everything) is composed. James is giving us a psychology not of consciousness, but of experience. In this, pure experience is undifferentiated; it is a 'primal stuff' (2003: 2). Knowing comes from the parts of this original experience relating to one another. One part here becomes the subject and knower and the other the object, the known. Here subject and object, like consciousness, are functions of experience.

James starts from 'percepts' and works to concepts. For him, the moment at which we have consciousness is the moment at which we recall the outer world when it is not materially present. That is, *memory* gives us consciousness. Here consciousness is 'an impalpable inner flowing' (2003: 4). What consciousness does in the more original chaos of perception is to fix attention on certain segments of experience, of this flow. This fixing of attention is not primarily representation. This is not a 'representational theory of perception'. Such representational theories violate our sense of 'life'. Such representational theories work from fixed mental images and exclude flow and connectives and intervening mental images.

Pivotal in this is the question of 'association'. In the pure experience of a room thus there is necessarily a diremption into two processes. One is that of the world of things, of external, physical reality. The other is the world of mental images. Each of these has a 'group of associates'. Here there are two different 'systems of association'. One is a physical system that includes the history of, say, a house, but also how the elements of the house work with one another to constitute a physical system. The other is our mental flow of associations. Both of these are 'diremptions' from pure experience. In the mental world of associations, the experience is 'the last term of a train of sensations, emotions, classifications, decisions, movements, expectations ending in the present' and the 'first term extending into the future'. This is a series including past and future of 'inner operations' (2003: 7). The same is true for what James calls the 'conceptual manifold'. Both percepts and concepts come to us initially as a 'chaos of experiences' (2003: 9). James's conjunctions are in this sense non-perceptual experiences. So is memory. Here the external world is stable. For James not only do the segments of our stream of mental experience 'couple' with one another. There is a coupling of internal and external worlds. Again, subject and object are 'functional attributes', that are realized in 'different contexts' (2003: 12).

There is a 'directionality' to this stream of consciousness by association. Knowing is always 'leading towards and terminating in a perception' (2003: 13). Knowing starts with and terminates in a percept. Starting with immediate chaos, 'the stable units get sifted out as real experiences with consequences'. Not only do thought and things come from pure experience, but thought and things are also functions. Here thought and things are in no sense polar opposites. In Locke, things have primary and secondary qualities. Primary qualities are, for example, mass, motion and volume, and do not entail the presence of an observer. Secondary qualities like colour, warmth and dampness entail an observer. For James, whether these secondary qualities are in the thing or the mind of the observer is anything but clear and distinct.

For James, it is the conjunctions of experience that give us cognition, that provide the bridge from perception to cognition. Experience, as we mentioned, is also 'life', of the manifold as 'confused and superabundant'. James understands Hume's rupture with metaphysics as a break with the 'trans-empirical'. Hume, as we know, woke Kant from his 'metaphysical slumber' (Meillassoux 2008). Kant, of course, saw himself as going beyond Hume's scepticism to argue that indeed we do have knowledge. In Kant, this necessitates a move from the imagination to the understanding. The imagination is very much like the Humean series of events connected by habituation only. Hume's break with metaphysics included a rejection of the notion of substance. Thus James notes that Hume refuses to relate facts to substances (2003: 22–3). In James's reading of Hume, substances would be trans-empirical particulars while facts are empirical particulars. In this, Hume breaks not just with formal and final cause but also with Aristotelian efficient and material cause. For efficient and formal and indeed material cause, Aristotle needed to draw on substance as a trans-empirical (metaphysical) term. Substance is a particular. It is the only one of Aristotle's ten categories that is a particular. All the rest are universals. This particular that is substance can be a singular or a common noun (or substantive): a singular substance like 'Socrates' or a generic substance like 'man'.

Substances are particulars that are qualified by universals. Socrates as a substance is qualified by old or young, by small and tall, by white-haired or bald or dark-haired. Socrates is thus a particular qualified by a universal, or by a series of universals: Socrates as a substance is a trans-empirical particular. Facts are empirical: they are not trans-empirical. Humean facts too must be experienced, but they are disjunctive; these facts are just disjunctive terms. Without substance, Hume gives us 'a philosophy of plural facts' (James 2003: 22). James also gives us such a philosophy of multiplicity. Without substance providing a causal connection, without, say, Leibniz's predicates as included in the subject, which are the qualities as integrated interior to the substance (see Deleuze 2006a), causal ties are pulverized. They are resolved into only a habitual sequence. Similarly, James observes that John Stuart Mill 'pulverizes all experience by association' (2003: 23). 'Association' is the key term here. With the disjunction of events, as in Hume and Mill, experience by association disappears. Still, notes James, psychologically, though not logically, we do associate events or ideas or things. James's psychology informs his philosophy. Empirically we actually do associate things. In effect, James gets to Kant's categories through associations, relations, conjunctions.

Knowledge in Aristotle's classical metaphysics is very much to do with substance. Kant breaks with substance for a new trans-empirical, i.e. the trans-empirical categories as organized through the transcendental unity of apperception, i.e. the subject. Kant is well aware that even though this subject is engaged in empirical, hence material, experience, it is itself largely metaphysical. Thus Kant saw the *Critique of Pure Reason* as a critique of metaphysics that worked through saving this important dimension of metaphysics. Indeed, Kant (1929 [1781]: 30) saw himself as performing for metaphysics what Newton had carried out in physics. In the Preface to *Phenomenology*, Hegel was acutely aware of this in observing that in Kant metaphysics became no longer a question of substance but was now a question of the subject.

The trans-empirical categories for Kant are not part of our minds. They are not part of experience. They are conditions of possibility of experience. For James, these categories are effectively dissolved back into experience as relations or conjunctions or modes of association. These 'transitions' are themselves empirically, i.e. psychologically, experienced. So we can have knowledge, we can have cognition. But we have it not as a condition of experience (à la Kant) but instead *through* experience. James (2003: 24) gives us a list of types of connectors, of associations, of relations of terms of experience. These are connections that are themselves non-perceived and impalpable facts. He gives them in order of distance from consciousness. The first is the 'with', which connects thought terms with physical terms; the second, which is a bit more intimate, is the time interval; the third is space adjacency; and fourth there is similarity. Fifth is relations of activity that put terms into a series involving change. Here we see the Humean series as well as causal ordering. Finally, and most intimate, are relations between terms in states of mind, such as memories and purposes. These are so intimate that these terms 'co-penetrate and suffuse one another'.

Jamesian cognition proceeds from immediate experience connected by these quasi-phenomenological connections that displace the categories. At the same time, knowledge proceeds less through the fixity of categories than through the dynamic of flow. Categories are rendered instead as transitions from 'next to next'. But knowledge is not realized until it realizes a *terminus*. This terminus is a percept: it is a percept, which is less cognitive fact than practical consequence. In such a context Hume distinguishes between 'demonstrative' and 'probable' reasoning. Demonstrative reasoning is, like in geometry, usually a question of mathematical truths. They are about relations of ideas. Probable reasoning is about matters of fact. James and pragmatism are more on side with Hume's probable reasoning. But with their relational paradigm and their insistence on a psychology, they break with scepticism and say that we indeed have knowledge.

Unlike in mathematics, this is not apodictic knowledge. It is not so much probable as it is contingent; it is hypothetical and thus can be improved upon or corrected. It is further knowledge that is always in process. It can terminate. But this termination is not in a proof, a demonstration, but instead in a percept. This terminus of knowledge as a consequence is the bridge from percept to pragmatics. These consequences then leave the sphere of theoretical reason for that of practical reason. These consequences, though surely perceived, are practical. Aristotle in *Nicomachean Ethics* made the distinction between the 'demonstration' of 'theoria', whose paradigm case was geometry, and praxis, which was instead a matter of 'deliberation'. In such a context James (2003: 45) speaks of 'verification'. There are two ways this is different from theoria: first such verification is not apodictic but instead provisional, and second such verification is in the facts of, not cognition, but practice.

Pure experience, writes James, is a series of overlapping and suffusing and *durcheinander* 'thats'. It is only with consciousness and memory that certain groups of 'thats' become 'any definite "what"'. The chaotic original stream of pure experiences starts to take on 'emphases' (2003: 49). Pure experience is 'unverbalizable'. Emphases, verbalizability and the 'what' emerge as pure experience undergoes diremption into thought and things. It is interest that decides what 'what' will be selected, and where emphases will be placed. James continues to observe that this verbalizability is less a question of propositions than of the relation between facts. James is at pains to disavow Bradley's dialectics, so that what Bradley and Hegel see as spiritual (*Geist*), James sees as the conjunctions that associate the facts of experience. These conjunctions, he insists, are also 'facts' (James 2003: 49). They are immanent. They are not so much trans-empirical subjects, verbs and objects but instead 'prepositions, conjunctions and copulas' that 'flower out of the stream' as 'naturally as do nouns and adjectives'. Here 'it is elements that have a practical bearing on life that are analysed out of the continuum, verbally fixed and coupled together' as immediate experience is broken down into 'subjects, qualities, terms and relations' (2003: 50). James is sceptical of the idea of 'the understanding', a pivot for Kant and for Hegel's (Bradley's) dialectics. The understanding, for James, is a function that then 'dips back into the stream of facts'. Thinking does not go on mainly in the abstraction from or subtraction from (cf. Plato, Badiou) experience, but is a question of addition, of the 'and' and conjunctions. It, with Deleuze's machines and connective syntheses, stays on the immanent plane of empiricism.

Pragmatism cannot deal with Bradley's Absolute, in which truth is a question of the best uniting the many and the one. Instead, for pragmatism, truth is about 'intellectual operators' and those that are 'most true which most successfully dip back into the finite stream of feeling and grow confluent with some particular wave'. For pragmatism, the truth of 'an intellectual product' is only in leading us 'successfully or unsuccessfully back into intellectual experience'. This questions whether 'our abstract universals are true or false at all'. James (2003: 52, 56) then repeats his list of relations of conjunction from co-terminous to contiguous, to likeness, nearness, simultaneity, in-ness, on-ness, for-ness and with-ness: this is the thing and its relations, these relations being ever so much more important than the thing's substance, its qualities and its in-itself. For James, in the final analysis, the 'word "is" names all these experiences of conjunction'. This 'is' which is 'and': 'and' is the stream, the temporality that is at the same time 'life'. They, along with the nouns and adjectives and abstract 'whats', flow from the stream and later return to the stream and grow confluent again. In this confluence they find their truth.

'Consciousness', we have noted, is a portion of experience that stands 'in determinate relations (which is also a relations of "reporting") to other portions of experience extraneous to itself'. 'To be "conscious" means not simply to be. But to be reported, known, to have awareness of one's being added to one's being'. Consciousness in turn is a basis for the self. The self for James is the continuous identity of each personal consciousness. The self entails 'the practical fact that new experiences look back on old experiences. They find them "warm" and appropriate the old experiences as "mine"' (James 2003: 65–9). So a new percept, say a pen or a madeleine, a new experience has past time for its content. And these feeling are the nucleus of 'me'. This is, then, an appropriation of the old experience by the new one. Only now do we get 'awareness'. This appropriative experience is also a fact of the awareness of self. And this is most importantly a question of 'associations'.

This leads on to James's discussion of affect, of 'affectional facts'. Affectional facts are very much on the borderlines of mental and physical facts. James introduces this by reiterating that 'there really is no difference between the material of thoughts and of things', the alter of whose 'extension' is little more than a filling of space. For him, the opposition of thought and matter is only a relation ('the with') and function of the same piece of pure experience. In this (James 2003: 72), the same piece of pure experience can stand for either the 'fact of consciousness or physical reality'. The 'inner' and 'the outer' themselves are 'only a result of later classifications arising from certain needs'. This said, there are affectional experiences, which are on the borderline of the mental and the physical, such as anger, love and fear. Pain is objective as much as it is subjective. These affections, to the extent that they qualify things, are not so much like Locke's primary qualities, which are independent of the observer – of solidity, extension, motion, number and figure. They are more like Locke's secondary qualities – colour, taste, smell, sound – of objects that produce sensations in the observer. Thus, affective facts are somewhere between perception and consciousness. Affective facts are mental so they do not 'act on each other by their physical properties, yet they act on each other in the most energetic way. It is by interest, by the emotions they excite, by their affective values, that their consecution in our several conscious streams is mainly ruled'. This is where value comes in. The value of an object, which is affective, is on this borderline. 'Desire introduces them (values); interest holds them; firmness fixes them' (James 2003: 79). Thus they are out there as the value of things, and they are at the same time 'mine', as they fit into my memories and my anticipation. This is close to Simmel's (2001) notion of value in *The Philosophy of Money*. Value, like beauty, is thus an 'appreciative attribute'. For James, the body is the space of affective facts.

> Our body is the palmary instance of the ambiguous. Sometimes I treat my body purely as a part of outer nature. Sometimes again I think of it as 'mine'. I sort it with the 'me', and then certain local changes and determinations in it pass for spiritual happenings. Its breathing is my 'thinking', its sensorial adjustments are my 'attention', its kinaesthetic alterations are my 'efforts', its visual perturbations are my 'emptions'.

The body is the mediator between the physical and mental world, it is the entity that intervenes between concept and percept (James 2003: 80, 117). The body stands in 'violent' contrast with the 'rest of our ambient milieu'; 'what occurs "inside" the body is more intimate and important'. The 'body identifies itself with our ego'. The 'soul' is at the same time 'life' and our 'breath'. Our images and memories act on the physical world only through the body. They 'seem to belong to our body', alongside our affective feelings.

3.2 Pragmatism: Activities

James's discussion of 'activity' is perhaps the pivotal link between radical empiricism and pragmatism. James, unlike neoclassical and

61

neoliberal economics and so much of sociology, speaks less of 'action' than of *activity*. Activity, as counterposed to action, means ongoingness and somehow embeddedness. Pragmatism's inherent vitalism is ingrained in such a notion of activity. Thus 'bare activity' is 'synonymous with the sense of "life"'. This idea of activity is at the heart of pragmatism's core idea of 'difference of fact'. Thus James formulates pragmatism's method in stating, 'there is no difference of truth that does not make a difference of fact somewhere'. The universals of truth may not be experienced but the differences in fact surely are. Without experience there are no facts. The point of pragmatism is change, and change entails not just experience but activity. James defines 'bare activity' as the 'bare fact of event or change'. Here the 'change that takes place is a unique content of experience' (James 2003: 83–4). There is something creative about activity and experience. Bare activity has no direction, no actor, is a sort of *'wilde Ideenflucht'*, is Kant's *'Rhapsodie der Wahrnehmungen'*. But in our world, activity comes with definite direction, with desire and a goal. Activity – as Nietzsche insisted – is always countered by resistances: the will has to overcome resistance. These resistances are what James saw as 'disjunctions'. Yet these activities have a certain *'Gestaltsqualität'*, so that the whole perception will drive and help define the parts.

Bare or elementary activity is, for James, bound up with the 'mere "that" of experience', a mere 'that' that is subsequently 'specified' into 'two "whats"', the what of thought and the what of things. For full pragmatism, you need this moment of the what, because it is its consequences that will produce change. This is at the same time the activity of *phronēsis*. It is the 'experience series' that 'gives the feeling of activity'. At the heart of radical empiricism is the 'experience series': Hume's and pragmatism's series of experiences. There is a difference between the feeling of activity and real activity because only the latter changes the world. This said, James's notion of activity is a sort of synthetic object that connects bits of experience in the series and forms part of the series of experience. We move back to Hume's *Enquiry concerning the Human Understanding*: 'in mental activity, the words physically to be uttered are represented as activity's immediate goal' (James 2003: 84, 89–91). To this James asks, 'where is the seat of real causality?' His answer is not at all in Kant's and Hume's physical causality, but in mental and provisional causality. Real causality also entails activity. It lies in the conjunctions that then make activity possible. Through these conjunctions, which also are syntheses, ideas are formulated. The deciding series is not the series of objects: it is the series of mental life, or experience before its diremption into two 'whats'. It is mental life as experience that terminates in activity. This moves not from universal to particular. It starts instead from a particular and moves to other particulars via conjunctions and syntheses. This is the seat of real causality. This is also the seat of what, for James, is freedom and the will. It includes the moment of effectuating real change. Hence thoughts work differently on each other than do things. Things work 'energetically' and physically on each other, while thoughts do a different work on each other through 'checking, sustaining, and associational activity' on one another. Effort is part of this. What sort of thoughts does James have in mind? In this context James joins Aristotle, for whom 'desires' are thoughts, and so are 'purposes' (James 2003: 96).

'Real activities', as distinct from just 'felt activities', 'are those that actually make things be'. They are 'creative activities' that must be 'immediately lived'. There is free will and novelty in each fresh activity situation. For James, 'humanism' must rise above common sense and embrace not just experience's and perception's 'that' but also consciousness's 'what'. Thus, in pragmatism, somewhere in the 'that' of efficacious causing and 'the thus', there are two kinds of facts. And these facts – the 'that' facts of experience and the 'what' facts 'of conceptual consciousness – must be experienced as one'. This is 'real effectual causation' in that it entails not just experience but also activity, featuring the 'conjunction (also as synthesis) in our activity series'. Finally, as mentioned above, these conjunctions emerge from the flow of experience to become 'categories', and yet 'it is the conjunctions that our activity series reveals'. In activity, it is the body that assumes centre stage. Our body is 'here and now'; it touches 'this'. In regard to our body all other things are 'there', 'then' and 'that'. So, it is the body that mediates the experience of the 'that'. For 'thoughts and feelings to be active', 'their activity emanates in the activity of the body' (James 2003: 89, 95, 97). James is clear, however, that the 'that' is not much of anything; it is not stuff. The 'that' is plural: it is the 'brownness or heaviness, flatness, intensity, space' (Taylor and Wozniak 1996). It is a multiplicity.

In this context, James's essay on humanism focuses on the bridge not from percepts to concepts, but from concepts back to percepts, and this is a driving idea of pragmatism. This points to the limits of such a radical-empiricist philosophy or psychology of experience, because pragmatism is a question of the service to humanity and experience as a whole, and by itself, is 'self-contained and bears on nothing'. In this context, we see how radical empiricism is not just a movement from next to next and its reasons or conjunctions. It is the connections between *very prominent* nexts, concepts and percepts. It is a chain that connects concepts to percepts, or thought to things. It does this through a set of psychological, including neuro-physiological, mechanisms. The concept must end in a percept to be effectual. Apperception must end in a terminus of perception, and sensation then to action. James insists that the relation of conception (or imagination) to sensation is analogous to that between sensation and reality. Conception (imagination) is to sensation as sensation is to reality (2003: 106). It is the action at the end of this series that is most important. Thus, the most important transitions in James are not from next to next, but from knower to known, from conceptual knowing to perceptual knowing. This is one image of thought, one 'next' knowing another. This may be the most important of experienced relations.

Let us step back a moment and consider the context of 'radical empiricism', which was 'James's metaphysics' (Taylor and Wozniak 1996). The essays first appeared in 1904 some fifteen years after the *Principles of Psychology*. The latter was a more positivist take on psychology, speaking of consciousness as a field, on the one hand, and the content of consciousness, on the other. James wanted a radicalization of both Humean empiricism and his own contemporaneous psychology. He did this through rethinking the 'new' scientific psychology as an analytic, associational empiricism. James's associationism pointed to a sort of 'penumbra' around consciousness of a habitual, trance-like, dream-like space of exceptional states. The latter development of this penumbra is central to radical empiricism and James's phenomenology of experience. It upset not only the content and consciousness notions of followers of Wilhelm Wundt's then dominant paradigm of scientific psychology. For Wundt, the primal fact was not experience but instead space. James also challenged the belief among positivists that cause was something between objects in the external world. Thus, we can understand James's contemporaneous *Varieties of Religious Experience* (Taylor and Wozniak 1996). In this we can see the influence on James of his godfather Ralph Waldo Emerson and his Swedenborgian father. In Emerson's transcendentalism we are to find truth in nature, in which God is not revealed but instead *perceived*. The Swedenborgian 'doctrine of the rational', like James's logic, rests on a deeper substrate of experience and use (Menand 2011). In James's psychology of religious experience, there is a mystical subconscious that is at once the source of logical thinking and religious experience.

64

James gave first voice to pragmatism as an idea at the Philosophical Union at the University of California, Berkeley in 1898. This was some eight years after *Principles of Psychology* had appeared, during James's transition from quasi-positivism to radical empiricism. Charles Sanders Peirce as well as Chauncey Wright were major influences on James, meeting regularly at Harvard's Metaphysical Club. Wright was a Darwinian, and Peirce schooled James in British empiricism. Peirce was an astute reader of James's later (empiricist) work, and wrote to James: 'to understand the world of thought as real is to assert the reality of the public world of an indefinite future as opposed to past opinions of what it was to be'. Peirce's pragmatism was, however, primarily about logic while James's primarily addressed action, and was an inspiration for the Progressive movement in American politics. Peirce wrote to James saying that Peirce's own work has always been both a logic and a phenomenology, but that phenomenology should be not a psychology but instead a philosophy. Peirce disapproved of James blurring the boundaries between psychology and philosophy, thinking that psychology should remain positivistic. Finally, Henri Bergson, ten years younger, was a James follower. James introduced Bergson to the American audience and they became friends, James overseeing the translation of *Creative Evolution* into English.

3.3 Dewey or Formal Pragmatics

James's career unfolded in a way that is quite parallel to those of Georg Simmel and Emile Durkheim. All three had a positivist phase around 1890 and after, and in the early decades of the twentieth century a more vitalist phase. And even for Wilhelm Dilthey, a vitalist current of 'life' was central to his idea of lived experience (*Erlebnis*). So Durkheim's *Suicide* and *Division of Labour* defined his positivist phase as did Simmel's *Soziale Differenzierung*. Moreover, James's and Durkheim's more vitalist '*Erlebnis*' work was inspired by or featured religion, James's *Varieties of Religious Experience* and, of course, Durkheim's *Elementary Forms*. But it was more than just the 'life' *problématique* that was essential to James; as important was pragmatism's focus on movement from the particular to the universal. This was also the case for John Dewey, who was much less close to David Hume than was James. We see this in Noortje Marres's book *Material Participation: Technology, the Environment and Everyday Publics*, which features Dewey and Water Lippmann's debates about public opinion and by extension the constitution of public spheres. Interestingly, Marres reads both Lippmann and Dewey as pragmatists. In this sense pragmatists, like empiricists, more generally argue against assumptions that social actors have full rationality. Such assumptions of full information are present not just in neoclassical economics and rational-choice theory but also, for Lippmann, in democratic theory, the 'original dogma of democracy'. Lippmann is sceptical of grass-roots democracy and gives us a theory of political and intellectual elites, in which specialists interpret and analyse the facts for political elites. This was articulated in his widely read *Public Opinion*, published in 1922, and reiterated in 1925 in a climate of further pessimism (with, e.g., the rise of Mussolini) with regard to manipulation and disillusionment with democracy in his *The Phantom Public*. Lippmann focuses on the particular, though, in arguing that the public does finally intervene in crises, often to throw the ruling party out of government, but even here only when led by political and interpreting elites in the media. So, in Lippmann there are pragmatist-like assumptions of limited rationality and a politics (and public) that works from the particular (crises) to the general.

Dewey is more optimistic about grass-roots democracy and civil society more generally. Dewey, unlike Lippmann, works from the opposition of state and the public. He does agree with Lippmann that modern technology – especially in cinema, the dime novel and the motorcar; that is, the media and consumerism – tend to distract the public and can lead to its intermittent eclipse. But unlike Lippmann or Habermas, as Marres emphasizes, Dewey will speak not of a public but only of publics. For Dewey and pragmatism, the truth of a proposition lay in its consequences. James is not focused on propositions, but instead on concepts. This is in a process that starts from the fact and the 'percept', leading to a formulation in concepts, which have consequences in other facts or percepts. In this process, which is always correctable, the truth of the (provisional) concepts will lie in this second set of facts. For Dewey and Marres (2012), these facts are 'issues'. Thus, Dewey's pragmatics diverge from Habermas's formal pragmatics in focusing on not the public but publics and in that political reasoning starts not from the universal but from particular issues. As in progressive economic theory, Dewey saw these issues as arising from 'negative externalities', themselves the consequences of political or market exchanges (Cobb 2013). Dewey's own epistemology moved on from positivism, which he understood as 'interactional' in the sense of the interactions and laws of Newtonian physics, to a 'transactional' paradigm, with assumptions of a sort of complex multiplicity in which there is no ultimate driving force, whether this is metaphysical or physical, such as in Newton and positivism. Marres's reconstruction of Dewey is particularly instructive today, in which a Jamesian radical empiricism is seen at the heart of a 'critical' theory, which is based on the potentialities of both humans and things. Marres, influenced by Latour, thus sees publics as also a question of technologies, of bits and pieces of nature as well as humans, in which publics are more or less conceived as assemblages. Dewey's transactionalism (and Marres's) is based on a focus on, as it were, intra-assemblage communication. That is, the relationship between agents is not so much a question of cause and effect but of communication. Thus, there is the contiguity of James and Bergson, while in the background is Gabriel Tarde's communicative constitution of collectivities.

Let us return to Habermas, who speaks of public spheres and the ideal speech situation in terms of a 'formal pragmatics', which is based on performative propositions. These performative propositions are validity claims that must be 'discursively redeemed'. Pragmatism, as distinct from formal pragmatics, starts not from this ideal speech situation of validity claims and discursive redemption, but from on-the-ground issues that are encountered. It starts out from facts: from the facts of perceived experience. Pragmatism's thoughts are not validity claims. For James, they are not even propositions, but concepts. And their validity, their truth and verification, comes not through argument or discursive redemption but in their consequences, again in facts and percepts. There is not one public sphere as in Habermas and, say, Arendt, but there are many publics. These publics are comparatively transient: they come and go with the consequences of conceptualization and political communication that intermediates between what are two sets of consequences. The initial consequences are the negative social and environmental externalities of markets, of production and state policy. A second set of consequences are those resulting from civic formulation arising from horizontal communication in addressing the issue. There is something transient about radical empiricist pragmatism in comparison to Habermas's formal pragmatics. In Jamesian radical empiricism, experience is about perceptions much more than conceptions. Consciousness and concepts are functions of experience, which is perceptual experience. Concepts are 'operators': 'truth' itself is an 'intellectual operator'. Truth must be 'effectual'. And a 'concept that does not end in a percept is ineffectual'. Consciousness is more or less an epiphenomenon of experience. We move from the 'that' facts of experience to the 'what' facts of consciousness and concepts. Pragmatist truth, then, is not a question of *Geltungsansprüche* or validity clams. Dewey's propositions are not claims. They are conceptualizations arising from issues, from perceived issues. Even if they take the form of performative speech acts as political interventions, they are not clams to anything. For James, again truth is not even propositional: it is a concept, an 'intellectual operator'. Its truth lies in the change it leads to, in its effectual consequences.

3.4 Some Conclusions

Our discussion of James and pragmatism can have implications for critical theory. In this book (also Chapter 4) we consider critique as contingency very briefly through 'Scottish' empiricism and in much greater detail above through William James's radical empiricism. Deleuze argued that Hume has effectively dismantled the modern subject as formulated in Kant's transcendental unity of apperception via a notion of the imagination or imaginary. For Deleuze, this is through the temporality of the series of events in Hume's imagination. In Adam Smith (2010), it is present in the *Moral Sentiments* in which our imagination extends into the space of the other. We can perceive only our own hurt. We must imagine the hurt of the other. We do so through putting ourselves in the place of the other. Foucault's Smith, as we noted above, is part and parcel of a technics – a posteriori technologies of the self – that contest the dominance and normative regulation of the a priori episteme of modern discourses

What leads to a technics for Foucault becomes very much a praxis in James and pragmatism. James's critique of metaphysics is at the same time a psychology, in which consciousness is comprised largely of the trans-empirical stream consisting of conjunctions and other connectives (see also Mackenzie 2010). These trans-empirical connections, however, are not perceived. They are in this sense perhaps also metaphysical. James's metaphysical 'ands' are what can make his radical empiricism very much of a piece with Deleuze and Guattari's transcendental empiricism. Such 'ands' connect together the particulars of Deleuze and Guattari's desiring machines, forecasting the machinic nature of twenty-first-century experience. Deleuze is well aware that this connectivity is virtual, hence also transcendental. Deleuze is inspired by Bergson, himself influenced by James. For Bergson (2011b), when matter takes on memory, the material becomes metaphysical. When matter takes on memory, matter takes on life. Thus *Lebensphilosphie* – in Nietzsche and Bergson – is also a philosophy of contingency. Life is inscribed in the particularity of the contingent. For James, as indeed for Bergson (2011a), this is also at stake in religious experience. James and pragmatism also break with cognitive experience in favour of praxis (and the religious).

Benjamin's theory parallels James in the way that it starts from the particular, say the kiosk in the streets of Eugène Atget's Paris, the arcade, or disused clothing in the surrealism essay, the everyday particulars of the city. Benjamin has a strong notion of the imaginary as his language of things works through not symbols but images. Benjamin's language of things, like Marres's take on pragmatics (above), gives agency to nonhumans. Like James, Benjamin in 'The Mimetic Faculty' gives a faculty that, unlike Kant's a priori faculties, is instead quite a posteriori. It works after the fact in its images of imitation. Benjamin's mimetic faculty is not an a priori condition of the possibility of experience: it is experience itself. This chapter is arguing that in today's times of contingency, William James's a posteriori and empiricist pragmatics may be particularly well suited.

The next chapter is about objective experience, about Weber's objectivism and the *Methodenstreit* between real positivism (allied with neoclassical economics) and interpretive social and human sciences. This is at the same time a methodological dispute between subjective and objective experience. There was effectively a much quieter *Methodenstreit* at roughly the same historical juncture. This was between James's religious experience and Durkheim's elementary forms of religious life. This is registered in the opening chapters, in effect a methodological prolegomenon to Durkheim's classic text. In these chapters Durkheim engaged in controversy with James and the British empiricist anthropologists. This controversy was on several levels. The first was empiricism versus positivism. James's radical empiricism – like Hume's – questioned causation and understood events as succeeding one another in time connected instead by conjunctions. Durkheim was self-consciously a positivist – though a complex positivist – and did think in terms of causality. He and Marcel Mauss understood that causality evolved from primitive classifications to more complex modern ones. In this knowledge, Durkheim operated like a modern social scientist; he operated – like natural scientists – in the register of causality. This is in the direction of objective experience, for the social-science observer. James and pragmatism, as just argued, as method worked very much a posteriori, whereas for Durkheim, society, or the social itself, was a sort of a priori. Once constituted through the symbols of religious life, it

69

took on a life of its own, determining, for example, how we know things. The rituals in the sacred thus constitute the classifications of the profane. This was Durkheim's sociologistic epistemology (Hirst 2013).

The above was part of Durkheim's sociological critique of James's and the empiricist anthropologists' psychologism. This was important for what a 'fact' is. For Hume, 'facts' were registered by the observer. That they were linked together in time, close to, invariably produced a convention whereby people spoke of them as cause and effect. But unlike 'physical' facts, cause itself was instead metaphysical, and we could not speak of cause without reverting to metaphysics, which Hume (unlike Kant) refused to do. For James, facts were not so much registered by the observer but by the individual psyche, the individual *consciousness*. Again, facts were connected not by causes but in a stream by conjunctions, 'ands' and 'buts' and 'howevers' and prepositions like under, over, but never by verbs such as cause or adjectives (qualities). The operative term here is consciousness, meaning of course the individual consciousness. Durkheim counterposed to this the 'collective consciousness'. Note, he did not speak of the collective actor or the collective subject as a purer positivist would, but about a collective consciousness. We recall consciousness is a term from subjective experience and phenomenology. What is produced from this collective consciousness are social facts. As in James's individual consciousness, facts need to be recorded by this collective consciousness as it engages with phenomena, with appearances. Again, in pure positivism subjects engage with objects, not consciousness with appearances. Thus, whereas objective facts of natural science and indeed economics will not vary from society to society, from culture to culture, Durkheim's social facts are mediated by specific collective consciousnesses of particular societies, which will make also social facts very different from one place to another. In twenty-first-century technological experience, when these facts are machine-mediated, they become 'data'.[3]

At stake for the social actors who Durkheim studies is that they engage more in subjective than objective experience. It is that collective consciousnesses engage in a collective version of subjective experience. Thus, economic anthropologists – in the tradition of Marcel Mauss's gift – work in the register of substantivist economics and not formalism, in which, like in Karl Polanyi, the economy

---

[3] This is not a relativism with regard to fact, and the importance in today's media of 'fact-checking'.

is embedded in culture. This is the case for the activities, and respondents, informants, historic and literary materials, that social and human scientists study. As for the social scientists themselves, Durkheim meant them to be objective. Durkheim is arguably the father of social, i.e. not cultural, anthropology – the tradition of Malinowski, Mauss, Fei Xiaotong, and, say, Ernest Gellner. This is different from the cultural anthropology of Boas, Geertz and postmodern anthropology in the US. Cultural anthropology is doubly Wittgensteinian: those they study are engaged in forms of life and subjective experience, and the anthropologists themselves are similarly engaged in forms of life and language games. In forms of life and language games, language is not propositional: it does not work in predications. Because of this theory, entailing theoretical statements is not possible. All we can do is to gloss cultural anthropology's thick descriptions. In social anthropology and Durkheim, though, we study collective consciousnesses and collective subjective experience; we as analysts are engaged in objective experience: we predicate, we theorize: we work not through language games but instead through predication. This is very different from the positivism that we will discuss in the next chapter. Here Max Weber was allied with the neoclassical economics protagonist of the *Methodenstreit*, Gustav Menger. Here, both the social scientist and the social actors s/he studies are engaged in objective experience. This was in effect a double positivism, whose origin was in the utilitarianism of John Stuart Mill. This was very different from the anti-utilitarian tradition that followed in Durkheim's footsteps, including, for example, Georges Bataille. It was Mill's utilitarian positivism – embracing Weber to the extent that he was involved, not in *verstehen* but in *erklären* – that gave us *homo economicus*.

— 4 —

OBJECTIVE EXPERIENCE: *METHODENSTREIT* AND *HOMO ECONOMICUS*

What is economic experience? What is experience in economic life? Some would say that the economy, as most of us know it, kills experience, destroys experience. If there is a dominant ideology in contemporary capitalism it is the ideology of *homo economicus*. *Homo economicus* has several assumptions: that we are utility-maximizing animals, that we are creatures of rational economic choice, that we have full access to all relevant market information and are able to select the best means available to our economic ends. In many respects, it reduces us to these characteristics. Economic man and woman are abstracted thus from everyday economic life. *Homo economicus* is an idea that is formed in the utilitarianism of John Stuart Mill.[1] It fully matures with the advent of neoclassical economics from about the 1880s. We have focused on experience as an a posteriori process; but *homo economicus* is not empiricist but based very much on a rationalist a priori. This a priori, as synthesized with matter, as Kant has taught us, gives us modern science – on the model of Newton's physics. If it is synthesized with not natural facts but social facts, then we have social-science positivism. Neoclassicism in economics and positivism in the social sciences is still – perhaps more than ever – dominant today. If Kantian cognition is a question of synthesis with natural facts, then neo-Kantianism, neo-Kantian positivism, synthesizes a social a priori with social facts. This chapter is as much about *method* in the social and human sciences as it is about economics. The first half is focused on the *Methodenstreit*, which was (and is) at the same time about

---

[1] There are many who make an empiricist reading of Mill. But to the extent that it is based on an axiomatic of utility and a basis for neoclassical economics, it is rationalist. *Homo economicus* itself is not based on any empirical men but again on an axiomatic.

economic activity and the nature of experience itself. The first half of the chapter focuses on the fundamental opposition between substantivist and formalist economics, which parallels the opposition between *Erlebnis* – that is, subjective and lived experience – and *Erfahrung*, or objective experience. In the second half, there is a focus on the transition from classical political economy to neoclassicism, from the a posteriori of Humean sensory experience and classical political economy to neoclassical utility and objective experience. This, we will see, is also a move from value as substance in the classicals to value residing in the subject for the neoclassicals.

In Chapter 2 we referred to Aristotle's distinction of episteme, praxis and technics. Episteme is a question of a priori knowledge as in Euclidean or Pythagorean geometry, beginning with axioms. Aristotle's technics instead starts from the particular, not from an axiomatic; it is a making in work and in art that is grounded in the experience of the particular. Chapter 5, on political experience, draws heavily on Hannah Arendt's idea of praxis, which again is a mode of political and ethical judging starting from the particular. It is in her case also a critique of a priori Platonic episteme-like politics that we encounter in Rawls and Habermas. Michel Foucault's entire work has been a critique of the modern episteme, of scientific and social-scientific discourse in the modern episteme. This modern episteme knowledge is, for him, a source of power, of governmentality and bio-power. Foucault's epistemic discourses predominate after the Kantian watershed, as modern sciences, social science and human sciences do synthesize with matter, with the facts of matter. Foucault also counterposed a *technē*, a technologies of the self, as up against episteme. If the modern episteme is based in the subject (as the ancient episteme had its basis in substance), then *technē*, self-technologies, are about not the subject but forms of subjectivity, which is at the same time a re-engagement with experience.

Foucault's *Birth of Biopolitics* gives us the discourse of *homo economicus*, which Foucault identifies with neoliberalism in economics. This, for Foucault, is the source of governmentality. He makes a clear distinction between neoliberalism of the Chicago School and ordoliberalism, on the one hand from liberalism, on the other from the liberalism of Adam Smith, Adam Ferguson and the Scottish Enlightenment. We will address this below. Here liberalism was not a governmentality or bio-power, but it was a biopolitics (Hardt and Negri 2009). It was not rationalist and a priori like neoclassicism/neoliberalism but instead empiricist, with a basis in David Hume. Smith as empiricist is an *a posteriori* thinker.

73

We will look at the birth of sociology in the work of Max Weber and at Weber's encounter with neoclassicism in Germany's *Methodenstreit*. Looking at Weber's types of social action, we can see that his idea of *zweckrational* action, which has been faithfully translated as 'instrumentally rational' – choosing the best means through rational calculation for given ends – very closely resembles Carl Menger's notions of utility. Does this mean that Weber and sociology are irreducibly positivist and experience-destructive? Or are things a bit more complex than that?

Let us start with this watershed at the birth of both neoclassical economics and of sociology. Karl Polanyi has made the distinction between substantivist and formalist economics. The distinctions are as follows: (1) Formalist economics presumes that markets are somehow natural. For Polanyi's substantivism, markets are institutions like any other, e.g. locality, state, family, religion. In this sense – and we will see below in the German Historical School – both classical political economy and neoclassicism (neoliberalism) are formalist. (2) Polanyi criticizes formalism's abstraction in which actors are diesmbedded from social and cultural relations. For Polanyi they are embedded. (3) Markets and other institutions are embedded, entangled with one another. (4) Substantivism features elements of the gift economy. Hence anthropologists from Malinowski to China's Fei Xiaotong to Marshall Sahlins are substantivists. (5) Most formalists – Smith, Marx, Weber – see the origin of capitalism in small traders (Weber's Ben Franklin) and manufacturers. For substantivists, these are part of the substantive economy. They see the origins of capitalism as exterior to national or urban substance, in the vast accumulations – concentration and centralization of capital – in fourteenth-century Venice. Here Polanyi's influences are Werner Sombart, who clashed with Weber on this, and Henri Pirenne, the major influence on Braudel and World Systems theory. The world system is the triumph of form over substance. Polanyi's emphasis is on who sets prices. In the mediaeval times that Pirenne wrote about, it is the guilds and city and organized religion who set prices. Price-setting by markets is more recent. But trade unions and states also set prices; think of China's central government and the Shanghai Stock Exchange. Aristotle in the *Politics* understood the three forms of association – *oikos* (household), tribe and polis – all as substantive in terms of economy. In the agora, it is not the market that sets prices, but instead trade and religious organizations as well as politics and notions of the just price. Aristotle's formalism comes in the unlimited accumulation of wealth exterior to the polis and the institutions

74

in long-distance sea-trading merchants. Aristotle associated such 'chrematistics' with rectilinear time, unlike the cyclical time of household and polis. This chrematistics was extra-institutional. What Aristotle understood as unnatural, Smith and moderns saw as nature and natural. Chrematistic, rectilinear time married to Christian redemption is, of course, the temporality of capital accumulation. It gives a rectilinearity to modern temporality in general. Below we will explore the debate, the *Methodenstreit*, between the formalists and neoclassicals around Carl Menger (and in large part Weber) against the substantivists of the German Historical School – Schmoller, Sombart, Simmel. The substantivists also embrace the first-wave institutional economics of Thorstein Veblen and John R. Commons. Neo-institutionalists like Coase and Williamson are formalists.

4.1 *Methodenstreit*: Formalists and Substantivists

4.1.1 Historical School: Subjective Experience and Institutions

So, who were the Historical School of Economics, who opposed Carl Menger and neoclassicism in the *Methodenstreit*, and what were they up to? Schumpeter in his *History of Economic Analysis* (1954) focuses on Gustav von Schmoller, the self-styled leader of what Schmoller called a 'historico-ethical' school. The *Methodenstreit* was occasioned by Carl Menger's 1883 book on methodology – his *Untersuchungen über die Methoden der Sozialwissenschaften und der politischen Ökonomie* – which was scathing – with strong argument – about the Historical School. It was followed by Schmoller's – quite political – response to Menger. Menger's close Austrian allies included Eugen Böhm von Bawerk, whose *Karl Marx and the Close of His System* became the benchmark neoclassical critique of Marxism. It was the Historical School versus marginalism, i.e. the Austrian School of Economics. It was in a sense Prussia – with their connections to something like *Staatswissenschaft* – versus Austria. For Schumpeter, Schmoller was arguing that the science of economics would come from historical monographs, like Schmoller's early book on clothiers and weavers of Strasbourg. Schmoller edited a series of documents on the public administration of Prussia and published work on mediaeval and late mediaeval bank credit. Werner Sombart, from the youngest generation of the Historical School, would deepen this focus on bank credit, especially in Venice and Italy, as the roots of capitalist society. This is important because it contrasted with Weber's *Protestant Ethic* as the cause or root of capitalism. It contrasted also with the Marxist historical materialism, in which the means and relations of production are the drivers of social change. Instead, for Sombart, and implicitly the earlier Historical School, capitalism's origins were in the sphere of circulation: in money and trade. Sombart was thus a precursor of Braudel, but also Gunder Frank, Wallerstein and Arrighi and world-systems theory. Schumpeter identifies the main elements of the Historical School. Primarily there was a strong relation to social policy. Hence their central role at the Verein für Sozialpolitik. Schmoller and his students were social reformers. Though of course non-Marxist, they were critical of the capitalist economy and markets. They contrasted their historical economics to what they saw as 'theoretical economics'. Schmoller saw marginalism thus as a 'speculative philosophy'; he opposed J.S. Mill as a theorist, and opposed Comte's sociological positivism and its 'naturalist' a priori (Schumpeter 1954: 807–11).

Schmoller's historicism did not want to see human beings as merely utilitarian or instrumentally rational creatures. The Historical School's reading of both marginalism and classical political economy was in this vein. The Historical School wanted a concrete focus on experience: not just on economic incentives but 'to study the whole of human motivation'. Weber's *Protestant Ethic* had a connection to the Historical School, which understood ethic also as ethics, again a focus on not just economic incentives, and even not just on an 'ethos', but on the ethical as a mode of extra-economic motivation. Schumpeter identified three generations of the Historical School. The older – Bruno Hildebrandt, Wilhelm Roscher and Karl Knies; the younger – Schmoller and his followers; and the youngest – Weber and Sombart and, we would add, Georg Simmel. Many readings of Weber – most influentially Friedrich Tenbruck – see Weber as a neo-Kantian positivist and in agreement very much with Menger. These readings focus on Weber's 'objectivity in the social sciences' essay and his critique of Roscher and Knies. Weber was the successor to Knies's professorial chair. But Weber had also self-identified with the Historical School. There was a certain evolutionary thinking in the Historical School, not Darwinian but more Hegelian, organic and idealist that was seen in, for example, Hildebrandt's work in terms of the evolution of economic civilization.

Schmoller and later Sombart were precursors of institutional economics, in which the market is an institution, alongside the state, and law, and family and religion. This for them was a rejection of what they saw as the abstraction of both classical political economy and neoclassicism. Schumpeter drew a parallel between Schmoller and Sombart and Veblen's and Commons's American institutionalism. This is very different from the new institutionalism of Coase and Williamson, which are neoclassical and neoliberal. Coase and Williamson look at the cause of institutions always based on transaction costs, whereas the first generation of US institutionalism saw institutions not as resulting from economic (trans)action, but instead as the basis of the economy. The old institutionalism was found in Commons's focus on law in his *Legal Foundations of Capitalism* and in Veblen's sociological economics. Commons takes the law to be as important an institution as the market. Commons was a follower of Henry George, whose ideas with regard to economic rents would have made him attractive to institutionalists then as it does to critical theory in China today in the work of Cui (2012).

Veblen's take on Schmoller in this context is interesting. Veblen only identifies Schmoller as an 'extreme' example of the Historical School – compared to more moderate members such as Roscher and Adolph Wagner. The Historical School and American institutionalists such as Veblen share a sort of inductivism, but the Americans were far more analytic. Though Smith's classical empiricism was inductivist in contrast to the neoclassical's utilitarian a priori, Smith's anti-historical and anti-institutional notion of markets as natural, his background in *tabula rasa* empiricism, also yielded a quite disembedded notion of the economic agent, much closer to an abstract formalism than to a substantivism.

Veblen (1919 [1901]: 263) takes Schmoller's *Grundriss der allgemeinen Volkswirtschaftslehre* to task for a naïve version of Baconian generalization in which 'simple enumeration' of examples will lead to 'eventual formulation of the laws of causation'. He disagrees with Schmoller's scepticism towards a natural-science-like treatment of the economy and his suggestion that economics should 'confine itself to narratives, and statistics'. Veblen (1919 [1901]: 258) contrasts the older historicist Roscher's 'historico-physiological method' with what he sees as Schmoller's 'philosophical-idealist method'. He reads Schmoller, I think correctly, as a 'late Hegelian' and a 'Romanticist', an evolutionism that is miles away from Darwin, but instead 'the unfolding of human spirit', the 'unfolding of life in organic nature', based on an 'inner necessity of the cultural course of human spirit'. This was unlike the sound, inductive, empirical generalizations, Veblen observes, of the elder Historical School.

Veblen (1919 [1901]: 263, 266, 276) sees Schmoller and his contemporaries as fixated on culture, looking at law, at ethics

(*Sitten*) and other factors that enter 'into the growth', the civilizing of culture. There are almost racist connotations in Schmoller's distinction of *Halbkulturvölker* and *Ganzkulturvölker*, in which the spiritual development of the working classes emerges, whose highest manifestations are 'sound, strong, spiritual and moral advancement'. Veblen finds it curious that for Schmoller the main economic factors are not land, labour and capital but instead 'population, the material environment and technological conditions'. In his *Theory of the Business Enterprise*, Veblen (1904) remarks how Schmoller (now with Henri Pirenne and Sombart) saw the business enterprise 'as an outgrowth of commercial activity'. Finally, there is a major emphasis, as readers of Weber's (1992) *Economy and Society* will be aware, on 'forms of household organization': in Schmoller's mediaeval research again on household structure, what Weber later called patriarchalism and patrimonialism. This is not just as opposed to feudalism as it is in Weber, but mainly thought on the lines of the ancient Greek *oikos*. Household organization was central to Prussian landholders and German ways of thinking economically – *Haushalt* is budget.

Veblen and Commons's Anglo-Saxon idiom has more in common with Bacon, Locke, Hume and Smith. There is a focus on sensory experience: they feature a posteriori thinking and empirical generalizations. Veblen and Commons see, consistent with David Hume's underpinning of repetition, the passions and sensory openness. The Historical School for its part has more in common with subjective experience, with *Erlebnis*, which has its roots in Kant's Third Critique. *Erlebnis* proposes, not the sort of universal subject of objective judgment, but a singular subjectivity which was at the heart of Schelling and Hegel's and Fichte's Romanticism and idealism. Thus Dilthey's *Erlebnis* is on the same page with the notions of experience in William James and phenomenology. Schmoller and his generation of the Historical School – and the previous and succeeding generation were much wiser – gives us a version of this kind of subjective experience.

In a book that addresses foundations of the human sciences, it makes sense to turn to Weber. Wilhelm Hennis and Keith Tribe focus on how Weber continued throughout his career to identify with the Historical School. Here there is advocacy of its 'descriptive-inductive method' in contrast to the 'theoretical analytic method' of Menger and the Austrians. Weber was Knies's successor to the Chair of Economics at Heidelberg, and his 1898 lecture course at Heidelberg was steeped in the Historical School and was also a precursor of *Economy and Society*. Weber's earlier studies were primarily in law: to take up the Heidelberg chair he had to learn economics very quickly. This lecture outline was not oriented to Menger's marginal utility. William Stanley Jevons never made it on to Weber's reading list. Economics itself had shifted from faculties of moral philosophy to faculties of law in Germany. Adam Smith, too, started out in more or less moral philosophy. It was François Quesnay who was first to identify himself as an economist, followed later by Smith. Classical political economy embraced Quesnay and A.R.G. Turgot as well as Smith, Ricardo and arguably Marx. The Historical School, especially the Older Historical School, worked from a contrast, not so much versus Menger and neoclassicism, but against classical economy as already an abstract-theoretical, an analytic, science.

German economics was in direct continuity with the cameralist tradition. 'Cameralism' was the German science of economic administration in the more or less absolutist state (Hennis 1988; Tribe 2008). It very much coincided with and took off from the French mercantilism of Jean-Baptiste Colbert. These were high civil servants: *Beamte* in the *Hofrat*. Such cameralism was instantiated in the princedoms of the Holy Roman Empire and again with William of Prussia, who established chairs of cameralism at Halle and Frankfurt Universities in the eighteenth century. Cameralism, as a science of administration, was divided into the three sections of public finances, *Ökonomie* and *Polizei*. The focus was the administration of the royal finances and systems of bookkeeping. The cameralists turned their efforts towards directing the state to mobilize resources (especially land) for the common good. In cameralism (*Camerawissenschaften*), we can see the *Wirt* in *Wirtschaft*. A *Wirt* is a landlord or a host, a *Gastgeber*, all this with echoes of household (*oikos*). Tradition is kept inside the modern unlike the much cleaner break with tradition of Anglo-French classical economics.

The German *Nationalökonomen*, like the cameralists, never became free-traders on the model of the French physiocrats or British political economy, but remained as a sort of *Sitte*-science, in which *Sitte* is customs but also ethics. Roscher's 1843 book was the foundational text for Historical Economics, and was entitled *Grundriß zur Vorlesungen über die Staatswirtschaft. Nach geschichtlicher Methode*. His influential text published in 1854 was *System der Volkswirtschaft*. So, German economics, like cameralism, remained focused on economic order. Keith Tribe's book on German historical economics was called *Strategies of Economic Order*. Rationalities of order of course are seen in Weber's formal rationality as well as in the rational bureaucracy even of the early Chinese state, which was never either the rule of law or an economic rationality.

Whereas classical political economy, surely from Smith, and probably from François Quesnay and the Physiocrats, began with the problem of value, German economics and Weber were focused on need. This is even the case in the marginalism of Menger. This partly parallels the shift from classical value to neoclassical need. When Hegel (1977: 14) in the Preface to the *Phenomenology* defined the modern as a shift from a thought based on substance to one based on the subject, this was truer than elsewhere for economics: classical political economy as based on substance, and marginalism on the subject. In physiocracy, this substance was wheat from agriculture; for Smith, it was labour and capital as the proportion of resources from profit that the merchant or entrepreneur devoted, not to consumption but instead to investment; and for Ricardo and Marx, this value substance was labour. Classical economics was very much based in Smith's adaptation of Quesnay's *Tableau économique*, which features the production and circulation of value through the social classes of a nation. In this sense, the 'wealth of nations' was a question of valorization, of accumulation of capital. When value (including capital as value) is no longer substance, then such valorization or accumulation is no longer at centre stage. Instead, it is the subject and his/her utilitarian needs that is pivotal. This is the economic actor of neoclassical economics, which then becomes no longer political economy.

4.1.2 Max Weber: Subjective Experience as Method, Objective Experience as Outcome

But historical economics from Knies to Weber was not concerned with just valorization; it was concerned in this sense not just with *homo economicus* (and Schmoller explicitly criticized Mill's *Logic*) but instead with the whole man. This is why Hennis's Weber understands economics primarily as a science of man. The Historical School saw classical economics and the neoclassicals, not as sciences of man but as natural sciences: in this sense, they saw classical economics as focusing on man in a state of nature on the lines of physics. They did not want a full materialism along the lines of Smith and Ricardo. They were influenced by Hegelian idealism. This also throws a bit of light on how materialism might be dialectical. Only Marx would have seen the Historical School and Weber as far too idealist, himself being more in line with Hume's and Smith's and Ricardo's materialism. So, where Franco-Britannic classicism and the Austrians started with value (based on subjective utility) as a priori, the question of how we get value in the economy, the Germans started with (not Physiocrat, but mercantilist-influenced) order, on the one hand, and 'need', on the other. Marginalism has utility in the place of need: the marginalists and J.S. Mill speak of units of utility. Need for the Germans was instead highly subjectivized. Subjective need thus is subjective experience and *Erlebnis* in contrast with utilitarian and neoclassical *Erfahrung*. Thus the sciences of man were *Erlebnis*-based. Hence Weber's *verstehende Soziologie* was very much *Erlebnis*, while *erklären* in his 'Objectivity' essay crossed over into positivist *Erfahrung*.

For the Historical School, there was a focus on needs and then goods as basic concepts rather than value. Tribe identifies a 'radical subjectivism' of needs, indeed not of the homogeneity but the diversity of needs. There is also a subjectivism of 'spirit'; that is, not economic incentives as motivating factor, but instead spirit as we will see below in Weber's *Protestant Ethic*. Menger himself, Tribe notes, never fully crossed over into marginal utility in the sense of Jevons and Walras. Menger's needs, as distinct from the utilities of Jevons and Walras, were not amenable to mathematical scaling but only to ordinal ranking. Full marginal utility analysis presumed ratio and interval scaling, and thus was easily mathematizable. This allowed some sort of *mathesis universalis* that Descartes and Leibniz envisioned. Menger's utility was thus needs-based. His ordinal scale of needs was ranked from the most vital to the least vital. He was looking for a balance of those needs to the sale of goods available. Proper marginalist utility, Tribe insists, is a continuous variable. The lack of homogeneity between goods meant they could be ranked with regard to the subject's preference. For Jevons, instead, utility was an independent and uniform standard of value (Tribe 2008: 75). Utility in Jevons, unlike Menger, was not tied to goods (in the Historical School's needs–goods couple), but instead to pleasure and pain, which could be formulated as a mathematical function. Here Menger could only give us marginalism in the sense of varying incremental levels of satisfaction linked to the choice of goods. Finally, for the Historical School there was not so much focus on exchange but also on Menger's notion of *Verkehr*, meaning traffic, transport, telegraphs and railways, on what we might today call logistics infrastructure (Rossiter 2016).

Menger published his *Untersuchungen über die Methode der Sozialwissenschaft unter der politischen Ökonomie insbesondere* in 1883 when Weber was nineteen years old. This reminds us how much economics was at the heart of social science in general. Menger started not inductively but from first principles, economic principles to build a *theoretische Nationalökonomie*. Weber goes a long way towards Menger in his 1903 critique of *Roscher and Knies: The Logical Problems of Historical Economics*. Here Weber, with Menger, spoke of abstract principles of economic action as not being inferable from historical research on individual economic phenomena. For Schmoller, Menger was too dependent on J.S. Mill's *System of Logic* (Gane 2012). Though Mill called himself an individualist and empiricist, his strong formulation of utilitarianism would seem to be based on an a priori of utility. Schmoller saw it as an a priori in contrast to his own a posteriori and inductivist method. For Schmoller, and Roscher/Knies, as Tribe (2008: 78) notes, the 'laws of the economy can be revealed through the study of the formation of economic systems'. For them, utility was not an a priori – as in Mill's 'abstract-deductive method' – but was only identifiable within the fabric of social activity. This was in an important sense a face-off between inductive and deductive methods, the deductivists as crystalized in Alfred Marshall's *Principles of Economics* published in 1891. Sociologists can recall how central Alfred Marshall was to Talcott Parsons's *Structure of Social Action*, as a lead-in to Parsons's treatment of Weber and Durkheim. Marshallian neoclassicism and the assumptions of the economic actor were central to Parsons's means–ends chains. Parsons's reading, indeed, of Weber was arguably Marshallian. So again, the *Methodenstreit* was that of *Erlebnis* versus *Erfahrung* as method: of 'ethical, realistic inductivism' versus 'abstract, theoretical deductivism'.

The point again is that for the Historical School and Weber, and indeed American first-wave institutionalist economics, economics was a science of man. It was not a natural science. Quantitative economics could not work for Weber because it left out great dimensions of economic life. Man is a complex creature and sciences of man could not be so strictly abstract-deductive. A science of man would have to deal with man's subjective needs, not objective utility. Historical School *Verkehrswirtschaft* did not deal with the isolated economy. It dealt with larger institutions and with material processes like transport and space. Classical political economy, with its focus on value relations – on value substance and valorization – could not deal with this. Neither could marginalism. As early as the 1898 lecture outline, Weber gave us a 'constructed "economic subject"' which was different from the empirical subject and could not work from motives that were in any way extra-economic. In addition to this question of motives of this economic man (which is probably more Mill–Menger than the classicals), there is 'complete insight into the prevailing [economic] situation and perfect economic knowledge' and 'an unfaltering selection of the most appropriate means for a given end [that is] absolute economic rationality'. Weber stressed this was unrealistic and 'analogous to a mathematical ideal' (Tribe 2008: 91).

Where does Weber stand in all this? First there is a focus on *Ethik*, as in *protestantische Ethik*, and the importance of ethics and probably ethics more than morality. In the *Philosophy of Right*, Hegel criticizes the 'morality' of Kant's imperative from the point of view of '*Sittlichkeit*'. *Sitten* are literally customs, traditions, use, folkways, but *Sittlichkeit* has been perceptively translated into English as 'ethical life'. *Sitten* and ethical life are highly embedded, more embedded in social norms of life than is the still partly abstract intersubjectivity of Smith's *Moral Sentiments*. So, we should think of the *Ethik* of Weber's *protestantische Ethik* as more or less embedded, not so dissimilar to *Sitten*. The extra-economic ethical works as a first cause, a motive of economic spirit as in Weber's Protestantism. There is a connection on this also to *Staatswissenschaft*, to the goals of the state as organizing and bringing order to the economy. In his Freiburg address of 1895, Weber maintained that 'social orders, however organized, are to be evaluated in regard to "the human type for which it optimizes chances of becoming the dominant type"'. This is an 'ethical type'. A 'setter of standards'. The state is of signal importance here. Weber and the Historical School read Smith in the context of 'natural law'. This is law in a state of nature, i.e. law without the state. In contrast to Anglo-French natural law, the German perspective is consistently from the point of view of statesmen or legislators. It is not in the natural law paradigm, but instead in legal positivism. Economics was even more abstracted from the state and everyday life with Marshall and neoclassicism. But in Germany up until the early 1950s, economics came under the canopy of *Staatswissenschaft*. This is consistent with Weber's view that economics was not a natural science but a science of man. In this context, Weber and other Historical Economists 'inquire into the quality of men who are brought up in given economic and social contexts'. In this national and *staatlich* context, Smith was seen as a 'cosmopolitical', the very antithesis of 'politics' (Hennis 1988: 117). Hence Roscher's *Staatswirtschaft* (1843) contrasted with Ricardo's *On the Principles of Political Economy and Taxation*, published some 26 years earlier, again based in calculation and 'cosmopolitical' laws, which had little to do with 'promoting human conscience, judgment and political responsibility'. So, economic policy, for Weber and the Historical School, never had, unlike for the British, purely economic ends or the *wealth* of nations. But it was meant to address life in its entirety and contribute to the moral–political problems of the whole. Thus 'human qualities are to be developed' through this: 'qualities of the soul', Weber writes in 1913.

A great part of this, as Wilhelm Hennis (1988: 132–46) notes, was already present in the predecessor to Weber's *Lehrstuhl*, Karl Knies. For Knies, sciences of man were to address the complete human being: 'to establish the moral foundations for everything that has force'. The human sciences were to investigate life as a result of 'real historical sense for the process of historical development and not simply the Englishman's sense of observation'. In 1883 Knies criticizes Smith and classicism for their 'assumptions of economics as unconditional and constantly uniform, derived from a general homogeneity of material means of production and human beings as purely selfish'. The *Nationalökonomie* would not only develop human *Innerlichkeit* but also understand this 'inner region' as also a *cause* of the outer region. The Church and religion were part of the development of this 'inner man'. Humans are driven not just by economic incentives, but for Knies also by religion as a motive force. In both the sense of ethics as cause and ethics as emerging from economic life, Knies tried to redefine political economy as an 'ethical science'. Hence, we are moving towards Weber with Knies's 'exact observation of historic life in its progressive development and the psychological study of man'.

Now enter the Historical School's youngest generation. In this context, Whimster (2007) focuses on Weber in comparison with Sombart and Simmel. Simmel's *Money*, Sombart's (1928) *Der moderne Kapitalismus* and Weber's *Protestant Ethic* were all published between 1900 and 1904. It was largely Sombart who put 'capitalism' on the agenda. The first two generations of the Historical School were less concerned with capitalism. It is Sombart who most problematizes the Smithian, Ricardian and Marxist valorization process. The younger Sombart was a Marxist and it was his *Der moderne Kapitalismus* that drove Weber to write the review for *Archiv für Sozialwissenschaft und Sozialpolitik* that became *The Protestant Ethic*. In the event, *The Protestant Ethic* drove all of Weber's sociology of the economic ethics of the world religions. The subtitle of Sombart's multivolume work is instructive: *Historisch-systematisch Darstellung des gesamteuropäischen Wirtschaftslebens von seinen Anfängen bis zur Gegenwart*. Sombart made the distinction between the enterprise, or *Betrieb*, and economy. Like institutional economists from Veblen to Commons, he was interested in the enterprise, the *Betrieb*. He noted that there were industrial enterprises in ancient Greece and

84

on a very large scale in the mediaeval guilds. But neither of these, because of rites and mores and restrictions, was primarily driven by the untrammelled profit motive. The breakdown of the guild structure was necessary in order to have capitalism. Capital could not exist, much less accumulate, where there were these restrictions driven by price and quantity fixing, by the framework of the guilds, by the master–journeyman–apprentice structure. Sombart observed in a later book, published subsequent to Weber's *Protestantism*, that the Jews, who were excluded from the guilds and thus were untrammelled, could be a vector for capitalism. But most importantly for Sombart, this happened in the Italian city-states, especially Venice, where capital concentration was necessary for long-term investment involved in long-distance sea trade. These were big capital outlays that brought very big margins. The ships and crews necessitated a huge centralization of capital for two- and three-year voyages. This was not possible inside the guild structure. Traders put this together with loans, followed later by finance, as Braudel (1992), Gunder Frank (1998), Arrighi (1994) and Wallerstein (1974) have written extensively on. This took place at the same time as the advent of double-entry bookkeeping also in Venice in 1494. This was Sombart's, Historical School, thesis.

For Sombart, the lifting of these restrictions combined with the means of double-entry bookkeeping allowed the unbridled acquisitive urge to flourish. Intellectually, the precursor was Aristotle's chrematistics; that is, unlimited wealth accumulation that could only proceed outside of the just price setting of the institutions of household, tribe, polis and agora (Alliez 1991; Berthoud 2002; Vogl 2014). In such unlimited accumulation, there was no ethic or ethics, even no ethos. For Sombart, the iconic figure was Jakob Fugger's long-distance trade and huge accumulations of capital. Weber countered this with Benjamin Franklin as paradigmatic capitalist. This was ascetic, anti-hedonistic, not primarily a question of acquisitiveness. It was a work ethic and most importantly an ethic of saving. Weber's Ben Franklin resembled Adam Smith's merchant, who limited the share of profits going to consumption in order to raise the proportion going to investment. Max Weber understood, as Tribe (2008) notes, marginalism as an economic science in terms of the optimization of resource allocation. In this, optimality is realized in terms of, not total, but marginal variation in want satisfaction.

This and its implicit potential mathematization can map onto Weber's *zweckrational* action in the later action theory, but formulated early as *homo economicus* in 1898. We recall Weber's 'Objectivity' essay, which advocated a social science that embraced *homo economicus*, positivist *erklären* and Historical-School *verstehen*. In *The Protestant Ethic*, Weber used a *verstehen* method to account for *homo economicus*, *erklären* outcome. Weber is looking to the singular subjectivity of the Protestant as a motive and cause, a psychological motive and cause of capitalist development. And this through what is an ethics that opposes acquisitiveness and even, in Weber's case, utilitarianism. Thus, Weber writes, 'the summum bonum of this ethic, the earning of more and more money, combines with strict avoidance of all spontaneous enjoyment of life' (Whimster 2007: 37). This is 'from the point of view of the happiness of, or utility to, the single individual it appears entirely transcendental and absolutely irrational'.

Simmel would have agreed with Sombart in that in modernity, with the trammels off, money becomes an end in itself. In this context, he develops the means–ends chains that are to be the basis of the later 1913 social-action theory, this having a profound effect on Parsons and on sociology more generally. Further, Simmel's *Erlebnis* sociology is very much a vitalism (Lash 2005). There is an energetics driving his *Philosophy of Money*. André Orléan (2014) has put Simmel next to Veblen in what for us is a substantialist economics, and is first-wave institutional economics, and by extension the critique of both classicism and neoclassicism. Simmel, unlike Weber (and for that matter both the classicals – Smith, Ricardo, Marx – and the neoclassicals), has a theory of value, based on neither substance nor the utilitarian subject but on the desire of the singular subject. Simmel looks at action as either being causal or intentional, hence teleological. In each case the realization of the action is driven by the expenditure of energy. The objects of Simmel's energetics of economic action carry the traces of such energy. Value, for Simmel, is when this energy of desire cannot achieve its object. We try then to realize or actualize desire. How? In means–ends chains and the now universal means, money is increasingly at the pivot of these means–ends chains, becomes the teleological means in this interweaving of purpose.

4.2 Classicals and Neoclassicals

4.2.1 Physics and Economics: From Conservation of Substance to Field of Utilities

Here we want to look at the counterposition of empiricism, of sensory experience in classical political economy to positivism and objective experience in neoclassicism. The German Historicists see mainly continuities between classicals and neoclassicals, as does the substantivist economics paradigm associated with Karl Polanyi and economic anthropology. Both, as we saw above, are, unlike the Historical School and the first-generation institutionalists, very much focused on value. The idea of value in exchange was present in Aristotle, especially in the *Politics*. This was a chrematistic notion of value where value in exchange was registered in money. Marx's *Capital* was very aware of this. One of the signal dimensions of Philip Mirowski's *More Heat than Light* (1991) is the explication of value as substance for the classicals – from Quesnay through Marx. In the neoclassicals, for their part, from Menger, Jevons, Walras, Marshall up until today, value shifts to the subject. The classicals were not dealing with an Aristotelian notion of substance. The source of their idea of substance (Mirowski 1991) was drawn from Cartesian physics. This is extended or material substance as opposed to the cogito or mental substance. The shift from classicals to neoclassicals thus was always a question of not the ancient but the modern episteme, in which value resided for the classicals in the object, for the neoclassicals in the subject.

This was also a shift from production, where value is determined for the classicals by first wheat in the physiocrats, then actually capital in Smith, labour in Ricardo and Marx. To repeat, Hegel in the *Phenomenology* noted the shift from classical substance to modern subject. Substance with its predicates to the subject, and its predicates, mediated of course by Christianity and God as subject. When God becomes subject, substance becomes very much matter. What Quesnay through Marx were addressing was really matter, though they used the word substance; for example, Marx's *Wertsubstanz* was not Aristotelian substance but matter.[2] The matter of modern physics, though this was, as we shall see, Cartesian physics. That it was Cartesian physics is important for the understanding of how capital works because (not for Newton but) for Descartes, this was conserved substance, with, as it were, energy conserved in the substance. Substance would be conserved as it was converted from labour to commodities, from the means of production or capital to commodities, right through the consumption of workers, merchants and entrepreneurs. This

---

[2] *Wertsubstanz* seems to me to be more than just matter. It stands in contrast to *Wertform* or value-form. *Wertsubstanz* embraces also use-value and, for me, the substance that we address in substantivist economics.

was present in Quesnay's *Tableau économique*, which greatly influenced Smith during his Paris years and is encountered again in Marx's *Capital*, volume II. Volume I of *Capital* is very much about labour substance and its exploitation, and volumes II and III are about extending circulation and reproduction through the *Tableau économique* of Department I and Department II. Value was thus conserved from production through trade and consumption. For all the classicals, this was production-driven – so the production-driven lineametric movement of substance or matter through trade, circulation, consumption was 'the true arbiter of the wealth of nations'.

For Mirowski (1991), physics sets up an episteme in which both classicals and neoclassicals are situated. For classicals this is value as Cartesian conserved substance; for neoclassicals, based on Laplace, Clark Maxwell and Helmholtz, it is energy that replaces matter (substance) in a paradigm of field physics and field economics. Both are based on a sort of energy: for the classicals, energy is substance; for neoclassicals, it is field. There is a change in the metrology, from a lineametric paradigm in the classicals to a field metric in the neoclassicals. Hence for the classicals, including Marx, there is Aristotelian exchange value based in money. But the moderns – from Quesnay on – were never going to be happy with this. Value had now to be produced. This could be from the land, as in physiocracy. It could be capital – the proportion of profit that was reinvested and not consumed – as in Smith. It could be labour, as in Marx (1967) and in David Ricardo (2004). In Aristotle, there was an anthropometric value theory. This will become the 'natural' basis of 'society' for Smith, but for the ancients and Aristotle, this kind of exchange and value is entirely unnatural. The 'provisioning aspects of social life' were divided into, on the one hand, what was necessary for both *oikos* and polis, both household management and polity, and, on the other hand, trade. And whereas *oikos* and polis were bounded and 'natural', trade was unbounded and unnatural. Trade, said Aristotle, brought together the differing estates as if they were equal, 'the husbandman and doctor', and disrupted the social structure of the polis. This is very much Sombart's view as we just saw, with Jews and long-distance traders who were excluded and separated from the guild structure giving the basis to capitalism. Note this is not Smith's local merchant. It is not local but very long-distance, hence long-time-period, trade that yields this necessary centralization of capital. Trade capitalism is thus long-distance trade capitalism. Long-distance and big ships. This is surely where capital on any kind of scale – in Venice and Amsterdam – accumulated. Some of this trade and retail activity was the province of slaves. This equalization through trade of statuses and of things – seen by Aristotle as an 'excrescence on the body politic' – was understood as static and not dynamic. There was a shift again from Sombart's mediaeval guilds (run on a quasi-*oikos* basis, with live-in apprentices and journeymen) and hence a 'natural' basis for the just price. From this there is a shift instead to a framework of contract that is based on the equality of things. The Greek polis had very little contract law, which was very much a Roman phenomenon. This equalization of value in objects required an 'arbitrary', a conventional, means of equalization of value. This means was money. Value, as intrinsically unstable, performing an unnatural function, would come under the label for Aristotle of not substance but accident. For the moderns, this materialist accident became the natural basis of social relations (Berthoud 2002).

For the moderns, Mirowski notes, such as Francis Bacon, there is a notion of conservation, that is now in a closed and bounded system of exchange: 'whatever is somewhere gotten is somewhere lost'. Here we are moving towards lineametric value and value conservation. This is present in William Harvey on the circulation of blood in what has become a sort of 'body-machine' and especially in Descartes, for whom all phenomena are matter in motion. It is this matter-in-motion idea of physics with Descartes and conservation of substance that is taken over by Quesnay. Now, with Descartes, the natural or matter, material substance is in motion. The natural is no longer Aristotelian stasis but motion. Thus, also we can understand the stasis assumptions of the above-discussed German cameralism partly based on the economy not as flow or motion but as Aristotle's household management. Harvey's idea was of the human body as a life machine and the coronary system as a pump. Correspondingly, Quesnay 'traces the circulation of generic value substance originating in agriculture through the three classes – landlords, farmers and artisans – of economic life. This was the move as well from natural philosophy to natural science (Mirowski 1991: 155). Now fast-forward to Smith, who is not happy with agriculture as the basis of all value. For Smith, wealth is a '*stock*', very different from Aristotle's chrematistics. The wealth of nations also is a stock. This stock is resolved into goods for immediate consumption, and resources for yielding revenue. The revenue-yielding stock from forgoing immediate consumption is capital: its prototypical proponent is the merchant (Mirowski 1991: 167).

Utility theory and the neoclassicals replace Cartesian mechanics with the Laplacian field. Laplace field theory was taken up by neoclassicals, most directly by Irving Fisher and Paul Samuelson. Laplace field theory in his *mécanique célestielle* was based on gravitation, hence field of potentials, a vector field. This was deterministic, based on continuous, and not discrete, variables, and presumed the stability of the solar system. Newton could not explain the stability of the whole, and opined that perhaps divine intervention was at stake. Newton also says we cannot discover the reason for the properties of gravity from phenomena. Newton used rather elementary geometry to describe his physics. He did not draw on his differential and integral calculus. Laplace uses the calculus to describe the vectors in the field. Similarly, Irving Fisher brings in the time dimension to the theory of price. A scalar is somehow an invariant under a transformation. A field is a vector space: a space of potentials. Newtonian gravitational potential is a scalar field. In calculus, the line integral of a vector field represents the work done by a force moving along a path. Here, conservation of energy is exhibited by the fundamental theorem of calculus. The rise of energy physics gave us the 'unification of the theories of rational mechanics, heat, electricity and magnetism'. This is 'syndetic: fragmented metrics are consolidated under a single all-encompassing yet reified invariant' (Mirowski 1991: 262, 271).

On the side of economics, it is value that is conserved: value as substance and now value as utility. It is the conservation principle that defines and fixes the identity of a system as it undergoes various transformations. In mathematics, it is the sum of potential and kinetic energy that is conserved in a closed system; in neoclassical economics, the sum of total utility, total expenditures. It is the conservation of utility, the conservation of expenditure or the conservation of their sum. Economists, observes Mirowski (1991: 273), similarly are thinking in terms of a preference field or a utility function and the distinction between the anticipation and realization of utility, i.e. potential and realized utility. Thus, field theory assumes importance in economists' theory of value. The format of a field (Laplace 2017) is 'a set of differential equations describing forces joined to some variational principle'. This is the beginning, freeing physics from dependency on matter. This works much better with neoclassical utility than with classical economics' production or endowment. The latter is more objective and less malleable. Again, key is the shift from substance to the mind, from external substance to the mind: to the mind 'as a field of force in an independently constituted commodity space' (Mirowski 1991: 196).

4.2.2 Scottish Enlightenment

Classical economics is rooted in the Scottish Enlightenment, which starts from an a posteriori empiricism that is very different from neoclassicism's a priori *homo economicus*. Hume sees man as a slave of the passions, the inclinations. Many have compared Smith to Mandeville's *Fable of the Bees: or, Private Vices, Public Virtues*. But unlike Mandeville, Smith has assumptions that human nature is benevolent. If we follow our inclinations, the invisible hand of the market will yield a positive outcome. The model of man is here not that of the rationally calculating animal of utilitarianism and *homo economicus*. Thus Deleuze's Hume is not at all positivist. Hume – with James and Deleuze – thus rejects the causation in favour of conjunction and replaces Kant's subject, Kant's transcendental unity of apperception, with the 'empirical multiplicity of perception'.

Hume and Smith are greatly influenced by a Scottish Enlightenment 'father', Francis Hutcheson, on experience. Hutcheson was Smith's teacher. Kant debated with Hutcheson and Shaftesbury's[3] idea of a moral sense and their aesthetics in both the Second and Third Critiques. Hutcheson thought mainly in opposition to Descartes' innate ideas, in regard to which he almost fully accepted Locke's position. What Locke calls reflection, Hutcheson understands as internal senses. Hutcheson disagrees with Hobbes's and Mandeville's assessment of the selfishness of human nature. Most of Hutcheson's internal senses are not cognitive. In reaction to Hobbes and Mandeville's assumptions, there are two internal senses – one of which is the *'sensus communis'* or 'public sense'. For Kant, the *sensus communis* becomes an a priori. For Hutcheson, it is empirical. Through this public sense we are pleased at perceiving the happiness of others and uneasy by their misery. We sense beauty through such an internal sense. It is a sense that is pleased by proportion, symmetry and harmony and depends on sight and hearing as external senses. For its part, the moral sense, with Shaftesbury, comes from the pleasure we take in the beauty of virtuous actions. It is also about benevolent feelings towards actions and affections in which we perceive virtue and vice.

For Hutcheson, a sense in general is a 'determinant of our minds to receive ideas independent of our will, to have perceptions of pleasure and pain' (Broadie 2001: 281). Again, influenced by Locke and Shaftesbury, for Hutcheson the 'operation of our external sense on

---

[3] Anthony Ashley-Cooper, 3rd Earl of Shaftesbury.

an object produces within us an idea of the object'. There is the move to Shaftesbury, for whom 'our internal or aesthetic sense operates on the eternal sensory idea, producing in us immediately an idea of the object's beauty'. Here, Hutcheson alludes to Locke's primary qualities of figure and number and secondary qualities of taste and colour. In primary qualities, the ideas work through resemblance, in secondary qualities they do not. Associated with Hutcheson's idea of beauty, in which inner sense operates on the material from the external senses, is the pleasure we take in the thing. The pleasure thus is not immediate but internally mediated. This operation is a passive operation. Beauty is 'the idea raised in us'. Our sense of beauty is 'our power of receiving this idea'. Hutcheson (2017 [1725]) states, 'The figures which excite in us the idea of beauty are those in which there is uniformity amidst variety'. This kind of pleasure is an association the thing arouses in our mind: much more like a Freudian association, or the Lockean association of ideas.

Hume is much more concerned with the possibility of disagreement on aesthetic judgments and wants there to be a standard of taste. This is to be an 'empirical method' where 'those who can enlarge their view to contemplate distant nations and remote ages are surprised by the great inconsistency and contrariety' of taste in art. This is Hume drawing his aesthetics and ethics in large measure empirically, from history, and this connected a posteriori with the conjunction. Hume gives mind and reason pride of place. But, at the same time, reason is indubitably a slave of the passions.

This said, a few points about this shift from empiricism to neoclassical positivism are warranted. First, much of positivism is not utilitarian nor *homo economicus*. Durkheim's positivism and his social facts are positivist but not at all utilitarian. They have little to do with Weberian positivism's *homo economicus*. This is because the key generator of Durkheim's social facts is the sacred itself. Utilitarianism is a question of the profane. Indeed, MAUSS (Mouvement anti-utilitairiste des sciences sociales) along with Georges Bataille is very influenced by Durkheim's sacred. Second, utilitarianism is not equivalent to *zweckrational* action. *Zweckrational* action, instrumentally rational action, might draw on J.S. Mill's *Logic*, but its *homo economicus* does not intend the greatest good for the greatest number as does utilitarianism. Yet the rational calculation of utility and units of utility has spread from utilitarianism to notions of utility and marginal utility in neoclassical economics and thus *homo economicus*. Finally, there are proto-utilitarian notions in Hutcheson and Hume: in Hutcheson's *sensus communis* and Hume's more nuanced notions – which separates the deliberation of judgment from the subsequent feelings of pleasure. But Scottish empiricism does not start with the rational calculation of utility. It starts instead with assumptions of the benevolence of human nature.

4.3 Conclusions: The Economic and the Political

We have considered ancient experience, and then subjective and objective experience. We have explored the objective experience of economic formalism – whether in classical political economy or neoclassical (neoliberal) economics. In terms of neoliberalism – which there is no space to address at length here – there are three strands. Those who have followed very much in the footprints of neoclassicism: its assumptions of marginal utility and the utility-maximizing social actor. We see this in Chicago School representatives like Gary Becker and Milton Friedman. Then there are those who do not accept the assumptions of utility maximization or perfect information and have been influenced by cybernetics: these include Hayek, von Neumann and Herbert Simon (Gane 2014; Mirowski 2002). Finally, there are the ordoliberals who Foucault saw as paradigmatic for neoliberalism because of their focus on the legal order. Other paradigm-case neoliberals such as R.H. Coase (1937, 1960), also from the Chicago School – which was the Chicago School of *Law* and Economics – operated with contracting notions, also extending neoliberalism's juridical model. What they all have in common – classical political economy, neoclassicism and all the schools of neoliberalism – is a certain formalism. It is this that was challenged by the substantivist economics of the Historical School, Karl Polanyi, the economic anthropologists and the world-systems theorists from Pirenne and Braudel to Arrighi.

But where are the politics in all this? This is where Hannah Arendt, whom we now turn to, comes in. Arendt, for her part, makes common cause with the substantivists in her distinction between work and labour. Labour is the homogeneous labour of abstract interchangeable units of labour time, which, like exchange-value, function only in reproduction: for Arendt, labour is the natural and biological reproduction of the household (Greek: *oikos*). Work for Arendt – and the paradigm seems to be Aristotle's technics – involves a new design every time; its products are singular and different from one another. Work contributes not to the natural reproduction of the *oikos* but is already incipiently political in producing the substance, the built fabric of the polis. We are on our way to Aristotle's *zoon politikon*, to what Giorgio Agamben (1998) calls *bios* instead of *zoe*, to the constitution of political forms of life. At stake for Arendt is surely not *die Politik,* which itself works from the model of labour and provides merely a space for instrumental action and the accumulation of capital. It is instead *das Politische*, not a formal but a substantivist politics. We are beginning finally to address political experience. Arendt's *das Politische* has next to nothing to do with Carl Schmitt. It is not a politics of friend and enemy. Arendt's *Politische* starts from classical, ancient experience. It is, with Aristotle, fully a posteriori, beginning from the particular and working towards the general. It is, again with Aristotle, based on language. Humans, for Aristotle and Arendt, are linguistic animals before they are political animals. To be linguistic is a precondition of *zoon politikon*. This is finally for Arendt and with Aristotle against Plato to engage in rhetoric, featuring deliberative rhetoric.

But Arendt's politics, unlike the communitarians such as MacIntyre (1981) or Milbank and Pabst (2016), are not just ancient polis-like virtues. There is always an ancient substrate of virtues and substance. But above this there is a modern transformation based on the freedom of the will. Arendt carries this out first as an Augustinian. Indeed, her challenge to Heidegger's mortality from her own politics of natality, or new beginnings, was based in Augustine (Kampowski 2008). But her modernity and political is then at the same time Kantian, in the knowledge that Kant – and the Kantian watershed at the beginning of fully modern experience – was not possible without first the City of God. If we had stayed with Leo Strauss (1978) in the Greek City of Man, this Kantian experience and the free will would never have happened. Yes, Arendt's politics are Kantian, but she stands resolutely against the objective experience of Kant's First Critique. And she also refuses the moral break with experience for the a priori of the Second Critique's categorical imperative. She starts instead from the aesthetic judgments of the Third Critique: that is, in a politics of subjective experience. If William James works from not concepts but instead percepts, Arendt's Third Critique politics are very much literally of the senses, of the five senses and more, and in this sense very much a politics of the body.

Arendt's modern politics in the end even breaks with Kant's Third Critique a priori (of judgment). Kant's Third Critique a priori is 'finality without end'. That is, in this context, political judgment should be like the judgment of a work of art: that is, not as a means to an end, nor as a pure end, but instead as what Benjamin (1977b) and Agamben (2005) see as a means without ends. Arendt will resist such a politics. Her (Kantian) politics have no a priori at all. Kant gives us a categorical imperative. Arendt will have nothing to do with anything categorical. Her politics are fully empirical. Hence, she has been adopted by anarchists and the democratic anarchists of, for example, Hong Kong's Umbrella Movement. Agamben's a priori politics are in many ways similar to Heidegger's a priori worlds and being in the world. Arendt's political worlds are thoroughly empirical. Agamben tells us, with his a priori of means without ends and implicitly Heideggerian worlds, that now we are all *homo sacer*. We have all been extruded from the political into something the equivalent of 'camps'. But we are not. We are not all *homo sacer*. Arendt's empirical and a posteriori politics tells us of the fragility of political worlds: of even Rome (and Augustine was also a Roman), of the Weimar Republic, of the rule of law and democracy. It is to the experiential politics of Hannah Arendt that we now turn.

— 5 —

HANNAH ARENDT'S A POSTERIORI POLITICS: FREE WILL, JUDGMENT AND CONSTITUTIONAL FRAGILITY

5.1 Ancients and Moderns

Arendt's singular great book is surely *The Human Condition*. You read *The Human Condition* and you are struck by the extent to which Arendt is Aristotelian. You are struck by her anti-Platonism and focus on experience. You see her focus on antiquity and wonder how anyone could see her as consistent with Habermas on public spheres and with Habermas's (and Rawls's) a priori conceptions of politics. The a priori starts from the universal and works deductively to the particular. Arendt with Aristotle is instead with the a posteriori and experience. With the particular. Aristotle, like Plato, foregrounds justice in his ethics and politics. Yet justice and ethics are not at the centre of Arendt's political. In Aristotle, justice is the core political virtue. We see more recently in, for example, Derrida (1994) that justice is the undeconstructible. Derrida on justice is quite opposed to Aristotle. For him, knowledge is Athens while justice is more or less Jerusalem. Derrida's justice resembles Levinas's ethics of ultimate and unconditional responsibility before the other, which itself seems to share assumptions with Kierkegaard's fear and trembling before an unknowable and invisible God. Justice is also Benjamin's 'divine violence' in contradistinction to law. Hannah Arendt, for her part, does not speak very much about justice. She is interested in action and politics. We will see below that her notion of the political and action is not just Greek. It is a 'reluctant modernity' that will segue through Augustine's will, whose unconditionality is at one with Kant's moral imperative.[1] The idea in Kant's idealism is the moral imperative; it is

[1] My empiricist interpretation of Arendt is rather opposite to Seyla Benhabib's, though

96

the unconditioned will, the subject as unconditioned will. The subject before it ever meets the object. Augustine's and Kant's pure will – and thus Arendt's political – is a lot different from Derrida's justice. Augustine's will is begun in Adam after the Creation, while Derrida's justice is much more a question of Abraham. The consequences of Adam's free will, i.e. original sin and the Fall, are the responsibility, the infinite responsibility, the infinite debt of Abraham and then of Christ.

But the undeconstructible itself then must be the a priori, here in Derrida the condition of possibility of thought and politics. A prioris are by definition in, for example Kant, metaphysical. We recall Kant's response to Hume's radical scepticism, to Hume's radical rejection of anything metaphysical, including the notion of cause.[2] Kant's response is to accept this and then to see causation, the other categories of the understanding as unified in the transcendental unity of apperception, as the a priori and metaphysical condition of possibility of knowledge. Yet this itself is based in the free will, the unconditioned nature of the modern subject. This is the basis of modern metaphysics so different from Aristotle's. Aristotle's was a metaphysics of substance, Kant's of the subject. Aristotle's substance is of course not unconditioned. It is caused. To be caused is to be conditioned. You need God and Adam and Abraham in order to have the subject.

This is also a problem with James's (Chapter 3) and Husserl's notions of experience. Whereas Kantian experience is that of the subject for the object, Husserl's and James's experience – as does all phenomenology since Hegel – mediates instead between consciousness and phenomena (appearances). Arendt, it seems to me, refuses metaphysics, including metaphysical notions of justice. For Arendt, in her empiricist vein, nothing is undeconstructible. All is empirical. All is fragile. Her paradigmatic examples are the fragility of Western liberal institutions in the face of Hitler's totalitarianism, and the fall of the Roman Empire. Her PhD thesis on Augustine was in the context of the fall of Rome and the emergence of the uncon-ditioned will: the fall of antiquity and the forecasting announcement of modernity. Not the Greeks but the Romans were, for Arendt, the political people par excellence.

for both of us Arendt does give us a politics of modernity. Paradoxically, my reading is closer to Benhabib's *Situating the Self* (1992).

[2] This is the lynchpin of Quentin Meillassoux's *After Finitude* (2008). Meillassoux uses Hume's awakening of Kant to reject experience altogether, in the direction of Badiou's Platonic and Cartesian rationalism.

EXPERIENCE

Arendt's concern is for the stability of worlds, of political worlds. With the Romans, she was aware of the dangers of plebiscitarian democracy. She was aware of the fragility of institutions. For her, institutions, including the polis itself, are constitutive of the political. Aristotle was well aware of this. For him, *oikos* (household management) and tribe and polis were associations or institutions. The rule of philosopher-kings was not the condition of possibility of justice. He and Arendt (unlike also Habermas and Rawls) are not looking for the conditions of possibility of anything. Aristotle looks at 158 constitutions of Greek city-states. He reckons that these states are more or less just, that they more or less provide a frame for eudemonia for the development of human capacities, of virtues, first among them as justice. He is aware that tyranny does not do this. Tyrannies are not in fact constitutional. If there are no constraints or few institutional constraints on executive power, then there is no constitution in any meaningful sense. City-states come and go. They are built and destroyed. Arendt is highly aware of the empirical nature of these formations.

Reminiscent of MacIntyre on the virtues some 25 years later, what we are given in Arendt is the *Nicomachean Ethics*. For MacIntyre, after virtue there is modernity. Arendt is much more on side with the Romans – with private law and contract, with property law, with representative democracy; that is, more liberal democracy. MacIntyre, like John Milbank (Milbank and Pabst, *Politics of Virtue*) in 2016, saw virtue in what was a critique of liberalism, in what can amount to an anti-liberalism, more consistent with today's – Milbank calls them post-liberal – politics. Arendt sees the mob at the door.

For decades, we have received Arendt largely through the juxtaposition with Habermas on the question of the public sphere. Indeed, her *Human Condition*, with its benchmark chapter on the private and the public, appeared only some five years before Habermas's *Strukturwandel der Öffentlichkeit*. Arendt has been reintroduced to readers in recent years through 'Italian theory' – through Negri and Agamben and Paolo Virno. Agamben has come to it from a slightly different direction than the 'multitudes' thinkers, the post-operaistas. The operaistas, with their focus on work, took up immediately on Arendt's distinction between work and labour, again in *The Human Condition*. Here especially Virno (2015) was prescient, reading Arendt's work as Aristotelian *technē* and thinking it through the juxtaposition of *technē* on the one hand and praxis on the other.

Agamben's Arendt has to do with Foucault on sovereignty and governmentality. Agamben and Foucault were concerned with *oikos*

98

and *oekonomia*. Foucault largely devoted the second volume of *History of Sexuality* to Xenophon and *oikos*. For Foucault and Agamben, governmentality is very much a descendant of *oikos*. Agamben proceeds then, especially in *The Kingdom and the Glory*, to contrast governmentality with sovereignty. Sovereignty, we then think, with Agamben would be something much more on the model of polis. In *Homo Sacer*, Agamben's *bios* is based on Aristotle's *zoon politikon*. For Arendt, the polis has little to do with sovereignty. She contrasts 'virtuosity' in the polis with the sovereignty of the modern state system, which for her would have been pre-eminently *oikos*. The Hobbesian ethos of sovereignty was realized in the Peace of Westphalia, which created a basis for the national system of sovereignty, consolidating the concept of sovereign states in international law. Arendt is aware of the instrumentalism of Hobbesian and Westphalian sovereignty. For her, virtuosity is at the heart of political action in speech and deed, in Pericles' performances in the context of the plurality: the plurality of a community of singularities in the polis. Sovereignty presumes not the monad-like singularity of Arendt, but instead an atomism in which every individual state is like every other: an atomism that defines instrumental rationality and Arendt's and Foucault's *oikos*-based notions of governmentality. Arendt's sovereignty is about, not the polis, but possessive individuals.

Whereas both political-science positivism and Habermas's and Rawls's ideal speech situation or original position are in an a priori mould, Arendt's politics are a posteriori. She does argue for work against labour. Here labour is a question of the natural economy of the household (*oikos*). Labour was for slaves and maybe women. But 'work' could produce for the needs of the polis. For Arendt, Marxism was a problematics of labour and not work. Marx's labour theory of value (Chapter 4) presumes an a priori of labour as substance. This substance is not work's concrete and singular activity, making craft objects or public buildings and infrastructure, but abstract homogeneous labour power. The Marxian blueprint for the communist society was also, for Arendt, governed by an abstract notion of the good, in a Platonic mould. Whereas labour, in its homogeneity and abstraction, proceeds from the general to the particular, work is more empirical, starting from the particular (see Chapter 2). Negri, Agamben and Virno situate this, not in Arendt's more classical Marxism, but in a neo-Marxism of difference, in which work is prioritized over labour. Arendt and the post-operaistas, as well as Bernard Stiegler and for that matter Foucault, are always aware of Aristotle's tripartite distinction of episteme, praxis and technics. All of the above see modern power, governmentality and instrumental reason as rooted in episteme. Indeed, positivism and neoclassical economics are based in episteme. The difference is that the Italian thinkers along with Stiegler (early Heidegger) and Foucault, with his technologies of the self, work from the contraposition of episteme and technics; for Arendt, we must think through praxis.

For her praxis is constitutive of the human condition. Praxis is what humans and not animals do. Man is *zoon politikon*. Man is fully human only in the polis. And the best polis – whether monarchy, aristocracy or democracy – is that which can offer space for the development of human virtues, the eudemonia of the virtues. Any of the constitution types featured in Aristotle's *Politics* could work as polis in fostering the virtues. Tyranny could not and neither could empire. Empire was a degeneration of the polis's constitution. Aristotle's tyranny or empire was governable by an arbitrary will. The monarch, in contrast, was constitutionally constrained. The polis's constitutions, unlike the arbitrary will of tyrant or emperor, were necessary to foster virtue. Aristotle's *Politics* is inspired by an empirical critique of Plato's *Republic*. The *Nicomachean Ethics* was partly a prolegomenon to the *Politics*. Arendt's *Human Condition* is much closer to the *Nicomachean Ethics*, yet she is concerned not so much with either ethics or questions of justice but instead with politics. Arendt was a contemporary of Leo Strauss at the University of Chicago. Nothing could be further from Strauss's mystical Platonism than what I will argue is her politics of experience. Strauss and Carl Schmitt were engaged in lifelong debate, Schmitt's idea of sovereignty and the sovereign owing a great deal to Strauss's nemesis Hobbes. Schmitt nonetheless understood the modern state as an illegitimate 'political theology'. For Schmitt, such a theology amounted to the destruction of the political. Arendt, fundamentally influenced by Augustine in her focus on a politics of 'new beginnings' or 'natality', will see the Augustinian and hence 'theologically constituted politics of the modern' – with Blumenberg – as legitimate. Problematic, surely: but legitimate and setting the frame for contemporary political activity.

It is important to situate Arendt's work in the context of Agamben and Walter Benjamin. There is a Kantian Third-Critique motif running through the work of all three of them. The Greeks did not have the sort of philosophical anthropology of the moderns. Yet justice, as a pivotal virtue of man and the polis, as distinct from the barbarians, and tyranny and the idea of *zoon politikon*, make it seem credible that justice would have been at the heart of an Aristotelian human condition. For Arendt, with whom these Greek origins must segue through Rome, Augustinian Christianity and Kantian judgment, the human condition is not justice but action or politics itself.

For Derrida, the undeconstructible is justice based on Benjamin's notion of divine violence. Agamben seizes on this in his juxtaposition of Benjamin versus Schmitt, of justice versus law. Here Agamben and Benjamin – though not so much Derrida – focus on divine violence or justice as a politics of pure means. This is the 'anarchist' Benjamin reacting to Sorel's *Reflections on Violence*. Here, violence as pure means or a politics of pure means is also a reference to Kant. In this regard, politics as a means to ends or instrumental politics would map onto the *Critique of Pure Reason*, a politics of pure ends to the Second Critique and a politics of pure means to the Third Critique. The Third Critique is divided into two sections, one on reflective (aesthetic) judgment and the other on teleological judgment (Gasché 2003). Teleological judgment's a priori is *Zweckmäßigkeit ohne Zweck*, or purposefulness without purpose, finality without ends. This is the very much the same as means without ends. Arendt's relationship to the Third Critique – which we will address at length below – is more complex. Its focus is on reflective judgment more than teleological judgment, and especially on reflective judgment's *sensus communis*. But she gives us elements – we will see – to bring reflective and teleological judgment more together in her notion of the political. In all these contexts, what Kant sees as an a priori, Arendt understands as empirical and a posteriori.

The Arendt–Agamben juxtaposition is worth taking further. Though he speaks of *zoon politikon* and *bios* versus *zoe* in *homo sacer*, Agamben's fundamental references are not Greek but Roman, indeed Roman and Christian. *Homo sacer* comes from Roman Law, and his Schmittian states of exception draw especially on Roman Law. His Paul book, the book on the monasteries, and the *Kingdom and the Glory* draw especially on Christian theology. Agamben, though anti-Christian,[3] is steeped in Christian influences. *The Kingdom and the Glory* promises to be, then, explorations of, in contraposition to *oikos* and governmentality, an exploration in sovereignty, as the very non-instrumental *gloire* of the king. Yet the greater part of the book is devoted to the examination of Christian theology and especially the Holy Family, the relation of God, Christ and the Holy Spirit. The Holy Family, he recognizes, is much more in the spirit of *oikos* than of polis.

---

[3] See Agamben's books on *Opus Dei* (2013b) and *The Highest Poverty* (2013a).

5.2 *Pax Romana* and City of God

In the essays collected under the title of *Between Past and Future*, we get a glimpse into Arendt's expanded political. Jerome Kohn (2006) in the introduction speaks of Arendt's admiration for the Roman god Janus. Janus is a god of beginnings, the most important of which was the foundation of Rome itself and the Roman Republic. This god of beginnings, unlike us mortals, can connect past to future: he has two sets of eyes, one fixed on the past and one on the future: so much different than we mortals who live mainly in the now: the now and here, *hic* and *nunc*. Rome was the world's first republic, unlike Greek democracy, the beginnings of parliamentary sovereignty. Rome lasted, including the Empire, which gave us technology, institutions and the *Pax Romana*, for nearly a thousand years. The Romans 'were the most political of all peoples'. Aeneas' descendants were to forge the eternal city, the everlasting public thing, the *res publica*, out of the fires that consumed Troy. There was no word for tradition in ancient Greek. For the Romans, tradition meant to 'hand down' this 'public thing', down the generations, from father to son. Greece had constitutions but did not build the institutions, the legal structures that – as Rome did – held together the citizenry. This was Roman justice, its *jus civile* underpinned a very different body politic from Greece. It was the basis from which Augustine wrote the *City of God*. Rome was quintessentially the 'City of Man', the this-worldly.

The *Pax Romana* resembles the *Pax Britannica* or even the *Pax Sinica* and today's threatened *Pax Americana* and *Pax Europa*. Augustine lived inside the *Pax Romana* and saw it crumble. Yet Augustine's City of God refused Rome's City of Man, putting things off till an apocalyptic, eschatological end. In contrast to Arendt's *Pax Romana* institutionalism, there is Augustine's City of God, which is by its nature anti-institutional. Compared to the Greeks, man for Augustine was created by God with free will. But the possibility to use this free will to attain redemption and the City of God was fully extinguished by Adam and Eve's original sin. Augustine needs to be understood with regard to his powerful Christology. This is in comparison with Pelagius, with whom Augustine was involved in dispute. Pelagius held that not all of man's free will – that is, his ability to act virtuously – was extinguished by original sin. Humans, Pelagius argued, were capable of virtuous conduct to the point where they could attain redemption. Thus, human good works could lead to redemption. For Augustine, salvation was based only on faith, not on good works. Man was here very much the passive receptacle of grace from God. But only from God via the death and resurrection of Christ. Thus, we do not counteract our sinfulness through virtuous action, but Christ who dies for our sins is our only redeemer. Through our reception of Christ, our faith in Christ – whether mediated by sacraments in Catholicism or the more direct reception in Protestantism – we can attain salvation. Man had free will in the Garden of Eden, we can exercise free will in everyday conduct; but we have lost it to the extent that it counts. And to count means to attain to the City of God. So, it's neither by law nor good works but by faith that redemption is possible. For Pelagius, God's grace was not fully extinguished in men's souls. For Augustine, it was. For all three of Catholics, Protestants and Eastern Orthodox, Augustine defeated Pelagius.

Augustine understood the implications of Pelagius' view. If we can attain grace and in salvation participate in the infinite holiness of God by our own efforts, we would not need Christ. Christ would just be a model of virtuous conduct and would not be the most important person of God. Then there could be no Christianity and no church. For Pelagius, then, we can achieve righteousness through our own efforts. But not for Augustine.

This discussion is to see how Augustine can work for Arendt. What is 'righteousness'? According to the OED it is the quality of being morally right. It is the quality of being thus 'justifiable', in that we have been judged as leading a life that is pleasing to God. This is the case in all the Abrahamic religions. The term righteous was introduced mainly by Tyndale's Bible as a translation of both the Hebrew tzedek and Greek diakios. There are also connections to dharma. Righteousness is an attribute, a quality of God in the Hebrew Bible, which is again consistent with the Sanskrit dharma as the right way of living. It is God's benevolence which through faith in Christ gives us the gift of salvation as participation in God's infinite holiness.

The two sides of this are surely Christ and the Church. Luther, very much the Pauline and Augustinian, was clearer about Christ than perhaps anyone else in his doctrine of sola fide; that is, justification by faith alone. For Luther, with Paul and Augustine, neither law nor works can lead to 'justification'. Sola fide and solus christos; that is not through God the Father but only through Christ. If we could achieve salvation through God, we could do it through our works, through virtuous behaviour. But this is incompatible with original sin and Christ being crucified for our sins. So 'justification', meaning judicial pardon by God, only works sola fide and solus

103

christos, only through faith and only through Christ. Only then can we share in the divine life of God, in the City of God. We cannot do this through Pelagius' works, or through law, through neither Pharisaic nor Roman Law. Paul as ex-Pharisee and a Roman as well as a Jew rejected both sets of laws for faith. And Augustine was the most important Pauline since Paul. And surely Paul, much more than the other Apostles, was, next to Christ himself, the most important Christian. God pardons or judges you through your faith not in God the father but in Christ. Hence your faith in the impossible in resurrection (Badiou 2003).

St Paul is the man of faith, of Christ and of the Church. We know that religion is not as important as Eusebia (William Tyndale), which is the spiritual relation with God. It is in this that God imputes (not infuses or imparts) righteousness in man. This spirituality is on the inside; religion itself only operates on the outside. Yet the Church itself is hugely important. And Paul and Augustine played such a key role in establishing the Church. In the New Testament, it is John and Paul, much more than Mark, Matthew and Luke, who give us a doctrine based almost solely in faith. Paul would marry the faith-based relation with God (the son) with the Church, as would Augustine. Only for the very few was spirituality sufficient: the rest needed the Church. Thus so much of the New Testament is about the Church, including the Epistles and the Acts. The four Gospels tell the story of Christ, with only John having the particular focus on death, resurrection and apocalypse. So much of the rest, and especially Paul in the Acts and Epistles, is about forming the Church.

5.2.1 Action and Work

So back to Arendt. We were looking at her 'institutionalism' of the *Pax Romana*. In this City of Man Augustine comes across as anti-institutional. All meaningful institutions (the Church) are to do with the City of God. The Greek City of Man, or polis, was institutional in the sense that the just man could emerge through the institutional meditations of household, tribe and polis. In Rome freedom becomes more formal and less substantive, hinging on property and contract law and representational republican government. Paul and Augustine dispense with all of this. Arendt's modernity will have to be equally institutional in supporting both the positive and substantive freedom of the polis as well as the negative freedom of *Pax Romana*. It is substantive and formal. This echoed Arendt's experience, in which the tradition of Western modernity, of rule of law and parliamentary democracy, based in the independent cities – the free cities (*'Stadtluft macht frei'*) of Western European feudalism and early modernity – collapsed with the rise of Hitler, with the tyranny of Hitler and Stalin. Yet, whereas Augustine chose the City of God, Arendt chooses the City of Man.

For us to get a handle on what Arendt means by action, which is at the heart of her idea of the political, Arendt is looking, among the Greeks, not at Aristotle who largely inherited the Platonic tradition, but instead at the pre-Socratics, in history and poetry, at Homer, Sophocles, Thucydides (Kohn 2006: ix), precisely because they did not see political activity as arising out of nature. Freedom and the new, 'natality', could not, would never, appear in the world naturally, and we remember nature is the basis of *oikos* or household.[4] Aristotle, for her, sees human agency too much on the basis of imitating natural processes and thus as a making, a sort of craft. This is *phusis* as nature, in the Greek experience of nature. Things of nature here did not come into being because of God's plan; indeed God did not create them. They came into being by themselves. This extended to man by Aristotle, in terms of man's teleology or final cause.

Making – and thus (not labour but) work – for Arendt operates according to a plan, a diagram through a blueprint through which 'the results of action are known in advance'. This is also part of her critique of Marx. Arendtian action and freedom have results that cannot be known in advance. If they could it would not be a new beginning. Thus, her notion of 'action' is as much Augustinian (and in this sense proto-modern) as it is Greek and ancient. The human condition is an anthropology and stands in contrast to a sort of 'animal condition'. Animals are mainly a question of species in which each one is pretty much identical to the other. Humans and human plurality are never collections of atoms but of singularities and this is also the human condition of beings reducible to one another ... distinct points of view in speech and action are indeed undermined by the necessities of labour. Action, to remind us again, involves both deeds and speech. Arendt extends this critique of labour as nature to Rousseau's natural modernity: for her, politics does not arise from a contract (Hobbesian or Rousseauian) in a primordial state of nature but from those that are already free. The polis, against both barbarians and households, stands very much distinct from nature.

---

[4] Thus, Leo Strauss in *Natural Right and History* (1965) could also be so against natural right. Natural right and nature would in this sense be making household and *oikonomia* the basis of how we live rather the political.

Arendt's mode of thinking politically will turn against both the universal and metaphysics. It 'arises out of incidents of living experience and must remain bound to them' (Arendt 2006: 14). Not metaphysics and not meta-discourse but commons sense, a *sensus communis* for which this world (as distinct from the other world of metaphysics) is what counts. Both metaphysics and Christianity give us devaluations of this world. For the political you need stability, both 'stabilizing force and a starting point from which to begin something new'. You need a mode of judgment that 'judges particulars in their particularity without subsuming under handed-down universals' (Kohn 2006: xx). The Romans gave us this stability with their thinking of tradition, unlike the break in tradition when you get the world destroying crimes of the totalitarian regimes that explode (Arendt 2006: 27) traditional standards of judgment.[5] This alludes to Kant on Common Law in which judgment means the referring of a particular to another particular from a previous case. And Arendt literally means the destruction of a world. The notion of world is important to her. Worlds here are a question of worldly goods, not Augustine's other-worldly ones or Jesus of Nazareth's, in which the good deed must be done in private, and not 'appear' in 'publicity'. Second, they are empirical worlds. The political is her world, while *oikos* is in nature outside of the world. These are not Heideggerian worlds as the condition of existence of authentic *Dasein*, but particular empirical worlds that are built and destroyed.

Animals only exist atomistically as members of a species, unlike human singularity. That is, only men are both mortal and natal. We are mortal and singular in our being towards death, in which, in Heideggerian vein, there is not death in general but always my death. We are singularities in our Augustinian being towards birth. In each case this is not biological, not the cyclical or circular time of biology and nature. *Zoe*, the animal or natural condition, has this cyclical time, while *bios* and the human condition of the political give us Augustine's rectilinear time. Yet the political is not part of a more or less deterministic historical narrative, as is sovereignty, but instead consists of 'single instances, the single gesture' of the virtuosos, the reason of whose action is immanent to that action. There is no human condition without memory, which gives us the stability needed for the political. Human words and deeds are mortal and only the human capacity for remembrance can make these last.

---

[5] Here we see again that Arendt's worlds are empirical and a posteriori worlds rather than Heidegger's a priori world as condition of possibility of authentic *Dasein*.

In which 'action has a *meaning* for the living, has *value* only from the dead'. All this is under threat in modernity, in which, as Rilke said, 'everything perishes'. Aristotle (and Arendt) put poetry and history in the same category because both make something lasting out of such remembrance. Poetry and history are not action itself, but record the action of the great in deeds and in words. For Aristotle, 'through the tears of remembrance', we get the 'essence of tragedy' in, for example, 'Ulysses hearing the story of his own life and feeling reconciliation, catharsis' (Arendt 2006).

5.3 After the Polis: Augustine and Free Will

It is Augustine, the subject of her PhD thesis, who gives to Arendt the modernity of her political. With Augustine, we see that the political is not just polis. It is action. It is action and world. Action is world building along with work. Work builds infrastructure for worlds that are fundamentally political. Worlds are empirical. They come and go. You need action to sustain worlds as well as build them. Eichmann and Hitler, the barbarians at the fall of Rome, are thus world-destroying. They destroy the political and debase the human condition. Arendt speaks of a German clergyman, who had the opportunity to confront Eichmann but would not do so, in terms of an absence of action. Action could have sustained a political world here, which was debased to a level far lower than *oikos*. Nazi totalitarianism is what gives us *homo sacer*, gives us 'bare life' (Agamben 1998). *Oikos* at least is life. For Aristotle, the *oikos* or household is the basic level of association, on a higher level is the tribe and the highest the polis. The telos, the final cause of the *oikos*, however, is the polis itself, is the eudemonia, the virtue- (or what today we might call capacity-) building workings of the polis. Bare life is excluded from all of this. Augustine was not just a Christian but also a Roman. And Arendt, as we saw above, praises the Romans – more than the Greeks – with their world-sustaining institutional development as the ultimate political people.

For many, Arendt's operative concept is natality: it is the capability to be born anew. If, with Heidegger, we get 'mortality' and being-towards-death, with Arendt there is natality, or being-towards-birth. Natality is understood as being at the heart of 'action', of the political, for Arendt, indeed of the human condition. Arendt's political is thus Greek, with the polis and virtues, made with Roman institutions and perhaps most of all *Pax Romana*, and is thirdly a question of Augustinian natality, which is Christian and fundamentally modern.

Hegel's transition from substance to subject, which is for him the transition from antiquity to modernity, runs through Christianity. If the pivot of Greek antiquity, its metaphysics and logic was the matter-and-form of substance and its predicates, then modernity's pivot, Hegel underscored, was the subject. Between antiquity and modernity, as Hegel with Arendt understood, and perhaps best shown at length in Blumenberg's masterwork, *Die Legitimität der Neuzeit*, the *Legitimacy of the Modern Age*, is Christianity. With Max Weber, Blumenberg's modernity is fundamentally Christian. This is a question for Blumenberg and Arendt of not the legitimation but the legitim*acy* of the modern. Against Carl Schmitt and also largely Nietzsche, for whom modernity is illegitimate as a 'political theology', for Blumenberg and Arendt modernity (although secular) is Christian-constituted, but nonetheless legitimate.

Arendt is aware that this Christian-constituted modern subject is Augustine's will, Augustine's free will. In Arendt's ancient Greece, action is not yet fully mature because there is not yet the ethos of the free will. Agency is a question of man, and humans, like other substances (including the political substance of the polis itself), are caused. Humans are constituted through material, efficient, formal and final causes. In Augustine's Christianity and after this in our modern, the subject and thus human agency are uncaused. What makes the will – from Christian to today's modernity – free is that it is uncaused. It is an uncaused cause, the unmoved mover. Unlike the Greek gods who are caused, the Abrahamic and Christian God is uncaused. He is completely free. The universe did not create Him. He created the universe. He then created only man in his image. How to reconcile uncaused God and largely uncaused man was at the heart of debates in metaphysics from Descartes to Leibniz until the question of this apparent contradiction and the question of theodicy was put to rest by the Enlightenment – by Voltaire – and confirmed in the origins of Kant's critique of metaphysics. Arendt, as we see below, is fundamentally Kantian. Augustine's free will is grounded in the other-worldly City of God, while Arendt with Kant gives us a subject whose will and potential for natality are rooted in the City of Man. With the move from substance to subject, the locus of potential, of potentiality, is also displaced. All classical substances are actual and potentials. Human substances are constitutively potentia (potentialities) for eudemonia, for the virtues. With the move from substance to subject, the subject is the locus of potential in the human faculties. Thus, as we saw with the impact of Amartya Sen's notion of justice (Chapter 4), in which the just polity is that which fosters the development of human capacities.

108

These faculties are in German *Vermögen*, which are at the same time powers or *Kräfte*; indeed, Marx calls labour or labouring power alternatively *Arbeitskraft* and *Arbeitsvermögen*, they include the cognitive faculty à la Kant, not to mention the faculty of reason, which is in Kant the faculty of the free will. For Arendt, as we will see below, the most important faculty, that perhaps mapping the most closely to Aristotle's virtue of justice in the *Nicomachean Ethics*, is the faculty of judgment.

Let us return to Arendt's Augustine to take further our grasp on action and the political. To rehearse from *The Human Condition*, whereas labour secures the means of subsistence of the household and work produces use-objects to create stable (political) worlds, action is different. Work's end is outside of itself. It needs a blueprint. Work is more craft than the rationalized episteme-infused contemporary R&D economy, but it does operate according to a blueprint that is outside of the work itself. Action instead carries its meaning in itself, in its own performance (Kampowski 2008). Action is a question, for Arendt, of 'virtuosity'. Arendt contrasts virtuosity with 'sovereignty', here understanding sovereignty as quintessentially modern on the model of Hobbesian and Westphalian national states. These sovereign states follow a means–ends instrumental logic, while the politics of virtuosity is not a politics of means to an end, nor even a politics of pure ends, but closer to what Benjamin and Agamben have understood as a politics of pure means, a politics of Third-Critique Kantian *Zweckmäßigkeit ohne Zweck*, of finality without end. The ever-invented nature of such virtuosity is the appeal of Arendt to the Occupy generation from Hong Kong to New York. This virtuosity is the performance of a Pericles in word and deed before the citizens of the polis. It is the value of rhetoric. Yet even in her political the actors are also the hearers of Pericles' rhetoric: the citizens as audience, who in their empirical plurality operate through putting ourselves in the place of others through and by communication.

Action not only carries its meaning in itself: it needs to work through appearances, not the least of which is the performance of the political virtuoso (Virno 2015). Action is rooted also in *natality*. Arendt, in *The Human Condition* (1958: 190–1), writes, 'the frailty of human institutions and laws and, generally, of all matters pertaining to men's living together, arises from the human condition of natality and is quite independent of the frailty of human nature'. This human condition is very much an anthropology. All anthropologies must be based on the *differentia specifica* that separate us humans from not just animals but from the gods. For Heidegger, neither animals nor gods (immortals), but only humans have mortality, meaning that each death is singular, as mine and only mine: the death of not the 'I' in general, but of this 'I'. For Arendt, neither gods nor animals have natality. The human condition is about such self-invention. It is like a 'second birth'. It is 'how we appear': our initial reappearance. As we speak and act, we appear in the sense of asserting our presence as we insert ourselves into the world, of disclosing ourselves. For Arendt, action is a *faculty*. It is a faculty 'ontologically rooted in the fact of natality' (Kampowski 2008: 258). Labour is possible for beasts and for us: labour and beasts live a 'biological process that is endlessly repetitive', 'it has no beginning, no end': no mortality, no natality. Action and new beginnings, for Arendt, are the 'quintessence of freedom'. They are perhaps the telos of the will. But the will cannot be action either. The freedom of the Kantian will is the unconditioned subject acting in tune with the public generalizability of your maxim without contradiction. But this is not the singularity of mortal and natal human being. So, we are born, for Arendt, not biologically but as singulars. This is a different kind of freedom and responsibility than in Kant's Second Critique. It is Kierkegaard's Abraham paying God back for Adam's irresponsibility. It is Kierkegaard's (Levinas's) unconditional responsibility to the God as Other. Abraham here was not just any 'I', but this 'I' who was Abraham. And God knew this. Arendt was also aware of Eichmann's responsibility as 'this I'. Arendt was Karl Jaspers's student, encouraging the Kierkegaard in her reading of Augustine.

Natality is at the heart of Arendt's statement that freedom is the principle of beginning in *The Human Condition*. This is her reading of Augustine's free will. This Augustinian will of natality features a distinctive temporality. Arendt opposed Nietzsche and *Lebensphilosophie*'s eternal return, which is a replay of the cyclical time of the Greeks, of the seasons. For Arendt, Nietzsche's will to power is no will at all. It obeys biological drives. This was also Augustine's critique of the neo-Platonists, who also gave us such a cyclical time. Cyclical time has no beginnings, no ends. No natality or mortality. This free will of natality and mortality entails such a move from cyclical time to rectilinear time. This is not metanarrative time or the time of Newtonian mechanics. It is the time of being-towards-death. Its birth leads to being. This time comes into being with the creation. That is the *ratio* of man, of Adam as free will. This creation of man is also the creation of time. Before this there was no time, but only eternity. In this sense, the human condition is time.

So, what then is action? Action for Arendt is 'a thing-having-its-end-in-itself', which we will see below is very much on the lines of Kant's Third-Critique finality without end. The new, or natality, is set up against the repetition of nature: against the 'unceasing, indefatigable cycle in which the whole household of nature swings perpetually' (Arendt 1958: 97). History thus is a collection of stories that can be told because new things happen. Action is a 'transitive' that passes over into the external world. These are the deeds and actions, 'deeds and events that are rare occurrences in everyday life and in history'. Unlike philosophy that works in the *sensus privatus*, history connects to the *sensus communis* through these stories of the new. Arendt is an Augustinian in terms of an implicit connection of the new and the free will, but for her, 'love and charity are anti-political' because they are 'unworldly'. Christian community is anti-political because it is non-public – if you give alms you must not say. You must not disclose. You must not appear. Philosophers and the Christians do not appear, do not speak transitively. Arendt's world – unlike Weber's Protestant or Augustine's City – is not other-worldly. Unlike the words and deeds in the polis or Rome, Christian speech does not disclose the 'who' of the speaker. Christian community, Augustinian Christian brotherhood is other-worldly. An other-worldly *sensus communis* – indeed a communion – is anti-political. For Weber, Eastern and Chinese religions are this-worldly (Kampowski 2008: 68). Ancient Greece is this-worldly. There is neither creation nor redemption, the gods only a bit transcendent. For the religions of China as in ancient Greece and Roman 'paganism', there is no creation. There is no creation thus no human *tabula rasa* of free will. Without creation and Adamic transgression, there is no redemption. There is nothing to be redeemed from. Other-worldliness and redemption are of a piece. With the Greeks, agency is caused. China's this-worldliness gives us the 'causation' of lineage, of ancestors and dynasties.

In her *Life of the Mind*, in the second volume on willing, we see Augustine as the first philosopher of the will. The pivotal question for Arendt is how the will can bring the new and 'change the world': how it can function in the world of 'appearances'. The world is less a transcendental condition of *eigentlich Dasein* than a world of appearances. The will's natality operates 'in a factuality which is old by definition', where it relentlessly transforms the spontaneity of its newness into the 'has been' of facts. For Augustine, the will incorporates the mind's activities, coupling memory with intellect, yet it always contains a struggle within it of *velle, nolle*.

A faculty or thing is only new for Arendt if it is *not* preceded by a potential. Thus, there is nothing new in Aristotle, because all actuality is preceded by a potentiality. Human reason is driven by a need to know the *causes* of things, thus Leibniz's sufficient reason as a self-evident first principle. For Leibniz 'no fact can be real or existent, nor statement true, unless there is sufficient reason why it is so and not otherwise' (Leibniz 2014: 107). But for Arendt and Augustine, the will must be uncaused. Aristotle cannot give us new beginnings or a will because of his notion of cyclical or circular based on the motion of heavenly bodies and the life cycle. Judaeo-Christianity gives us rectilinear time. There is creation *ex nihilo*. God does not create the world as a potentia. When there is no sufficient cause, no potentiality precedes it. For Aquinas, God acts not by the necessity of his nature but by the will: the *velle*, *nolle*, the willing and nilling. Human willing is not explicable by preceding causes: Arendt's prime example is Aeneas and the uncaused freedom of the founding of Rome. God creating the world is the paradigm of new beginnings: a new experience of temporality, based on such foundings, on new beginnings. Arendt in *Life of the Mind* invokes Augustine, for whom 'time and man were created together, and this temporality was affirmed by ... birth, the entry of a novel creature who as something entirely new appears in the midst of the time continuum of the world' (Kampowski 2008: 150–3).

This brings us back to the contraposition of substance and subject. Substances are caused by Aristotle's four causes. Subjects are not caused. Also in the move from antiquity to modernity the notion of freedom changes. Freedom, to the extent that it exists, in antiquity is a question of the 'I-can'; after Christianity, freedom is modernity's 'I-will'. From the I-can of I am not a slave so I am free or I have the means to be a free citizen of the polis. The 'I-can' is externally oriented while the 'I-will' is going on in the self. The pre-Christian 'I-can' is an objective state of body and mind, while the 'I-will' is subjective. Thus, Jesus of Nazareth invoked only one of Moses' Ten Commandments, 'thou shalt not covet', the only one of the Commandments that is related to inner life. The transition is in most narratives (e.g., Foucault) effected by the Stoics who were rooted in the 'I-will', a will again that is split and can obey or disobey itself. Whereas for St Paul it is the law of the spirit versus the law of the flesh, for Augustine this takes place inside the will.

5.4 Politics as Aesthetic Judgment

Arendt wrote the first two volumes of *Life of the Mind* – *Thinking* and *Willing*, corresponding to first two critiques. *Judging* was never written. Yet she always insisted that Kant's Third Critique was close to her own idea of action. This is a notion of action that is less ancient than modern. While most of her other discussions are about action, her full discussions in *The Human Condition* are in the frame of the polis. But Arendt is highly aware of the post-Christian tradition that is modernity. For Aristotle, even the gods have causes. The Christian (and Jewish) God in contrast is uncaused, and so is man who is created in God's image. A multiplicity of theological debates from Augustine through Leibniz (and indeed implicitly Max Weber) dispute the seeming contradiction between an omnipotent God and man's free will. Yet the figure of man is also an uncaused cause and thus the will is already there as a cornerstone of the modern subject. It is the cornerstone of the Kantian watershed in which the basis of the First Critique's subject of knowledge is the Second Critique's freedom of the moral and practical will.

Where is Arendtian action in all of this? First, her idea of action is (though perhaps reluctantly) very much modern in its acknowledgement of natality and Augustine's unconditioned will. What are the other building blocks of such an Arendtian modern political? They are first the stability bequeathed to us by the Roman institutions of private contract and property law, republican and thus parliamentary government, and legal–rational bureaucracy, the elements of modern rule of law. To this we would need to add, with Otto Preuss and more implicitly Weber, not the ancient but the proto-modern mediaeval independent city-state, which was based very much on the productive structure of the guilds.

Yet it is not the Augustinian will of the Second Critique but the aesthetic judgment, teleology and *sensus communis* of the Third Critique that is the key to the modern political. This would be impossible without Augustine's and Kant's free will. The Third Critique is comprised of two halves: one on aesthetic or reflective judgment and the other on teleological judgment. Arendt will work both of these, though the first more than the second. This is unlike the recent concern with teleological judgment of Agamben, Benjamin and others. The a priori for judgment in general is *Zweckmäßigkeit ohne Zweck*, which is that, not of reflective, but of teleological judgment. Teleological judgment would thus be a condition of reflective judgment. Arendt mainly works from the opposition of judgment and morality. Without the will, we would not have judgment. Without reason as synthetic, we would not have judgment. Judgment is fully modern. Thus, right at the beginning of these lectures she distinguishes between what is purposive (*zweckmäßig*) and First-Critique mechanical causation (Arendt 1982: 13). She also brings in straightaway that judgment is about community: 'it is about not man but men in the plural'. The polis itself, she is aware, is purposive, teleological (its teleology is human *eudaemonia*) and gives us a plurality. She is aware that the *object* of judgment is teleological, organic not physical (Newtonian) nature as in Kant's blade of grass. She is writing with one eye on Kant's late political pieces ('Perpetual Peace' and 'Idea for a Universal History with a Cosmopolitan Purpose'), where history too is seen as a part of nature – meaning biological and not physical Newtonian nature – and is thus also purposive. Its purpose is the universal cosmopolitanism that will allow us to develop all our faculties.

She observes that Kant wrote a metaphysics of morals and of nature, and that metaphysics is by definition beyond experience. Judgment by contrast is grounded in experience: in subjective not objective experience, but in experience all the same. Objective experience needs the metaphysical a priori categories brought together by the transcendental unity of apperception to operate. The question here is if judgment itself needs to be metaphysical. Or can judgment only be empirical? Kant's judgment requires an a priori so is also metaphysical. Arendtian judgment is empirical. Judgment for Arendt, more than Kant, involves the imagination and communication. If perception presents, the imagination instead re-presents. The imagination in Kant can operate transcendentally (Stiegler 2010). But the imagination does not have to be transcendental. In Hume and Smith, it is empirical. Arendt's imagination is closer to Smith and Hume. Thus, Arendt takes the a priori in both Heidegger's world and Kant's imagination (and judgment) and makes it a posteriori: she takes their transcendentals and makes them empirical. She takes what is for them metaphysical and transplants it to the realm of experience.

She insists that the 'judgment of particulars' has no place in Kant's moral philosophy. Moral reason, she says, is 'identical with the will'. The 'will utters commands, imperatives' while judgment arises from pleasure and delight (Arendt 1982: 5, 15). If moral reason is unconditioned, it must rule out 'inclination'. Judgment may be disinterested, but it still arises from inclination; it is conditioned. It arises from in the world, from 'on the earth'. After 1789, the 65-year-old Kant becomes interested in institutions, something Arendt notes that the pre-Critique Kant took no interest in. Most of the questions that Critique Kant addresses arise from pre-Critique Kant, who wrote, for example, already on the Sublime and the Beautiful. We must recall that the pre-Critique Kant is a rationalist. As a rationalist, with Leibniz and Descartes, he accepts the validity of theodicy and proofs of God's existence. But Kant is also living in the Age of Enlightenment. And Enlightenment thought, not just the Scottish but also the French Enlightenment, is not rationalist. It is very much influenced by Locke and empiricism. Kant awakens from his metaphysical slumber quite late in the Enlightenment, when a number of others have already woken up, in, for example, Voltaire's destruction of Leibniz's theodicy. Idealism itself would not have been possible without the Enlightenment. Not just Kant, but Hegel and all idealism must understand cognition via a priori, synthetic judgments. Synthetic judgments synthesize with matter, with the empirical. Rationalist cognition operates through a priori, analytic judgments with no regard for the empirical. Empiricism in contrast is a question of a posteriori synthetic judgments and thus works fully on the level of the material. Kant accepts Enlightenment empiricism but then re-grounds it in the ideal. Pre-Critique Kant had already addressed cognition from a more or less purely metaphysical point of view. Critique Kant awakens through Hume and Newton, yet needs to save knowledge from scepticism and Hume's demolition of causation. Kant saves knowledge by bringing back the metaphysical categories: hence the ideal, the non-experienced, as the condition of possibility of experience. The ideal in this is first explored in cognition in the categories (featuring causation) as brought together by the transcendental unity of apperception. Most importantly, this unity of apperception – which is not empirical yet operates empirically – itself has its basis in the completely free (thus fully unempirical) will of the moral imperative. Of what Kant calls the pure practical will. The pure practical will works not cognitively but practically. Its precursor is not Aristotle's episteme but instead praxis. It is indeed Augustine's will. This is the space from which Arendt and Arendt's modernity are operating.

'The Roman' in Arendt is focused on institutions (law, representative government, rational administration) as both built worlds – we build worlds in the paradigm of natality – and in the preservation of worlds. Kant's late, political thought is interested in institutions. This is very unlike and more grounded than the pure practical will of the moral imperative and much more, as Arendt underscores, in line with Third-Critique judgment. This is in a sense not unlike Plato's moving from the pure a priori of *The Republic* to the institutions of *The Laws*. In the late political writings, Kant is interested in constitutional law, and by implication in the rule of law. Arendt, too, in her 'Roman-ness' and her support of the rule of law against totalitarianism, is ardent about constitutionalism and the rule of law. She with Kant looks at the American political body via considerations

115

of the 1776 Revolution, and here, too, teleological judgment raises its head where 'every member should be purpose as well as means'. This is nature as teleology as a 'guarantee' of perpetual peace. Thus, also the very late 74-year-old Kant in 'The Strife of the Faculties' sees 'a great purpose of nature working behind men's backs'. Thus, enlightened yet self-interested individuals are less important than the human species whose teleological nature this is.

The three elements of Arendt's Kantian-infused thinking on the modern political are: (1) organistic teleology and purposefulness: (2) the imagination (addressed below); and (3) communication/communicability. Arendt continues and look at Kant's 'What Is Enlightenment?', written as a journalistic intervention in 1784. Arendt pits herself very much against this essay. The Third Critique is still too far away, penned in 1790, because each of Kant's three Enlightenment 'whats' has nothing at all to do with politics. Arendt with justification reads the 'what should I hope?' as addressing mortality and immortality. The 'what should I do?' is about 'not action but the will' of independent selves, though Kant is becoming aware of the importance of 'sociability/communicability' (Arendt 1982: 19). Still Kant does not ask 'how do I judge?', though this, Arendt thinks, may be implicit in the Second Critique in that, 'although moral duties are by definition free from inclination', 'without inclination there would be little point in constructing myself'.

Arendt insists on the empiricism of the political. Even Aristotle, for her, in the last instance presumes that *bios politikos* was there for the sake of *bios theoretikos*. Philosophy, for her from Parmenides, has been about 'the delusions of sense experience' (1982: 21–2). Parmenides travels to the heavens 'to escape the opinions (doxa) of mortals'. Willing, unlike action, is free from sense experience. Before Parmenides and since Pythagoras, philosophy has been about withdrawal in a sect, a cure for life, a cure for living among men. For the Romans, in contrast, being alive was to be among men. The episteme-minded Greeks' philosophy was for the young, while for the eminently political Romans philosophy was for the old. From Pythagoras, we have the soul's immortality: we have forms and the incorporeal as causes of things in this world.

Even the late and institutionally minded and judgment-driven Kant cannot escape from the dictates of pure practical will. Even in the 'Idea for a Universal History from a Cosmopolitan Point of View' the end is 'a universal': it is 'an escape from the particulars' (Arendt 1982: 26). What the Greeks do for thinking, Kant and the moderns (following Augustine) do for willing. When Kant considers why man, among all animals, exists in his anthropology, his answer from the *Critique of Judgment* is that 'man and every rational creature in the world, as a moral being can no longer be asked for what end he exists, for he is an end in himself'. Yet Kant's man or 'better man' is social: 'his true end is sociability'. So, Arendt sees this contradiction in Kant: that of the Second-Critique pure practical will versus the sociability, the communicability of the Third Critique and indeed neither thinking, nor willing, but instead judging.

The Critique Kant, like the French empiricist Enlightenment, is ruthless against theodicy. You can't justify the Creator in the face of experience of evil before the tribunal of reason. This is even more the case for Arendt, for whom theodicy relies on the 'argument that if you look at the whole, you will see that the particulars, about which you complain, are part and parcel of it and as such it is justified in its existence'. For the pre-Critique Kant in 1759, thus, 'the whole is the best and everything is good for the sake of the whole'. The *Critique of Pure Reason* (an important part of which is the new rejection of theodicy) thus is experience. Pure reason is the anti-experience and its critique is experience. Indeed, experience makes the thinking faculty divide into the spheres of the understanding and reason (without experience). Kant must reinvent Augustine's free will as reason and as the basis of his whole system.

Yet Kant needs something that links the empirical reason of the First Critique to the pure practical Critique of the Second. He needs a link connecting Newtonian empirical science, which for the most part expels metaphysics from cognition to the Second Critique, which contains the majority of metaphysics left over after the triumph of empirical knowledge. He needs a link from the sphere of necessity, which needs to obey the laws of mechanics, to the Second Critique's sphere of freedom. And this is judgment. Arendt's Kant begins by talking about – not philosophers or scientists – but doctors or lawyers' judgment in applying rules to cases. Here Kant is already incipiently thinking of communities of men. Here, with Jaspers, Kant distinguishes between science whose truths depend on experiment and repeated experiment for validity, and a philosophy primarily concerned with communicability. For communicability, you need a community of men. Kant is already straining to 'bring philosophy down from the heavens'. Philosophy descends from the heavens first through Socrates, not dogmatically putting as polar opposites truth on the one hand and doxa or opinion on the other. Socrates, like Aristotle, begins by examining opinions, and presuming that anyone 'can render, can give an account'. To give an account, Arendt notes,

117

is far different from to prove. To render account is what Athenian citizens asked of their politicians, to hold them accountable. In speaking of accountability and community, Arendt is at the same time speaking about publicity. For Kant, almost every maxim that violates the moral imperative entails secrecy and the absence of publicity. Populist politicians do not give accounts, are not held accountable. Critique, and especially its empirical element – as distinct from dogmatism – entails publicity. Arendt (1982: 43) sees Kant's community on the lines of her plurality, in which each must take the viewpoint of others into consideration.[6] This public plurality means we must put ourselves in the place of others. Judgment must be enlargement, by using our faculties of imagination – and here we have echoes of Smith's moral sentiments (see Chapter 4) – to compare our judgment with possible judgment by others.

Arendt reads Kant's two late political essays on 'Perpetual Peace' and 'Idea for a Universal History' as a prism for Kantian judgment as a mediation for action and the political. Teleology in Arendt's Third Critique characterizes both the object and subject of judgment. In Kant's two late essays, written more or less contemporaneously with the Third Critique, it is not the work of art or nature, but the political that is the teleological subject or object. The biological purposive organism becomes humankind on a world scale: humankind as brought into association in leagues of nations for perpetual peace. But the aesthetic judge and the political judge from the cosmo-politan point of view are not actors, but only judges, judging from a distanced point of view. This is how Kant can approve of the French and American Revolutions as a spectator, and not preach resistance to authoritarian Prussian rule. The judger is not an actor but a spectator taking into account the views of other spectators. Judgment is from the general point of view of the spectator rather than the partial point of view of the actor. It is not the active but the contemplative that experiences the pleasure of the beautiful. Kant originally was going to call the Third Critique the 'Critique of Taste'. Arendt focuses on such a notion of taste that, for her, 'tames and clips the wings and gives order to the thought of genius'. Taste, for Kant, already gives unity to the imagination, intellect and spirit. Yet only the genius is inspired by spirit: the genius, who 'no science can teach, no industry can learn'. Genius is about communication but before that representation. It 'consists in expressing the ineffable element in

---

[6] So, Arendt's public, like Kant's community, is neither secret nor private as a '*sensus privatus*'.

118

the state of mind (*Gemützustand*) that certain representations arouse in all of us, but for which we have no words and cannot without the help of genius communicate to one another' (Arendt 1982: 63). The key word again is 'communicate'.

Kant famously quotes Cicero who distinguishes between, on the one hand, making and the genius as a maker and, on the other hand, judging, of which even the ignorant are capable. The latter are rooted for Cicero even in the uneducated in 'common sense'. And it is common sense, which is pivotal, a clue to Arendt's plurality, as distinguished from the 'private sense' of the logical faculty that can work without communication. Arendt thinks seriously about 'sense', about what constitutes a sense. She proceeds to think through literally the five senses, what she calls the five 'faculties of sense'. Sense, she observes, is a question of perception. Among the five senses, perceptions of sight, hearing and touch are easily communicable, while smell and taste are 'inner sensations', so 'private' and incommunicable. Sight, hearing and touch are thus 'objective senses', capable of making a representation of something that is absent. The faculty of the imagination takes up the objective senses straightaway and easily because of this capability. The imagination is that which is capable of making a representation, of making present something that is absent. Bringing the 'there and then' into the 'here and now'. But this faculty is possessed by neither, literally, taste nor smelling, in which the 'it pleases-or-displeases is immediate and overwhelming' (Arendt 1982: 64). Only taste and smell are discriminating by their very nature. Further, only taste and smell relate to a particular qua particular' (1982: 66). Taste and smell are hyper-empirical. The imagination and its schema are somehow mediations between the particulars of taste and perception and the universals, the concepts, of the understanding. Yet they never get to these concepts. *They are made universalizable, not by concepts, but by a sort of sixth sense, by the* sensus communis. Through their communication and communicability. Thus, for Kant 'the beautiful interests us only when we are in society'. We are not contented with an object unless we can 'feel satisfaction in it in common with others'. Judgment takes by definition others' possible judgments into consideration.

Here again we can see Arendt's empiricism and a posteriorism in comparison to Kant. Kant gives us experience in his break with metaphysics. But he then circumscribes this empiricism with so many a prioris that this empiricism becomes instead a positivism. We addressed neo-Kantian positivism in Chapters 3 and 4 in regard to Durkheim and Weber.

119

In Kant's First Critique, judgments can be, on the one hand, a priori or a posteriori, and, on the other hand, analytic or synthetic. If rationalist (metaphysical) judgments are a priori and analytic and empiricist judgments a posteriori and synthetic (with the material of experience), then a priori synthetic judgments are the foundations of positivism. Kant gives us a series of a prioris, the most fundamental of which is the subject as Augustinian free will in the Second Critique. The second, cognitive a priori is the necessity side of the free will, i.e. the transcendental unity of apperception, unifying all of the categories, featuring causation. The third aesthetic (and teleological) a priori is the *sensus communis*, which itself, as political, works teleologically as a finality without end. It does so as a common sense without the mediation of the concepts of the understanding. The third aesthetic a priori connects through the *sensus communis* both finality without end and reflective judgment. Or, better, the *sensus communis* is the basis of both finality without end (teleological judgment) and reflective judgment.

For Kant, this is an a priori, a supersensible world (and in this sense Weber and his interpreters Schluchter and Habermas are correct to speak of a 'religio-metaphysical' era – and this is because religion and metaphysics are both other-worldly) prior to modernity. Arendt rejects these remnants of metaphysics in Kant. The world – that is, worlds – are never supersensible or other-worldly. Unlike Weber or even Heidegger, she will not speak of a supersensible world. Moreover, she will never with consistency speak of a world but instead of worlds – a Greek world, a Roman world, a liberal world. Heidegger and Weber, in contrast, speak of not worlds but world. Religions are thus never 'other-worldsly', and Heidegger's *Dasein* is not 'being in the worlds'. Arendt's worlds, unlike Augustine's city, are never supersensible. They are not a priori full stop. They are instead a posteriori.

Arendt's *sensus communis* is thus not transcendental. It is empirical, and it is plural. The *sensus communis* is a question of the Kantian imagination. It operates on the imagination of a plurality. It is a sense whose function is more communication than representation. In fact, it communicates representations. But these are representations of the imaginary, not mediated through concepts of the understanding. It communicates nether neither through concept nor through a maxim. To communicate not through a concept is to communicate instead through an image or a schema. To communicate not through the maxim makes the *sensus communis* very different from the free will. The process of representation-communication is determined partly by the object and partly by the community itself.

Moral judgments are valid even if not communicated. Judgments of taste are only valid through communication. We cannot reflect on the object until we imagine it. And even then, reflection takes place through this *sensus communis*, through its communications. The *sensus communis* is an extra sense, yet like an extra mental capacity that fits us into a community. And further, a *sensus communis* without speech. It 'takes account a priori of the mode of representation of all other men'. Here we must 'abstract from "charm and emotion" if we are seeking a judgment that is to serve as a universal rule' (Arendt 1982: 70).

Taste via perception is not communicable. For this you need a representation by the imagination. As represented, we gain a distance on the object and take up a disinterested position towards it. At this point the sensation or the representation is communicable. The object of perception is not yet beautiful. It can please/displease in immediate taste, but is only beautiful once we gain disinterest. We cannot communicate it until we gain this distance of disinterest as a spectator. You do not *taste* a meal as a group or through representation: you taste it immediately. You fully enjoy the meal when you communicate it. Only in common. So, you need both representation but also the mediation of communication for an object to be beautiful. Kant speaks of the common sense as a sixth faculty of sense. It is the least immediate of all, less so even than vision and hearing. Yet it is still in important respects a sense. It is a sense (the sense) that works only through communication, through communicability. No communicability is possible without both representations through the imagination and a community of spectators with which one communicates. What pleases in perception is gratifying; what pleases in the imagination is beautiful. Only then do we have the operation of *reflection* (that is at the heart of reflective judgment and what makes it reflective). Only then – after representation and disinterested communication – do we have a judgment at all. This judgment can then become reflective. When it becomes reflective, we relate the judgment to a maxim or a rule. And this rule, unlike the rules of cognitive or moral judgments, is not pre-given. To work through a concept would mean working through a pre-given concept of the understanding, a category such as causation. This is what Kant calls 'determinate judgment', and stands as polar opposite to reflective judgment. Determinate judgment working through a concept such as cause takes place in the realm of necessity. Moral judgment with a universalizable maxim takes place in the realm of freedom. Reflexive judgment bridges these two realms. It is neither determined, as for

121

Arendt are the lives of animals, nor is it completely free, which for Arendt is only for the gods. Reflective judgment is for humans: it is the human condition. Lacking a pre-given rule or maxim, to reflect in reflective judgments is to find the rule. The rule is to be found in and through the *sensus communis* itself. It will work through the imagination of the *sensus communis*, and the imagination shifts out of the now (*nunc*) to imagine the past and future. The collective imagination of the *sensus communis* can find the rule in the community's past – and Kant here uses the example of past judgments of English Common Law. Or it can find the aesthetic rule, for example, in an imagined or anticipated future.

The *sensus communis* is a *Zweckmäßigkeit ohne Zweck*, a finality without end or a means without end. It operates, as we saw in Kant's late political writings, as, not a mechanism but an internally driven organism. With no external end and not as a means to an end, its past and future are not external to it. It does not happen in time; it is instead its own temporality. Thus the a priori of all judgment – of teleological and reflective judgment (of the two halves of the Third Critique) – are one and the same thing. But this is Kant. What are they for Arendt? First, we need to note that this *sensus communis* is more or less co-extensive with her notion of world. Arendt's world is the political. Heidegger's world is about *Dasein* and things. In this sense, his *Being and Time* was already *Technics and Time* (Stiegler 1998). Arendt's world is an intersubjectivity. Heidegger never addressed this intersubjectivity. Nor could Husserl give us what needed to be – for him and Heidegger – a transcendental intersubjectivity. Arendt's world, unlike Heidegger's, does not connect subjects with objects: it is instead intersubjective. Arendt's world is not an a priori but an a posteriori intersubjectivity. It is empirical. It is built partly through work and the external blueprint of the infrastructure needed for the political – hence Roman technology with its dams, bridges, aqueducts, roads, amphitheatres and thermal baths, its 'Roman operating system' (Koolhaas 2001) was the political par excellence. But it is built anew from the inside through praxis, through action, the action of virtuosity. It needs Augustinian and thus Christian new beginnings, natality: it thus needs the free will. If the polis's telos was eudemonia, the modern polity's telos is freedom. It needs freedom as its telos. But though it has freedom as its horizon, the modern polis is not itself freedom. It is not built freely. Once Augustine's and Second-Critique Kant's free will is in place, it needs modulation, fundamental modulation towards judgment. Willing must become judging. It needs shifting from the abstract a priori of the categorical imperative to what is quintessentially uncategorical. It needs modulation towards the *sensus communis* of political communities. But, most important for us, this *sensus communis* needs further modulation: from what Kant saw as transcendental to the Arendtian empirical. As empirical, this *sensus communis* is fragile. Today's liberal *sensus communis*, not unlike the Kantian idea for a universal history from a cosmopolitan point of view, is now under such threat that the cosmopolitan order Ulrich Beck (2006) alluded to is in profound danger. The risk society itself is at the gravest risk

So, what have we got here with Arendt, and Arendt's Kant? Kant's political writings of 1784–96 are caught between the Second and Third Critiques. There is an evolution of history towards the cosmopolitan driven by the purposefulness of Third-Critique teleology. Yet the telos of this natural – as distinct from mechanistic – teleology is freedom: it is Augustinian and Second-Critique freedom. This is not the telos of the polis that drives all association – including family and tribe – for Aristotle. But it is the free will of the individual. It is not the just man that is most important to be realized in the polis: it is instead the uncaused cause of the free will. And Arendt's modern political is driven by neither justice nor morality: it is driven by the political itself. Freedom is its telos but its driving force is the political itself. And it is here that we find action in Arendt.

Action is a faculty for Arendt, as is the *sensus communis* alongside the will and other faculties, including of course the imagination. Arendt, as we have seen at length in this chapter, is in many respects an empiricist: thus her (Third-Critique) judgment starting from immediate empirical perception. Cognitive (i.e. not aesthetic) judgments, as synthetic and a priori, privilege the a priori; that is, the concepts or categories brought together by the transcendental unity of apperception. But (aesthetic) judgments start with literally perception – unlike cognitive reason, that is, from the beginning a priori – and they move step by step until the a priori (Kant's *sensus communis*) comes into play. They start from, not the more objective (sight, hearing and touch) of the five sense organs of perception, but from the most subjective of the organs of perception, the tongue and nose. It then must work its way to the *sensus communis* through a representation: through the imagination. In the first edition of the *Critique of Pure Reason*, the imagination and its schemata are a necessary mediation between perception and the understanding. In Arendt's Third Critique, the understanding is fully circumvented. Working up towards aesthetic judgments of beauty before we even represent an object, we can gain pleasure from it because of the accordance between the understanding and the imagination. But that same understanding does not subsequently mediate the judgment itself. This happens after the re-presentation in the imagination. Only then with sufficient distance and disinterest of representation can the *sensus communis* come into play. Because it operates through the a priori *sensus communis*, Kant's faculty of judgment is an a priori faculty. For Arendt, both *sensus communis* and judgment are faculties. But again they are *empirical*, a posteriori faculties. A priori faculties are metaphysical as Kant at length recognizes. As metaphysical they are the basis of Idealism, of which *The Critique of Pure Reason* is the inaugural text. *The Critique of Pure Reason* is also the inaugural text full stop of critique. Rationalism and idealism both partake of the metaphysical. The difference is that whereas rationalism (Descartes, Leibniz) steers clear of experience, of the empirical, the material, idealism synthesizes with experience, with the material. Positivism here takes its cues from idealism: which is why Durkheim as positivist and the positivist half of Weber were constitutively neo-Kantian. Arendt's faculties and judgments, her worlds and the Arendtian political are fully a posteriori. She philosophizes, or better thinks, with Kant and against Kant. Compared to Kant and positivism, Arendt too is radically empiricist.

5.5 Conclusions: From Politics to Technological System

Arendt's politics of experience are themselves a foundation, taking in the integral classical substantivism, and incorporating it into a modernity of new beginnings, of a subjective and aesthetic sensibility of the bodily senses, the subjectivity of a plurality of points of view that are constitutive of her paradigm of not objective but subjective experience. Of the empirical and a posterior fragility of the rule of law and our democratic institutions. Are Arendt's insights sufficient to take us forward in what is a technological age, an age of decentred geopolitics with the rise of China and India? Especially, can it cope with contemporary machine-mediated technological experience? What is, then, the nature of such *technological* experience and what are its implications for the human and arguably post-human sciences?

Gilbert Simondon and Bernard Stiegler give us a prism on technological experience that can possibly take us forward (Hui 2016). Both Simondon and Stiegler have roots in phenomenology – in Husserl, Heidegger and Derrida. Phenomenology was, we saw, paradigmatic for modern subjective experience. If in objective experience

124

subject engaged with object, then in phenomenology (and subjective experience – and this is very clear in Heidegger's (2012) early lectures) – it is consciousness which engages with appearances. What Simondon and Stiegler do is put technics or the technical system in the place of consciousness. Derrida was already part way there in his putting writing in the place of consciousness.

What does this mean? It means in the first instance that *individuation* is technologically driven. If consumer and now digital capitalism tend to homogenize us and reduce us to interchangeable atoms, then individuation gives us the chance of becoming singularities, each different from every other. How does this happen? We came across individuation in our discussion of Aristotle in Chapter 2. Plato, for his part, had no notion of individuation. You have the forms on the one hand and the 'deluded material world' on the other. It is only when form combines with matter to yield substance that there is individuation. In this process, each substance becomes different from every other. Individuation is a process that yields substantial forms. This is Aristotle's hylomorphism, which Simondon famously defines himself against. In hylomorphism, *hyle* is matter and *morphe* is form. In Aristotle's near materialism, it is matter that drives form, the substantial form is what it is for humans what you are, but it is driven by material causes like your parents. Hylomorphism reaches its apogee with Aquinas, for whom it is God that individuates souls, as forms and substantial forms and their difference become very much souls.

Not just Simondon but the entirety of modern Western thought rejects hylomorphism. From Galileo to Newton to Cartesian physics to Kant's First Critique, substance as matter/form thinking is rejected for, as we saw, objective experience and an understanding of nature in terms of mechanism. Individuation disappears for an interim, but then subjective experience brings it back with each consciousness being different from every other. Hylomorphism makes a reappearance, not the least in Husserl's phenomenology. It is not, however, thought mainly as a process. This is what we get in Simondon. Simondon (2007) gives us an evolutionary process, in which physical individuation is followed by biological, collective (social), psychic and technological individuation. In technical individuation, it is the 'technical system' that drives both social (collective) and psychic individuation. The question then becomes, what is driving this technical system? The answer is that it is a self-driven system, it is a self-organizing system, it is even a self-building, an autopoietic system (Maturana and Varela 1980). Then we need to ask what is driving this self-organization?[7] The answer is, for Maturana, as for Prigogine and Stengers (1989), its structure. And what is at the heart of this structure? For Stiegler this is memory. Memory is already very important in Husserl's phenomenology. During the here and now, the *Jetztzeit* of perception for Husserl, there is a moment of past and future; the moment of the past is primary retention. We can only be presented with an already past moment – that is, the moment of a past perception – through a secondary memory, a secondary retention. For Freud, as Stiegler (2004) is highly cognizant, there is such a driving of the system, by this, time unconscious memory. Freudian individuation is symbolically driven by desire: to counteract the influence of drives that militate against individuation and bring about *la misère symbolique* in today's digital capitalism. For this, the imagination is necessary. But when this past is recorded, in writing (Derrida 2001) or another technology, it becomes what Stiegler calls tertiary retention. It is this kind of technical memory that drives experience in the age of technology. It drives the technical system, like computer memory or RAM.

For Simondon and Stiegler we are technical beings, in that through evolution it is the technical system that drives both social and psychological individuation. What they are saying is not, like object ontology or the new materialism (Bennett 2009; Harman 2002), that we are ourselves objects. They are also not saying à la Haraway (1991) and Mirowski (2002) that we are cyborgs, or a fusion of technological and human beings, but that we as psychological and collective beings are part and parcel of the technical system, and in this way we are technical beings. This process of simultaneous and mutually overdetermining individuation, for Stiegler, is also thus a process of 'trans-individuation'. In the next chapter I will understand this trans-individuation, with Maturana, as the 'coupling' of two such technical systems, two systems of what I want to understand as technological forms of life. In coupling, these systems communicate and exchange information, images and symbols. They thus individuate one another. Technological forms of life work through two very different logics, both of them about technology and forms of life, life as symbol constellations. Here technology works through a mathematical logic of the algorithm: the conversion of Gödel's mathematical science by Turing into the register of engineering. Forms of life work though the language games and everyday performative speech acts. Forms of life may be technically driven but they are still forms of life, meaning as

---

[7] I am indebted on this point to conversations with Jihyeon Kim.

much as matter. They are the formal, rule-bound, precise language of predication of set-theoretical mathematics transformed into, of course, the algorithms of engineering, themselves coupled with these undefined and imprecise language games.

When two such technical-cultural systems (and cultures are forms of life) encounter one another, there are two possibilities. One is war and strategies of friend and enemy that we see in so much of encounters of such cybernetic systems and that we see again in the logic of the 'Anthropocene'. The other is communication: it is structural coupling of memory and exchange. It is such communication that in Walter Benjamin's German was rendered as a *'mitteilen'*, a sharing with.

— 6 —

FORMS OF LIFE: TECHNOLOGICAL PHENOMENOLOGY

6.1 Forms of Life: Transformations of Performative Language

6.1.1 Forms of Life and Exclusion: Homo Sacer's Experience

Politics has, with migration and the other at the forefront, become increasingly a question of the experience of the excluded. Political theorists have come to focus on this. Some, like Roberto Esposito and Giorgio Agamben, have understood this in terms of *forms of life*. Both of them draw on Carl Schmitt but then take the side of those excluded from political forms of life. Esposito, for example, understands politics on the model of biological life, in which borders are immunity reactions to the virus of 'the stranger'. Esposito's *Immunitas* (2011) is based on the idea of *munus*, the root of immunity and community. *Munus* means gift, in the context of public office. If community is based here on the outside through the constitution of the social body so that it is immune to the virus of the migrant, immune reaction, then, on the inside is based on some sort of gift-giving, mutual gift-giving.

Political forms of life and their community define themselves against the outside, and here we can begin to see where Schmitt comes in. But they also have an internal logic of gift-giving or the gift economy, that we saw in Polanyi on subjective experience and substantivism above. This interior, these forms of life, are on the one hand gift-giving, but at the same time they are a community of virtues – of virtues as internal and external goods – whose governing virtue is justice. Justice is the glue of forms of life that we enter as political animals. Giorgio Agamben gives us forms of life that include and exclude: they include with Aristotle as *zoon politikon*

128

or *bios* and they exclude with Carl Schmitt as *homo sacer*. Forms of life include and they exclude, as friend excludes enemy. *Homo sacer* is likely to live in camps – in concentration camps or refugee camps: he is excluded, constituted and lives in a state of exception. A state of exception to both the forms of life and rule of law. The basic opposition is between *bios*, or political forms of life, and *zoē*, who is bare life: who is *homo sacer*. Bare life is outside of forms of life altogether. The template for Agamben's political life is the very unjuridified Greek polis, a community that was only very minimally structured by law. But *homo sacer* does not emerge then. Antigone is not *homo sacer*. *Homo sacer* himself arises from the highly juridified Roman polity. It is Roman Law that gives the rule for *homo sacer* as he who can be killed without punishment for his killers.

Agamben's *homo sacer*, himself a template for the political experience of the excluded, works from two principles: on the one hand, 'sovereignty', and on the other, 'governmentality'. You would think that sovereignty is about Hobbes, and governmentality Foucault. But in fact, both are about Carl Schmitt. The integral political community as a form of life is Schmitt's friend and is the principle of sovereignty. Sovereign is he who makes the decision determining friend and enemy, and at the same time deciding who is *homo sacer*. But law is not a question of sovereignty: it is a question of governmentality: what Foucault called juridico-discursive power. The juridical dimension of Roman Law and later contract law and property law of the modern state is not a question of sovereignty but instead of governmentality. Schmitt, while no fan of what we call legality or the rule of law, was a jurist and endorsed a certain juridification. And a law that decrees that 'the other' can be killed with impunity is hardly the rule of law. It is, instead, the excluding action of forms of life, thus sovereignty. Thus Agamben can say *homo sacer* is both decreed by, yet an exception to, the law. He is constituted by both governmentality and sovereignty.

Schmitt read, not sovereignty, but instead governmentality as 'theological'. He saw the theological, or 'political theology', in the rule of law, and in particular in Hans Kelsen's notion of pure law. Leo Strauss also saw Kelsen as enemy in his *Natural Right and History*, and in some ways out-Schmitted Schmitt. For Strauss, natural right was already the worst kind of formal proceduralism, whose precursor had again to be Augustine of Hippo. Augustine's free will was the basis of, for Strauss, the City of God, not the City of Man, and then later was the theological basis for natural right, which Strauss rejected in Locke, Rousseau and Hobbes as an effective replay of the theological, which took a turn for the even worse when it became 'history' in Hans Kelsen and Weber, and degenerated into a legal positivism, a full 'proceduralism' that was a space just for the pursuit of instrumental interests. Strauss wanted instead law based in substantive reason such as in Plato's *Laws*, with an admixture of mystic Judaism – which for him would not have been theological. Jurist Schmitt and classicist Strauss were very much on the same page when it came to political theology. Schmitt saw the economy, too, as somehow theological: a theological politics constituting *die Politik* against *das Politische* of the state of exception. The difference with Agamben is that whereas Schmitt sees the theological–governmental and the political as sovereignty and state of exception as engaged in mortal combat, Agamben sees them as allies in the creation of *homo sacer* and his experience. Schmitt, much more than Leo Strauss, saw this as a struggle also against the economic. Thus, Schmitt was especially hostile to Walter Eucken and the ordoliberals, whom Foucault addresses at such length. Schmitt de facto agreed with Foucault's analysis that ordoliberalism was about a particular version of the rule of law, or more accurately the *Rechtsstaat*, what Weber called legal-rational domination. Hence the ordoliberals were against state-of-exception decrees by the executive and for a legally regulated economy, in which law would guarantee competition, by not permitting monopolies either by big business corporations or by very strong trade unions. Hence the resurgence of ordoliberal influence in post-Keynesian Germany with Gerhard Schröder's flexible labour policies. Ordoliberal law-based anti-statism was both anti-Nazi and anti-Keynesian. The point again is that Agamben's forms of life – in a Schmittian vein – through exclusion in combination with juridical structured governmentality, constitute the subjective experience of the excluded, of *homo sacer*. Agamben, of course, is developing a politics of *homo sacer*.

Thus, Schmitt was against formal-rational law, which he saw as a replay of a theological and transcendental God. Schmitt substituted for God's *nomos* instead the *nomos* of the earth: in place of God was the transcendental and impartial arbiter of formally rational law and governmentality. Agamben also broaches issues of theology and economy in his least penetrable book, *The Kingdom and the Glory*, which was a very Schmittian attack on political theology. Agamben's (2013a) notion of forms of life is of a piece with Aristotle's *Nicomachean Ethics*, in which forms of life constitute the political on the lines of the polis. Agamben distinguishes sovereignty from governmentality, which seems to coincide with the distinction of polis, on the one hand, and *oikos* (as household management and economy), on the other. In this, governmentality is external to and understood in counterposition to the political: it is *oikos*. Agamben's (2011) *The Kingdom and the Glory* is subtitled *For a Theological Genealogy of Economy and Government*. This book appears to be about not governmentality but sovereignty, indeed the integral – and very non-instrumental – power of the king in his glory. But the subtitle does not lie. Because the *Kingdom and the Glory* very much echoes the doxology regularly following the Lord's Prayer, which is at the basis of the economy, and government. In *The Kingdom and the Glory*, the Trinity – Father, Son, Holy Spirit – is a Holy Family principle of *oikos* and hence economy. So, the kingdom at stake in *The Kingdom and the Glory* is not any secular political kingdom but is instead God's kingdom. This is like in Graham Greene's novel – *The Power and the Glory* – of a similar name, 'For thine is the kingdom, the power and the glory, forever and ever, amen'. This is God's kingdom and God's glory, literally a political theology. Agamben is referring, if sometimes obliquely, to Carl Schmitt's political theology.

For Agamben, the polis and sovereignty open the question of justice while governmentality is a matter of law. On justice, Agamben aligns with Walter Benjamin's 'Critique of Violence'. We remember *homo sacer* is doubly constituted: first, by law and governmentality, but second, he is constituted by biopolitics.

Thus, *homo sacer* comes from the state of exception, not from governmentality but from sovereignty and what Agamben (and arguably not Foucault) understands as biopolitics. Agamben understands biopolitics to be rather opposite to governmentality. They are instead literally biological, even racial: they are the way, in a *nomos*-of-the-earth vein, sovereignty as forms of life excludes the other, excludes *homo sacer*. Justice here is on the side of neither sovereignty nor governmentality, but instead on the side of *homo sacer*. With Benjamin, these are a politics of neither means to an end, nor pure ends, but instead justice is understood as pure means. Italian *operaista* writers such as Hardt and Negri (2001) speak of formal and real subsumption in Marx's *Capital*. In Agamben's and Benjamin's politics of pure means, there is no subsumption of particular by universal, neither by the means-to-an-end of capital, nor the pure ends of the dictatorship of the proletariat. There is, instead, neither formal nor real subsumption, but no subsumption at all, in an anarchist rendering of political forms of life, of a community of difference as a coming community.

6.1.2 Language and Forms of Life

Let us think further about forms of life as a politics and indeed a language (as Benjamin does in his 1979 essay 'On Language') of pure means. Means, especially means without ends, are a 'how', the 'how' of a culture, of how a culture leads its life, they are a way of life. Both in terms of the culture at stake and the human-scientific observer, this 'how' is a methodological issue. It is a method of leading one's life and a method in the sense that the observer will be looking for the how rather than either the why (cause) or the what. This means without ends resembles Aristotle's praxis: whereas in episteme and its a priori a universal subsumes a particular, and in technics what is made can be separated from the making, hence ends separated from means, praxis must contain its own end, and is thus for Virno (2015) like the virtuoso or diva whose work is never recorded, hence never separable from the singing.

For Agamben, forms of life – although consistent with Wittgenstein's notion – is to do very much with praxis: surely not with Platonic episteme, nor in the first instance with *technē*, in which there is an external end, set for example by the craftsman's polis-situated clients. Praxis must instead contain its own end. It is to produce nothing outside of itself. If forms of life are comprised of 'hows', then so are language games. Language games are formed of 'hows'. Propositions are about 'whats'. They are about the truth-value of propositions or predicates. This is indeed the language of logic, logico-philosophical language. In objective experience, sociology itself asks what questions and the why or causal question. Are causal questions predications? Well, categories are predicates in Latin. And of all of Kant's categories – mode, quantity, quality and relation – cause is a relation that can be predicated of a substance, and can have more or less truth-value. But this is the formal language of logic and, indeed, we will see, of mathematics, and not the language of forms of life, not the language of language games, not the language of performativity. This kind of language is not understood in terms of its truth-value, but in its 'how'. *Philosophical Investigations*, which is the *locus classicus* of forms of life, of *Lebensformen* and the energetics of life, is the *héritier* of lived experience, *Erlebnis*, that Wilehlm Dilthey first spoke of. Wittgenstein's *Tractatus Logico-Philosophicus* was in the spirit of Weberian objectivity, of positivism, of experience as objective Kantian *Erfahrung*. *Philosophical Investigations* (Wittgenstein II) is about lived experience and forms of life. The 'what', of course, is a 'saying', and indeed most things cannot be said. The how, on the other hand, is a showing. Like pointing to the bricks a builder needs (Last 2008).

For Aristotle, the human *differentia specifica* was first language and then political praxis. In language, Arendt and Aristotle, in alliance against Plato, recognize the importance of rhetoric. Dialectic for Socrates and Plato is a dialogue between two, while rhetoric presumes a multiplicity. Rhetoric is not just false and merely a Sophist means of persuasion. For Aristotle and Arendt (Chapter 5 above), especially political rhetoric – and Arendt's models are Pericles and Achilles – often contains important truth contents. Yes, you must persuade your listeners but listeners also have a good nose for the truth in terms of the content of your language. The quality of argument is important: that is, fact checking and looking at values and what can follow from what in deliberative reasoning. But it also matters *who* you are, who the speaker is, i.e. the character of the speaker. Who is permitted to speak is as important as what is said. And so is the backstory and the identity of this 'who'. Rhetoric has been seen as handmaiden to, or conversely as opposed to, dialectic. Dialectic is a question of the two in which the one has the truth and the other will approach it as his or her doxa is changed into truth during the exchange through argument. Rhetoric is not about the two; it is about plurality or multiplicity, but instead through on-the-ground practices, reasoning from particular to general, deliberative praxis in the polis. Deliberation, and Aristotle's 'deliberative rhetoric', are ever more important, of course, in our age of plebiscitary authoritarianism more generally. Edmund Burke contrasted deliberation, on the one hand, and inclination, on the other. Aristotle had a hierarchy of rhetoric: the lowest level was ceremonial and ritual and pronounced in, e.g., funeral orations; the second was legal or juridical and the highest deliberative.

Dialectic also presumes that we will arrive at the universal, which then will subsume the particular. But political forms of life presume, not the universal, nor even the particular, but instead the singular. Dialectic often works in the register of universal and particular, while rhetoric in the register of the singular: in the register of the political as a collectivity of singularities. This is Arendt's multiplicity of points of view, which constitutes plurality in her notion of the political. Indeed, the Platonic forms are universals that are forever in time and omnipresent in space. Aristotle's forms, thus Aristotle's substances, are singularities, each one different from every other. Form is glued to matter as substance. And it is form or formal cause that gives to substances their singular shape. Political forms of life are a partly rhetorically constituted collection of singularities.

Arendt is scathing about 'the social', which she counterpoises to the political. The social for her is *oikos*, what Foucault sees as governmentality, and the subsumption of the political singular under the universal. Arendt's social is very much that of social-scientific positivism. But what kind of social is at stake in forms of life? But what kind of experience is there in the more embedded, substantive, forms of life? But Wittgenstein does use the term 'forms of life': twice in the first 20 pages of *Philosophical Investigations*. In both cases it is subsumed under the more general, for him, theme of 'language games'. Wittgenstein's forms of life, though, are less political than they are social and cultural. Forms of life, too, are not objective but subjective; they are also not universal–particular but singular. *Philosophical Investigations* starts with a quote from Augustine's *Confessions*, in which Augustine is thinking about early childhood. The first sentence then from Augustine: 'When grown-ups need some object and at the same time turned towards it, I perceived this, and I grasped that the thing was signified by the sound they uttered, since they meant to point *it* out'. They signalled to him through facial gestures their acceptance, investment of affect or rejection of the object. 'I gathered from gestures and by means of facial expressions, etc. indicating the affections of the soul, when it desires and when it rejects. Once I got my tongue around these signs I used them to express my wishes.'

Philosophical Investigations stands to the *Tractatus Logico-Philosophicus* in a way resembling Aristotle's rhetoric to his logic. The logic is substance and predication resembling the propositional format of the *Tractatus*, though the *Tractatus* is organized to a greater extent to latching onto the outside world. Forms of life are different. Aristotle's idea of form is about a 'what'. It is that which distinguished something from everything else. Wittgenstein's forms are about the 'how'. This is not the ethical how of how we should lead our lives. But instead, the more factual or social or better cultural how, of how not individuals but cultures – not so much polities – lead their lives. They are ways of doing, of eating and sleeping and storytelling. This is how *Philosophical Investigations* defines language. It is how we are different from animals. Wittgenstein writes that it is not important to say that animals do not talk because they lack mental ability. Instead, they simply do not talk: they do not use language. 'Giving orders, asking questions, telling stories, having a chat are as much a part of our natural history as walking, eating, drinking, playing'.

Language is a way of doing as is eating, drinking, storytelling, chatting, and ordering, exclaiming, being delighted. They are means of doing these 'hows'. In this sense, they are a language – like in Benjamin's essay on language – of pure means. But Benjamin is thinking of literature and poetic language. Wittgenstein is thinking about the language of everyday life. Wittgenstein keeps speaking of 'ostensive' (*hinweisend*) language both in training and use. *Hinweisend* means to point, to refer to. To point to something means to be in the world with it. In contrast, statements about something presume a two-world model. The seventh main proposition of the *Tractatus* is that 'whereof you cannot speak, you should remain silent'. Showing or pointing in this sense is not speaking. Thus, can be understood Michael (not Karl) Polanyi's dictum that 'we know more than we say'. Wittgenstein says, compare these above language uses with how logicians like Frege or the young Wittgenstein understand the structure of language: with Frege's 'truth-value' of assertoric sentences. In saying that language is thus part of our natural history, Wittgenstein is saying that language is no different than other ways of living. Language thus is not at all about describing life. Language is life. This is not the Saussurean notion of language. Benjamin's critique of such 'semiotic language' is that it is instrumental language – as well as the language of law, predication, the common noun and judgment – in regard to which he counterposes the language of pure means. Wittgenstein does not discuss means and ends. Yet clearly Saussurean language is separated from life. Meaning is about the differential relationship between signifiers. Language is lifted out of life. There is surely a problematic relationship with the referent in Saussure, but in Wittgenstein the referent is not important at all. Language and life are on the same contiguous level.

In this sort of sense, we see commonalities between Frege, Wittgenstein I and Saussure. And Wittgenstein II, like phenomenology, breaks with this. Wittgenstein II, like Arendt, is more a posteriori and 'anti-theoretical' (Lash 2015). What has meaning for Wittgenstein II? It relates to expressions that are not at all propositions or predications. And what constitutes these expressions? For Wittgenstein II, the meaning of a sentence, even if that sentence is primarily a pointing, is possible only if the expression is a move in a language game. No language game, no meaning. He writes that 'to imagine a language is to imagine a form of life': that the speaking of a language is 'part of an activity', a 'form of life'. Here it is the language game rather than the individual sentence that is most important. Wittgenstein writes that an 'ostensive definition'

135

(explanation and use), the meaning of a word, is possible only if the role the word is supposed to play is already clear. That you must already know something about games and even chess 'before you can ask what the king in chess is called'. That 'it only makes sense for someone to ask what something is called' if he/she 'knows how to make use of the name'. This again is prioritizing the form of life over the sentence or the name of the thing. The form of life is a background, a context for the meaning, hence the use of the thing. Anti-positivist forms of life, modern as distinct from Aristotle's ancient forms of life, are the social understood as the background, a stock of knowledge, unspoken assumptions, usually unarticulated. As Wittgenstein II says, you cannot articulate the rules of chess unless you know how to play chess. This is again the primacy of the 'how' over the 'what'. No 'what' without a 'how'. In the second half of this chapter on technological experience, we speak of horizontal and open-system technological experience and vertical and closed-system experience. We discuss the former in the context of Alan Turing on chess playing and 'imitation games' and John von Neumann on strategic moves and game theory. We will discuss them in contrast to Wiener's vertical and closed-system cybernetic command and control. In Turing, von Neumann and Herbert Simon, there is a focus on chess playing, on moves in playing chess. There is a question of moves in simulation, of dissimulation and moves against dissimulation, in cracking the codes in World War II. Von Neumann unpacks supply and demand in neoclassical economics into game-theoretical bargaining moves in an auction. Are open systems in markets and forms of life a question of moves? Are these moves in language or more generally 'symbol games', in which the symbols can be also numerical, geometrical or even religious?

Knowledge in Aristotle's *Metaphysics* was about the four causes of substance as well as the categorial predications of substance. But in modernity, with Kant, it was the subject that was doing the predicating, and knowledge was about matter, not about formed matter – that is, substance – but matter and movement and cause. Now form or any possible equivalent of form was transposed on to the subject. The subject in modernity's classic dualism – more the subject in Kant than in Descartes – would know matter and the formed matter that was substance has disappeared into form as subject and matter as object. Form and powers of predication in the subject are the basis of natural-science knowledge and by implication of all positivisms. What Wittgenstein does is put form back into life: form becomes modes of living. As for the subject, she is no longer objective but situated in forms of life. And the predications of natural science and, by implication through the human sciences – and perhaps even more than in sociology in economics and philosophy – becomes instead the natural language of language games and forms of life. For Wittgenstein, language games are forms of life. And predication, objective statements and the subjects of logical positivism and analytic philosophy become just one of many language games. Form is restored to life but in a way that is very different from classical forms of life. Thus, in a sense Husserl repeats Hegel's replacement of the subject–object couple with the consciousness–appearance couple. It is from this 'more primordial' consciousness–appearance relation that subject–object bifurcation derives. Thus subject–object experience as in positivism is displaced by consciousness–appearance experience in phenomenology. What Wittgenstein effectively does, and phenomenological sociology more explicitly does, is to replace consciousness with forms of life.

6.2 Technological Forms of Life

6.2.1 Communicational Forms of Life

But what about in the contemporary age in which forms of life are threatened by globalization? In which one form of life will often relate to another as if it were a virus, in terms of an immune reaction (Esposito 2011). What about in an age such as ours, which is importantly post-human, informational and comprised less perhaps of language than of information, communication and data? Our forms of life have become informational, from genetics, through information machines, up to the social sciences themselves. For example, in economics the problem of information in analysts such as Simon and von Neuman and Hayek has replaced the distribution of scarce resources. In both cases forms of life were arrayed against episteme. In the ancient, a combination of anti-episteme praxis and technics gave us political forms of life, which were rhetoric's combination of *technē* and praxis. Each time, as episteme power and the epistemic – first as pure episteme and second as synthesis with nature and positivism – is opposed by forms of life.

In the communication age the same thing happens. Now neoliberal power asserts itself on an informational model. No longer is economics on a neoclassical *homo economicus* model, in which each person 'is the brain', in which a Newtonian classical mechanics model of market and commodity – inaugurated by Benthamite utilitarianism – and consecrated by J.S. Mill's first use of the term *homo economicus*, is the all-seeing unbounded rationality of *homo economicus*. Now the informational model of Simon and Hayek and von Neumann's game theory replaces the Newtonian model. Now systems become self-organizing on the lines of control, command, communications and intelligence, or C3I. Now big data and databases – themselves nonlinear systems of self-organizing data – are king in neoliberalism. Now no longer is neoliberalism driven by the last breaths of finance capital. Since the 2008 crisis now the characteristically communi-cational-forms-of-life digital capital – of Apple, Google, Facebook, Amazon, Airbnb and Uber – takes the driver's seat. These are forms of death in which nonlinear power, generated to start with from the RAND Corporation and Frazer Aircraft, takes the helm (Mirowski 2002). Before we had the full rationality of 'economic man', but now we have only the bounded rationality of Herbert Simon's economic and also algorithmic simulation. With *homo economicus* no longer at the helm, the market is no longer a mechanism for the allocation of scarce resources, but an information-processing mechanism.

What is counterposed to this mode of cyborgization and not actor networks or even matter free of humans? Instead, we have not the new materialism but the cyborg experience and the technics and politics of Mirowski and Stiegler and Simondon. Now forms of life have become fully technological: phenomenology becomes machine phenomenology. The political bond of classical antiquity and modernity's social bond are displaced by the communicational bond of technological forms of life. Now what was first rhetoric and is later language games becomes reduced to the thinness of the communications of social media; rhetoric becomes visual rhetoric. TV stars become politicians. Experience itself becomes technological as we work through an a posteriori mode of political resistance. Neoliberal power takes on a new a priori and is counterposed to resistance in what is now a transformed a posteriori of techno-social experience.

What was the old rhetoric in the classical started, as Aristotle said, from ceremonies, from the ceremonial: first in ceremonies, then in law, then finally in the political. But it was the ceremonial that first came to assure the social bond. The original social bond of Marcel Mauss's gift constitutes the social as ritual. Then, with Lévi-Strauss's exchange of women, it went beyond the ancestral solidarity of the clan to form solidarity at the level of the inter-lineage, and incipiently of the tribe and the creation of a proper symbolic. But what happens

138

to this symbolic, conscience collective that is the glue of society – when we come to communicational forms of life? This symbolic becomes dependent on noise, on chatter. At stake is this noise itself, this meaninglessness of endlessly exchanged messages and pictures and sound in groups of between seven and eight and ten people on Facebook and WeChat, etc.: this noise that can give us a communicational solidarity whose thinness can be made up for by its extensity and can form a basis for resistances of both technics and praxis in the communication age.

What happens in communicational or informational forms of life, whose condition is of course the cybernetic revolution, the move from a Newtonian to a cybernetic, a Turingian episteme? Turing is inter alia the inventor of the algorithm, which drives of course communicational, technological forms of life. Turing makes two moves in this context. First, he follows Gödel in the break with Cantor and Hilbert's 'deterministic' set-theoretical mathematics for Gödels incompleteness. Secondly, Turing translates Gödel's algorithms from the register of mathematics' propositional statements to the performativity of computing. At stake is Gödel's undecidability, from which in a consistent axiomatic system some propositions are not provable, and all propositions are only provable in an inconsistent axiomatic system. Turing transforms this logic of logic into the logic of the algorithm. Turing's final transformation of language starts from Gödel. Here Gödel's predications become Turing's performatives, the commands of his algorithms. And this final transformation of non-propositional language – from rhetoric, to language games to, now, algorithms – becomes the basis of our present communicational forms of life.

6.2.2 Entropy or Negentropy

I want to draw on Mirowski's *Machine Dreams* at some length and in some detail to develop the idea of technological experience and technological forms of life. And how much its assumptions were rooted in questions that were thrown up by thermodynamics, and in particular the question of entropy. Indeed, all of technological experience is one way or another of dealing with this. There is no computing, no machine experience without the problem of entropy. We will see machine experience is not a question of Wiener's negentropic signal, which is information, but a question with Turing, von Neumann and Shannon of the *entropic* nature of machine intelligence. Machine intelligence in Turing and von Neumann is deceptive. It simulates randomness. In the film *The Imitation Game*, the good guys Turing and the Brits beat the bad guys by being more evil than they are (Fuller and Goffey 2012). This is a question of the second law of thermodynamics formulated in 1854 by Lord Kelvin, William Thompson, which specified the connection of heat and temperature in relation to energy and work. The first law of thermo-dynamics holds that energy can be exchanged between physical systems as heat and work. The second law understands entropy as a quantity: a quantification of a state or order of a system that expresses useful work, which can be performed. We find such entropy in systems from heat engines to chemical systems. The founding figures of thermodynamics are Pierre Duhem, Ludwig Boltzmann and James Clerk Maxwell. Thermodynamics is always about quantities: about differences in quantity in heat energy. Clerk Maxwell showed that this second law was displayed only as a statistical regularity. In thermodynamics and in computation, it is often a question of statistics, entailing a certain measure of indeterminacy. The second law is also saying 'heat cannot pass from a colder to a warmer body'.

Energy exists in any body in thermodynamics in the form of heat. Negentropy designates the battles of life against the dissipation of heat death: of negentropy against entropy. Maxwell's demon made heat pass from a colder to a warmer body. This negentropic demon monitored two gas chambers and made it so that heat could pass from the colder to the hotter chamber. The demon operates the portal, the door between the chambers. The door and demon are also assumptions in cybernetics and hence in machine-mediated and machine experience. For William Thompson, the demon cannot create or annul energy. But just like a living animal, he can store and reproduce energy. He can operate thus on individual atoms to reverse the natural dissipation of energy. Maxwell saw that in Darwin there was progressive development, while in thermodynamics there was decay and dissolution. Yet he spoke of a third possibility, of neither progress nor decay but stability, of homeostasis, from Claude Bernard and physiology, which is a property of a system in which a variable like temperature is actively regulated to remain constant, sometimes through negative feedback.

In this context, Mirowski (2002: 50) looks to Leo Szilard, who with Enrico Fermi created the nuclear chain reactor and wrote the letter for the Manhattan Project's atomic bomb that Albert Einstein signed. Szilard was a student of Einstein's under whom, with von Neumann, he studied statistical mechanics. We are moving from Maxwell's

FORMS OF LIFE: TECHNOLOGICAL PHENOMENOLOGY

demon, to intelligent beings counteracting the decrease in the entropy of the thermodynamic system to allow, for example, the construction of a perpetual motion machine. Taking on the assumptions of Einstein's observer, who now is situated in a 'reference frame', we note that the act of measurement itself costs energy. Yet Szilard was aware of the demon-like effects, the negentropic effects, of the investment of information. Negentropy here is associated with information and with *memory* for the first time in the physical sciences. What is to provide the feedback, the intelligence, the negentropic loop if it is not system memory itself? It is system memory that does the organizing in self-organizing systems that give it its structure. Put another way, memory is its *structure*. Sloterdijk (2004) is perceptive in terms of what it is that makes a self-organizing system self-organize. In sociology, we see simple functional systems in Parsons. This systems force of organization comes from outside the system. In Newtonian physics, this is simple external cause. In functionalism from Spencer through Parsons until today, there is a Darwinist paradigm at stake. Here the cause or force of organization of systems comes from its environment. In the case of a society comprised by subsystems like the family, the Church, etc., the cause of organization of a subsystem is the whole of the system. It is the function that it plays in the larger system. Thus, unlike in mechanics and on a biological paradigm, the whole causes the part. This is functional causation, as explicated by, say, G.A. Cohen (1978). But here this functional cause is still external cause. What Sloterdijk is on about is that excess of self-cause beyond functional and mechanical cause. It is this excess that is driven by the system's structure. The system's structure thus does the organizing for the system. Moreover, the structure is involved in the structural coupling of second-order cybernetics (Hayles 1999). Thus, in Humberto Maturana's *Autopoiesis and Cognition*, there is structural coupling of two or more autopoietic systems. At stake are not so much relations of a single evolving system with its environment, but a co-evolutionary paradigm that Donna Haraway (2016) has understood in terms of 'sympoietic systems'. What we see in Szilard is that the structure through which these systems couple and exchange energy and information is memory itself: memory, in its most general sense as machine memory or plant memory.

So, memory is a faculty not just in humans but manifested by a system, a system where entropy-fostering (self-)measurements occur. We see this in Karen Barad's (2007) focus on measurement and the device in quantum physics and in her understanding of how we 'meet the universe' at the intersection of matter and meaning. In cultural and media studies, arguably the two basic and fundamental texts are Stuart Hall's essay on television discourse and Claude Shannon's engineering theory of communications (Hall 1973; Shannon and Weaver 1963). In these, Hall gives us a theory (not inconsistent with Wittgenstein) of meaning and Shannon a theory of 'matter'. In a similar sense technological experience, or technological forms of life, is this meeting of matter and meaning. Much of the 'new materialism' (e.g. Bennett) leaves the meaning out of the equation. This is the great insight of Barad's technological phenomenology, in which we (meaning) meet the universe (matter) halfway. For Barad, meaning meets matter through the mediation of Nils Bohr's quantum physics device: his two-slit wave–particle measuring device. Similarly, we encounter the matter of everyday life as mediated through a plethora of such devices in the internet of things (Jung). Technological phenomenology is very much a forms-of-life phenomenology. In place of the observer and her mind on the meaning side of Barad's equation are the forms of life of a culture or community. This is putting together Maturana's structurally coupling autopoietic and co-evolutionary systems with Francisco Varela's Buddhist-influenced forms-of-life phenomenology. We bring together Wittgenstein II from the first part of this chapter with technology from the second part. We are in agreement with Haraway's (*Staying with the Trouble*, 2016) flat and open and horizontal sympoietic systems as an alternative to what Haraway sees as Latour's (2014) Anthropocene of Carl Schmitt's and Gaian vertical and controlling systems. This is, implicitly, Haraway's second-order cybernetics critique of Latour's first-order cybernetics.

To return to our narrative, Leo Szilard's machine memory is negentropic, and illustrative of the cybernetic problem of 'the reinstatement of order'. This, for von Neumann and Turing, will become a question of computation, of the mathematical logic of computation. Later, Schrödinger in a pamphlet 'What Is Life' in 1943 would speak of 'code' in the place of Maxwell's demon (Mirowski 2002). Thus, code enters along with memory in the battle against entropy. Code, genetic or otherwise, but especially algorithms, will provide the anti-entropic thrust. In biology it is particular proteins that counter the laws of physics (Parisi 2004) in coded reproduction. For Wiener, self-organization is through negentropic feedback loops, feedback mechanisms, which change mechanical matter into more or less vibrant matter. Live matter, without mainly being self-organizing, is already vibrant matter (Bennett 2009), in Darwinian or functional explanation, already on an organismic paradigm. What we are interested in here is not just life but self-organizing life.

FORMS OF LIFE: TECHNOLOGICAL PHENOMENOLOGY

Schrödinger with code, and Szilard, with memory feedback machines, 'bootstrap random information', organize it and feed it back to bring systems to higher levels of order. These work via statistics (cf. statistical mechanics) as well. Again, the inspiration is thermodynamics and, not classical mechanics, but statistical mechanics. Statistical mechanics develops with the shift from the focus of classical mechanics on force, mass, motion and gravity to one on heat and the theory of gases. In Bernoulli's kinetic theory, gases consist of a great number of molecules moving in all dimensions in a world of mechanically colliding particles. Their impact on a surface is gas pressure, which is heat: the gas pressure of a system is its kinetic energy. Maxwell later saw this as a distribution of molecular velocities. This gives us physics' first statistical law, which Boltzmann subsequently formalized as statistical mechanics in the context of his formulation of entropy in the Second Law of Thermodynamics. Statistically speaking, most systems are in a state of disorder: close to the maximum disorder of gases in a system at equilibrium. This is a state in which field potentials are negative. This entropic state of states, tending towards such disorder, is most probable. For Boltzmann, collisions have a law of probability following from such random collisions. And, conversely, a dynamically ordered state – one in which, as Boltzmann noted, molecules are moving at the same speed in the same direction – is almost infinitely improbable.

Such laws of probability and statistics function also in information entropy and negentropy. Thus, statistics become (Mirowski 2002: 57) the means through which, for Wiener, signal could be precipitated from out of noise. For both von Neumann and Wiener, the model is partly the statistical feedback algorithms in a torpedo, whose context was US military strategy. The question in such strategies is how much of this signal is down to random movement and how much is down to what Mirowski calls 'Maxwell's Other Demon', a duplicitous, strategic demon, sometimes giving itself off as pure entropy or randomness but that has its own strategy. Maxwell's Other Demon is the key player in von Neumann's game theory and more generally in game-theoretic economics. Wiener, for whom information is negentropic, creating signal out of noise, invented the term cybernetics. The first Macy Cybernetic conference, inspired by Wiener, in 1946 featured 'teleological mechanisms'. Wiener understood cybernetics to be at the heart of what he called the second industrial revolution. This is the cybernetics of C3I – command control, communication and intelligence (Haraway 1991).

143

Wiener's cybernetics, initially with Turing and Weaver, were opposed to David Hilbert's axiomatic determination. Wiener could not believe in the existence of a 'closed series of postulates of logic, leaving no room for arbitrariness in the system' (Lin and Wong 2016). Statistical thermodynamics instead made common cause with Gödel's incompleteness. To closed-system axiomatics, Wiener counterposed an 'automatic device using error-sensing and negative feedback to correct performance with inbuilt encoding by a heterostat for feedback loops'. The I in C3I is of the enemy, and communications are in, for example, evasion-targeting as a set of communications subject to feedback corrections. For Wiener, the cybernetic paradigm also applied to the nervous system (Pickering 2011). Here, McCulloch and Pitts proffered a model of the neuron on the lines of computational power. For Wiener, the nervous system was a 'device' 'which makes decisions on the basis of decisions it has made in the past' (Mirowski 2002: 62). Thus, again, it is memory that is feeding back into control. Wiener defines information with regard to thermodynamic entropy, measured as 'extracting "signal" from "noise" in a communication channel' (Mirowski 2002: 62). This, as we will see, is very different from von Neumann's automaton, which is not looking to extract signal from noise but instead 'for the maintenance of the complexity of organization, and the use of randomness itself to bring about further (complex) organization'.

Turing was also involved with the idea of simulation. In 1948, he wrote a chess program. The Turing test indeed measures simulation. The entire artificial intelligence (AI) paradigm of computer science is about simulation. Mirowski writes about a cybernetic regime in economics. He has distinguished two types of cybernetic economists. Those like Herbert Simon who were basically concerned with simulation, and those like von Neumann (and indeed Turing) whose computational thinking was framed by logic and mathematics. For his part, Turing is starting in part from games: from machine-simulated chess games. And chess games and game theory are not very far apart (von Neumann and Morgenstern 1944). In Benedict Cumberbatch's Turing film, *The Imitation Game*, the imitation game itself was the Turing test, which registered the possibility of machine intelligence. If you, on one side of the curtain, could not tell whether it was a machine or a person on the other side from its responses to the conversation, the machine passed the Turing test, i.e. the imitation game. The point regarding von Neumann, and to a lesser extent Turing, was the mediation of computation with game theory. Once game theory and dissimulation come to centre stage, the idea of information changes radically. Wiener's and Szilard's idea of information was one in which computation was a bootstrapping of random information to achieve higher levels of organization. Von Neuman's game theory and then Turing's machine (the UTM) was not, like in Wiener, a question of Maxwells' 'good' demon, but of its evil other (Fuller and Goffey 2012).

6.2.3 Incompleteness: From Predications (Science) to Algorithms (Engineering)

At the heart of this is incompleteness. We have introduced von Neumann's entropic game-theoretical framework. Von Neumann was, as a young man, a Hilbertian, and thought it was always possible to design an axiomatic to solve Hilbert's *Entscheidungsproblem* (decidability problem). Along with many others, the somewhat more mid-career von Neumann switches to Gödel. Turing, for his part, was from the start a Gödelian, assuming that there is no algorithm possible to solve Hilbert's *Entscheidungsproblem*. We note that Turing uses the word algorithm. Computer scientists use Hilbert curves, but Hilbert himself did not speak notably about algorithms. Gödel, for his part, saw algorithms as operations generating theorems from an axiomatic. For Gödel, mathematical procedures took on the sort of colouring of an algorithm. It is important in this context to distinguish between mathematical and technological statements. Mathematical statements are constatives, while algorithms are always performatives. We say this knowing the blurredness of boundaries between the two types of statements. Our point here is to distinguish the scientific episteme – of a priori synthetic (and analytic) judgments – from technological activities. In Kant's sense, mathematical statements are a priori analytic, and scientific statements from natural or social sciences, which presume experience and the empirical, are a priori synthetic judgments. Technological forms of life and technological experience are questions less of judging at all, but instead of making. They are about performatives, about engineering, about making. Constatives are true or false. They are truth-evaluable. Performatives are not. An axiomatic consists of statements, propositions or equations like a = a that are taken as true, self-evidently true. From these statements, we can prove true theorems. For Gödel, the algorithms mediated between these two kinds of constatives. They were not constatives themselves. They were not truth-evaluable statements. They were instead procedures or operators. Within mathematics they were performatives. In Mandarin, an algorithm is a *suanfa* (算法), a method of calculation. An algorithm is always a method. Methods are not true or false. A method like ethnography or survey analysis may proceed from research questions or hypotheses and lead to true findings. But the methods are never true or false themselves.

In the transition from Gödel to Turing, problems of logic and mathematics are converted into engineering problems. Thus, Turing gave the first detailed design of a stored-program computer. The program is a set of algorithms, and these may be stored in the computer. There is, on the one hand, the Turing machine and, on the other, the universal Turing machine. The Turing machine is an abstract machine that manipulates symbols on a strip of tape according to a set of rules. This is a mathematical model of computation. The machine proceeds according to instructions. Let us note that Turing's focus on rules, even algorithmic rules, was despite their incompleteness, and the dimension of undecidability is very different from the more hermeneutic (late Wittgenstein) notion of experience we have looked at in this book. Indeed, Michael Polanyi, younger brother of Karl, engaged in debate with Turing over the possibility of non-rule-based tacit knowledge, over knowing how rather than knowing that. M. Polanyi – also an influential critic of positivism – influenced Hubert Dreyfus's Heideggerian disagreements with AI. Turing and our idea of technological experience or technological forms of life are a third mode of experience, cross-cutting and short-circuiting positivism and phenomenology. The result is something like machine phenomenology that is encountered in Simondon, Maturana/Varela, Stiegler and Niklas Luhmann and, more recently, Karen Barad. Turing is partly already there.

These are questions of rules. Algorithms are not true–false statements or truth-evaluative. But they are also not like procedural rules, regulative rules or constitutive rules. John Searle makes the distinction between regulative and constitutive rules in *Speech Acts* (1969). Here you need constitutive rules in order to speak the language at all, whereas regulative rules are more about what you can and cannot say. The same sort of distinction could be made between constitutional law and public and private law that fall under it. All these rules, though, tell you what you can do and what you must not do. Neither constitutive nor regulative rules are constative but instead performative. Constative statements are not rules. They are truth-evaluative. Legal and linguistic rules are about praxis. Algorithms, Turing-type rules, are not truth-evaluative and in this sense not in the realm of episteme – either in Euclid's (analytic) or Foucault's (synthetic) sense. Algorithms are not about episteme but instead about making: in the register of engineering and technics. So let us revisit once again Aristotle's famous distinction between episteme, praxis and technics. Episteme is about constative statements that – whether analytic as in mathematics or logic or synthetic as in the natural and social sciences – are truth-evaluative. These constative statements are not basically rules. Speech acts in the realm of practice and technics are not truth-evaluative. The rules of praxis (practice) are constitutive or mostly regulative. They are about a doing. Whereas the rules of technics are not regulative but instead generative. They are about a making. The shift from Gödel to Turing, to repeat, was one from the constative and truth-evaluative analytic judgments of mathematics to the generative rules of such a technics.

In this sense, cookbook instructions are not praxis rules. They are not about the 'can' or the 'must/must-not' but about the 'how-to'. Further, for Turing they are incomplete and undecidable. Algorithms are incomplete generative rules. Turing demonstrated the uncomputability of Hilbert's *Entscheidungsproblem*. A Hilbertian computer scientist would ask for an algorithm that takes as assumed a statement of first-order logic together with a finite set of axioms beyond first-order logic's axioms. The *Enscheidungsproblem* in computation begins with Leibniz's attempt to build a calculating machine, one that could manipulate symbols in order to determine the truth-value of mathematical statements.

Turing, with Alonzo Church, formally defined an algorithm as 'effective calculability'. Not calculations but the possibility or faculty of calculation. And not any calculability but only those that are efficacious, put into performance. We recall the *Entscheidungsproblem*. Turing defines what an algorithm is with his Turing machines. For any given algorithm, a Turing machine can be constructed that simulates the algorithm's logic. This is Hilbert's premise that Turing challenges and sets limits to in terms of computability. To prove incompleteness, Gödel assigned numbers to logical formulae and thereby reduced logic to arithmetic. Turing's machine could capture Gödel's effective methods in the, now not mathematical, but mechanical procedures of its algorithms. A central processing unit (CPU) in a real computer is the electronic circuitry that carries out the instructions of a computer program (algorithms) by performing basic arithmetical and logical (control, input/output) operations specified by instructions (the algorithms). The processing unit and control unit are separate from the storable components such as main memory and input/output circuitry. A CPU comprises an ALU (arithmetic-logic unit) and a process register that supplies operands to the ALU and stores results. The operands are symbols like '3' and '6' and the operators are symbols like '+' and '='. Only a stored-program computer can have a CPU. Von Neumann's EDVAC (Electronic Discrete Variable Automatic Computer) later used the same space for storage and treatment of CPU instructions and data. The tape of the Turing machine comprises symbols in squares. The Turing machine uses sequential memory to store data. Sequential access memory, as opposed to random access memory, reads stored data in sequence.

Turing's machine had unlimited memory capacity in its infinite tape marked out into squares; on each square a symbol is printed. The machine can read and write the symbols one at a time, using the tape head. The main point for us is that the Turing Machine with its undecidables and incompleteness was not based on Maxwell's good demon but on his evil, his entropic, demon (Mirowski 2002). In this such entropy was also the simulation of randomness through duplicity. Turing's coder–decoder beat the Germans in effectively being more evil than the Germans.

6.2.4 System Encounter: War Games or Sex Games?

Von Neumann was hugely influenced by David Hilbert's programme of axiomatization. Hilbert sought to solve the contradictions in Georg Cantor's set theory through finding the axioms from which these seemingly inconsistent theorems can be derived. An axiom is classically a statement that is self-evident and so well established as to be accepted without controversy or question. In modern logic, it becomes simply a premise in the context of a system of statements. Axiomatization is to work back from the more local statements to the fundamental axioms. Hilbert himself did this for Euclidean geometry. The young von Neumann thought that economics was not yet a candidate for axiomatization. But he worked on axiomatization of set theory, quantum mechanics (QM) and game theory. He wanted to use Hilbertian space to axiomatize matrix mechanics: to axiomatize states in matrix mechanics. Matrix mechanics itself comes from quantum mechanics. The canonical formulation of quantum mechanics pertains to Werner Heisenberg noting that electrons were no longer moving in the orbits of classical physics and further that the intensity of radiation quantities is not, as in classical physics, sharply defined. Von Neumann followed Max Born – who had developed

148

matrix mechanics with Heisenberg – in a matrix algebra explanation. Matrix mechanics understood that in QM particles, there was not continuous emission of radiation. Photons and emissions were not continuous but discrete. The matrix describes the motion of a QM particle. This motion, for example for Niels Bohr, concerned the discrete nature of every state and the quantum leaps between states. A pure quantum state was understood in this context as a 'ray' in Hilbert space. A quantum state, for its part, is the state of an isolated quantum system, and gives a probability distribution of each observable for the outcome of each possible measurement on the system.

Hilbert, very much the Kantian in terms of apodictic knowledge, saw physics and geometry as ideal fields for axiomatization. Von Neumann, as he breaks with Hilbert for Gödel, wants to extend this to games. Ernst Zermelo had already extended the application of set theory to chess, in which the value of a feasible position for one of the players can be mathematically (objectively) decided. The problem again of entropy in measurement, as Bohr later noted, was pivotal. Following from Einstein's situatedness of the observer and observer effect, it was asked, what can offset the rise in entropy in the act of measurement? The answer for Bohr was the collapse of entire wave packets. Quantum mechanics and not classical mechanics featured the superposition of such states, system states. A quantum is the minimum amount of any physical entity involved in an interaction. This magnitude of such a property is discrete. Thus, a photon is a single quantum of visible light and of all other forms of electromagnetic radiation. And the energy of an electron is also quantized: in certain discrete values of an atom's electrons. Thus, Max Planck spoke of quanta of matter, of electricity, gas and heat. That energy is radiated and absorbed in discrete quanta. Einstein showed radiation exists in spatially localized packets: that is, quanta of light. Thus, particles are discrete packets of energy: matter is packets of energy, with wave-like properties.

Thus, in QM there is the discrete, not the continuous of classical mechanics, and the existence of states, discrete states with statistical probabilities, unlike the determinism of classical mechanics. Von Neumann was crossing over from mathematics to physics and then computation to economics. Quantum mechanics' probabilism was opposed to Newtonian classical determinism. Thus, the centrality of statistics now is not positivism, but brings in anti-determinism as against Newtonian and Kantian determinacy. Von Neumann adapts Gödel's incompleteness theorems, whereby 'for any self-consistent

149

recursive axiomatic system powerful enough to describe the arithmetic of natural numbers, there are true propositions about naturals that cannot be proved from the axioms' (Franzen 2004: 71), i.e. from the accepted axioms of set theory. A theorem in this is a provably true proposition.

Let us bring this back to technological experience, which we are understanding as experience through not negentropic, but instead entropic, information machines. Through machines shot through with statistical indeterminacy and incompleteness, with machines that are already alive in Einstein's sense that matter is energy (Bennett 2009). This matter, with Jane Bennett, is vibrant and indeterminately self-organizing. This is experience through a prism of cybernetic understanding of information as intelligence, through the dissimulation of games. Let us take this back to Maturana and autopoietic systems. These are self-making systems, in which self-making is indeterminate. This pertains to a technological (hence algorithmic) and forms-of-life phenomenology. The set-theoretical statements and predications – i.e. axioms and theorems – have become performative: have become the also dissimulating mathematical instructions dealing with the information intelligence of the environment. But, more importantly, they engage with the intelligence information of other nearby systems. Here system memory is structure that drives self-organization through algorithmic rules. Systems encounter other systems either, on the one hand, through dissimulating war games or, on the other hand, through structural coupling. This is the difference between first- and second-order cybernetics – from Wiener through Turing and von Neumann to, nowadays, Latour, based on a military model with origins in atomic bomb strategies and Arpanet, etc., and what might be called third-order cybernetics. This order of cybernetics is more biological, is about coupling rather than war games, and we see it in Maturana but especially in feminist media theory – Hayles, Barad, Haraway, Parisi and of course Prigogine and Stengers and Lash and Lury (2007). Here, with Turing, whenever structural coupling takes place, it is not deducible from the machine's axiomatic. The structure is memory, and the way the structure drives the system is through algorithmic procedures. The structures may couple through algorithms. The outcome is system change or literally reproduction.

Gödelian notions of computation would 'query whether some predictably terminating algorithm could determine whether a given number was the code for a sequence of formulas (Mirowski 2002: 119). As Hofstadter (1979) remarked, 'Gödel incompleteness can be applied to any Turing-complete computational system'. Breaking with Hilbert's axiomatization of games, von Neumann asked 'how self-organization of information and communication through processes of struggle could ideally result in a kind of order' (Mirowski 2002: 121). For its part, Claude Shannon's notion of information is much more in line with von Neumann and Turing than it is with Wiener's negentropic understanding. In von Neumann and Turing, complexity was already the key question rather than Wiener's problematique of signal versus noise. At issue here is artificial intelligence. Information is machine intelligence. If economics adapts von Neumann and Morgenstern's type of game theory, then humans or humans with computers in markets adopt a sort of machine-intelligence paradigm of dissimulation. A machine is intelligent if it can dissimulate so that you cannot tell if it is a machine or a human. Cryptography is intelligence, as is game theory: it is intelligence as spies see intelligence. It is also the intelligence of decrypting. This is in a C3I system in which the 'I' is intelligence, and in which the three Cs only work to the extent that the 'I' is functioning well. This is different, for example, from Philip K. Dick's VALIS, in which God is a vast active living intelligence system. For Dick, intelligence has to do with mind in the very broadest sense. Communication in this is opened up to include, for example, how a mechanism, an automaton, is equipped to track an aeroplane, a warplane, for guided missile technology. Warren Weaver, who was the main mediator of research funding from the military to von Neumann and the others, was a key player on the National Defence Research Committee and always on the lookout for electronic and digital solutions. Weaver and von Neumann brought computing technologies into building the atom bomb at Los Alamos. Weaver was a decisive influence in the Applied Mathematics Programme and thought that computing would have an effect on mathematics itself, pushing in the direction of discontinuity and discreteness (Mirowski 2002: 174). After all, 0s and 1s are discrete, as are algorithms.

Shannon and Weaver's (1963) text, which has provided the dominant paradigm for information and communication down to the present time, was driven by Shannon, in regard to whom Weaver was mainly a popularizer (see Roch 2009). Shannon and Weaver take on Wiener's probabilistic ideas and move them in a different direction. They are more influential for their theory of communication than for information. Their model of communication is based on information source, message, transmitter, receiver, signal, noise, channel and the probability of error in encoding and decoding. For Shannon, information entropy is a measure for uncertainty in a message.

But before addressing Shannon, let us once again accentuate the notion of technological experience in this book. We have discussed this in the context of other work in cultural studies and women's studies. It is significant that perhaps the three most important and influential texts in media theory and cybernetics have a connection to feminist theory: these are both Haraway's early and recent works, Katherine Hayles's post-humanism and Karen Barad's work. This is not to forget the work of Jane Bennett and younger scholars like Luciana Parisi. Many have noted Shannon's 'semantically impoverished' notion of information and communication. For Niklas Luhmann, in contrast, semantics is implicitly at the heart of his technological communication (Luhmann 1989).

A system, for Luhmann, connects to its environment semantically. This is of a piece with Maturana and von Uexküll (2010), in which nonhuman perception is cognitive and a question of meaning. The point is that the meaning has less to do with the perceived than with the perceiver. Hence, Maturana's famed observation that when a dog bites you, it's not about you, it's about the dog. Hayles's (1999) distinction between first-order and second-order cybernetics is very much about a paradigm shift from Wiener to Maturana and Varela. Luhmann's sociology is of course a sociological take on Maturana. Hayles says that second-generation cybernetics is much closer to the body, much more bodily. And there is a clear shift from a military paradigm and military context to a biological context also seen, for example, in Parisi's *Abstract Sex* (2004). Entropy in Parisi and Lynn Margulis's Gaia hypothesis is counteracted less through self-organization than it is through reproduction – also in von Neumann's automata – and communication that is understood as 'coupling', in Maturana and Luhmann as 'structural coupling'. The dual agent or the intersubjectivity of Turing and von Neumann and Shannon is friend versus enemy, it is a hostile intersubjectivity, while the intersubjectivity, or at points inter-objectivity in Maturana, Luhmann, Hayles and Parisi, is not military but biological and, of course, Maturana and Lynn Margulis are biologists (and Varela a neuroscientist). Key here is exchange of information and for that matter energy exchange at the level of structure. Once you bring back the semantics (with Luhmann and Varela and more recently Karen Barad), you are moving perhaps necessarily to a technological phenomenology.

Varela was more phenomenological than Maturana. So, in this sense, biologically as distinct from militarily, we can understand Hayles's embodiment. But what can this semantic mean? And how can it be algorithmic? Wendy Chun (2013) and Adrian Mackenzie

(2006) have understood algorithms as working not just as performatives but also as the background language of forms of life. The crossover to the semantic is necessary for human scientific notions of techno-social experience; that is, cyborg as distinct from strictly machinic à la Shannon and even von Neumann.

For Shannon and Weaver, the idea of information in their communication theory is 'not what you do say but what you *could* say'. Information and communication in Wiener is the signal, what you do say. In Shannon and Weaver, 'information is a measure [and for them and others, entropy, but not communication, is always a measure] of freedom of choice'. Freedom of choice when one 'elects a message' (Hayles 1990: 51). The state theory of quantum mechanics comes in here, because for Shannon and Weaver, 'information applies not just to individual messages but to the situation as a whole', whereby the situation and not the signal is 'the unit of information'. For us this state, this situation, would cross over with Wittgenstein's forms of life or cultures. Focus here is on the discreteness and disjunction of the state or situation. For Shannon's 'real theory of meaning', which is still semantically impoverished, language is designed with a view to things 'not that people say but they might *wish* to say, and thus must deal with its task *statistically*'. This reaches out, of course, to statistical mechanics and explains the thermodynamic behaviour of a large system – this is statistical thermodynamics as distinct from classical thermodynamics – in which temperature, heat and entropy arise from the naturally uncertain state of the system. Here, Mirowski (2002: 169ff.) notes, we connect the laws of mechanics to everyday practical experience in the sense that our incomplete knowledge is the uncertain state. Weaver thus spoke of the 'disorganized situations with which statistics can cope, yet [these situations] show the essential features of organization', what Weaver called 'organized complexity'.

Again, it is this situation, this state, this discrete state that is what technological forms of life are when understood via Wittgenstein semantically. They are not the speech acts or the performatives. They are the condition of possibility of performativity, the language games that make the speech acts possible. And such also is technological experience. It is not exactly *Erlebnis* against Kantian *Erfahrung*. Now *Erlebenis* and *Erfahrung* are no longer distinguishable. *Erfahrung* becomes an indeterminate, discrete state. It is not Dilthey's *Erlebnis* or Benjamin's *Shockerlebnis*. It is not a one-off. It is a state, a situation, a form of life in which singular *Erlebnisse*, in which shock experiences in life and in art, are possible.

Shannon wrote his MA thesis on electronic switching circuits and their description by Boolean algebra. In Boolean algebra, the values of the variables are not the normal continuum towards infinity, but instead they are the truth-values of true and false, 1 and 0. As importantly, these values, these operands, do not work by the main operators of addition and multiplication (e.g., $y = 3x + 7$), but alternative operators of conjunction and disjunction. We are back, of course, in the conjunctive experience of William James and Deleuze's reading of Hume. Thus, there is conjunction and disjunction in modern programming language, digital electronics and set theory and statistics. You can manipulate expressions in the algebra of sets and translate them in Boolean. BITs themselves are such binary digits. This again will seem to be the translation of Gödelian algebra into the language of algorithms. Remember Shannon is an engineer, speaking the language of performativity and algorithms, and not a scientist speaking in descriptive statements. Thus, Shannon gives us a two-element Boolean algebra, a 'switching algebra'. The first ideas for this information theory came from his Bell Labs-published 'A Mathematical Theory of Cryptography'. Shannon and Weaver's *The Mathematical Theory of Communication* was published some fifteen years later.

Shannon gave us a mathematical dimension of information based not on Wiener's assumptions of continuity, but instead on assumptions of the discrete. Here, Shannon from cryptography gave us an idea of information very much like Turing's disinformation, on the blurring of the 'distinction between natural randomness and information evasion, entropic control and stealthy (Mirowski 2002: 69–70) dissimulation, communication and misinformation'. Thus, opposing Wiener, for whom larger uncertainty in 'the case of a large set' means less knowledge, hence less information, for Shannon, information is produced where 'choice is made from a set, the larger the set the more information' (quoted in Mirowski 2002: 70). Shannon, like the others, was also obsessed with the human brain, hence his core idea regarding coding information for transmission is to do with human and animal transmission of information along nerve networks, a noisy redundant system. This, for Shannon and for von Neumann, is an evolutionary model. In this sense, 'thermodynamic entropy is a measure of the number of ways the unobserved therefore probabilistic microdynamics of molecules can make up a measurable macrostate like temperature'. Translated into symbols, this for Shannon means 'a given probability of a particular symbol showing up, and a measure of the likelihood of strings of symbols' (Mirowski 2002: 72). Thus Shannon's 'symbol transducer' is a

154

'device capable of decoding and recoding strings of symbols as inputs and outputs' that 'may have an internal memory so that its output depends not only on the input symbol but also on its past history' (Mirowski 2002: 71).

All roads here lead back to Gödel and his efforts in a sense to reverse Frege's attempts to reduce arithmetic to logic. Gödel's contention is that 'for any formal system adequate for the expression of number theory or arithmetic, assertions can be found that are not decidable within the formal system'. Here Gödel assigns numbers to statements in the formal system to 'construct the proof on the creation of formal procedures for the computing of Gödel numbers for specific propositions from the Gödel numbers of the axioms' (Mirowski 2002: 79).

What Mirowski wants to give us is a computational, a machinic, economics. What he does give us – with von Neumann – is something much larger than this. It is a whole sociology, an entire technological sociology, a machinic sociology. He wants this to be completely machinic. I want it to be properly cyborg, fusion of human and machine. He wants forms of life to be fully computational. I want – with Maturana and Varela – a forms-of-life phenomenology that is at the same time machinic. This is not first and foremost about performativity, but about the forms of life that make performativity possible. Wiener gives us performativity; Shannon and von Neumann forms of life: the algorithmic as forms of life. At the heart of this is von Neumann's theory of automata. And we need to remember they are not negentropic, but entropic. More Freud's death drive than his sex drive (or ego). So, what are these automata? Von Neumann here developed a logical theory of automata as 'abstract information processing entities, exhibiting self-regulation in interaction with their environment' (Mirowski 2002: 536). There von Neumann and Mirowski ask: (1) What are the prerequisites for self-regulation of such automata? For von Neumann, it is the architecture for sequential digital computers (note: contemporary computers have not a sequential, but a distributed, connectivist architecture). (2) What are the prerequisites for self-reconstruction of an abstract automaton of a given level of complexity (cellular automata, probabilistic automata)? (3) Does a universal automaton exist that can 'construct' any other given automaton like Turing's Universal Machine? (4) Are there regularities and formal methods of resistance to noise (i.e. entropic degradation) in the process of self-replication of automata, the evolutionary problems of automata producing another of greater complexity?

Mirowski rightly insists that economics needs 'not a mathematical theory of machines, but a machinic model of mathematics'. At stake here is not science but engineering. Science and mathematics make descriptive statements. Engineering works through algorithms, through performatives and their surrounding technological forms of life. Mirowski, through von Neumann, wants to extend this to all social relations, which can be seen as algorithms in the sense that institutions can be seen as computational. In this, institutions are information processors: data processors. In this, markets are evolving computational entities. They are 'linear bounded memory automata', because it is memory that processes information. Memory processes information through algorithms. Forms of life themselves are a question of memory. For Michael Polanyi and his ideas of tacit knowledge, we know more than we can say.

Pivotal for Mirowski and von Neumann are market automata, and particular algorithms for particular markets. The question then becomes for them and for Turing, under what conditions the algorithm halts, and the corresponding question about the possibility of the infinite tape. That is, to determine whether a computer program (i.e. an algorithm) will finish running or will run forever. What is halting? A very simple example in pseudocode is the program: 'print: hello world'. After the output, the program halts. But what about a general, the most general, algorithm that would never finish running, and would run forever? Turing has an answer for this. It is that 'a general algorithm to solve the halting problem for all possible program-input pairs cannot exist'. It is that the halting problem is in fact undecidable (Mirowski 2002: 545). This is, for Mirowski and for von Neumann and Shannon/Turing, not a Cowles, Bourbakiist mathematics but a 'constructionist mathematics'. There seem to be assumptions of finitude in Turing and von Neumann's critique of set theory as opposed to the infinity of Russell, Frege, Cantor, Hilbert and Bourbaki.

6.3 Conclusions

This chapter starts from political forms of life, in Aristotle and Carl Schmitt, and then moves on to the more embracing notion of forms of life in Wittgenstein, based in language: in performatives, but more fundamentally in the games which are the forms of life that make performatives possible. This entails a break with positivist modes of distanced and objective experience to lived experience, in which experience is immediate and infused by life and life energy. Performatives are in this context moves in a language game: thus, a form of life is largely a question of such moves. Then we move to machine experience, machine-mediated experience and nonhuman experience more generally. Moves in forms of life are in terms of rules, often implicit, that human beings do not need another rule to use. Forms of life also are memory, collective memory which, via these rules – which are often only customs and not formulable – generates such moves. Forms of life are largely a question of meaning. Technological forms of life, in contrast, are a fusion of matter and meaning. Memory is now in great part machinic. Memory is mediated by algorithmic rules, which are on the one side linguistic and on the other mathematical. Moves have become in major part machinic. This is all very much a question of, it seems, a new episteme, a more or less mathematical episteme that emerges with Cantor's set-theoretical mathematics and Hilbert's axiomatizations, but then becomes incomplete and indeterminate in Gödel and Heisenberg. This mathematical episteme turns into a technics, as cybernetics and computing transmute these constative utterances of science into the performative moves of engineering. And cybernetics is about engineering. What are the implications for experience? For Whitehead, all matter, from electrons up, are beings of experience. For Bergson, all matter has memory. For Benjamin, not just humans but things communicate. Though animals and plants may carry out all of these activities, encounter their world through meaning and are even possessed with perception and imaginaries, it is only human beings in the main that are symbolizing beings. That is, human beings and their intelligent machines, whose pervasion makes symbolization and domination and control increasingly mathematical. Yet, the very entropic and probabilistic dissipation of these systems makes technological renewal, indeed, in Arendt's sense, natality, possible.

More broadly speaking, we have identified two modes of technological forms of life. One is based on a military model and is vertical and about control. Cybernetics in Chinese is *kongzhilun* (控制论), in which *kong* is control, *zhi* is system and *lun* doctrine; that is, the doctrine of control systems. The origins of technological forms of life are also in cybernetics. These control systems have to deal with inputs from their environment and then issue outputs. It is in between input and output that algorithms play their role. Hayles (1999) and others make a distinction between first-order and second-order cybernetics. As we discussed above, first-order cybernetics on a military model focuses on the C3I of control, command, communication and intelligence. Second-order cybernetics works much more in a logic of coupling and reproduction, in which open systems couple with one another in the exchange of information. Whereas, for example, Wiener and Shannon worked from the military model of vertical, closed systems, a number of feminist theorists including Hayles (1999), Barad (2007) and Haraway (2016) have, with Humberto Maturana, focused on such structurally coupling systems. Techno-social forms of life can work either way. And here we remember that nature, too, in, for example, Latour (2014) and Haraway is very much conceived as genetic along with other information systems. Techno-social forms of life can, with Latour and Carl Schmitt, work on the vertical and military model of what Latour calls the Anthropocene. Or it can work on Haraway's paradigm of horizontal and structural coupling systems. Technological forms of life can go either way.

In the next chapter, we shall keep our eyes on 'technological experience', but shift registers somewhat not to how we experience objects but to how objects or things themselves might experience. We do so through the prism of Chinese thought and Chinese art, drawing especially on the thought of François Jullien. But first we need to ask the question, how is experience different in the context of Chinese thought? How is experience different in largely the absence of the Kantian epistemological or aesthetic subjects? That is, when there is really not a lot like Western experience. How do we experience not just in the absence of Augustine and Kant, but without even the a posteriori of the polis? Chinese thought has never obsessed with the *qu'est-ce que c'est*, the 'what is it that it is', of Western thought. It has never primarily asked the question of either epistemology or ontology. It has focused not on epistemology's predications of the appearance of the thing, not on ontology's thing-in-itself. There are borrowed words in Chinese for, say, substance, *shiti* (实体). But there is no notion of substance per se as in Aristotle as formed matter, or mattered form is *xingshi* (形式), another borrowed word. So, no classical experience – because neither substance nor polis, no modern subjective or objective experience. China never had a polis because there was never the partial break with lineage in the ancient Chinese city (Li 2014; Weber 1966).

In Aristotle, there is not a huge break between epistemology and ontology, between substance, on the one hand, and the predicates that defined and classified things. You needed epistemology to have ontology. Ontology is about the being, the substance, the nature of the thing beyond its predications. But to have ontology you needed to have a relation of awe and wonder as to what indeed was a thing. This break comes in modernity with Kant's distinction of the for- and in-itself. And, indeed, thus objective and subjective experience. Even

158

for ontology you need to have predications, propositional formal language and precise definitions. These are all the language not of forms of life but of the early Wittgenstein of the *Tractatus*, which is a *tractatus logico-philosophicus* with its foregrounding of logic in what can be said. As a *tractatus* or treatise, it is a systematic elaboration of principles. It stands in contrast to treatises that came before it, the *Tractatus Astrologico Magicus* and Spinoza's *Tractatus Theologico-Politicus*. *Philosophical Investigations* breaks with saying altogether for instead showing or pointing. In *Philosophical Investigations*, which is anything other than a treatise, there are no principles, there is no system. There are vague and confused usages rather than definitions. It breaks with logic as does speech-act theory more generally. The closest to forms of life and language games we get in Aristotle is rhetoric, which itself is more or less analytic and predicational, the most predicational of which is deliberative rhetoric, and the least predicational of which is ceremonial, which begins to approach the rites and music of the Confucian Classic.

Technological forms of life, we observed, were on the one hand language games (the opposite of formal language and the least rule-bound of any language use) and, on the other, mathematics, or, more accurately, applied and engineering-driven mathematics. Mathematics is not technological: engineering is. This technologization of mathematics makes logic and mathematics itself performative. The more formal language is, the more closely it approximates mathematics. Mathematical predications are the most formal, the most clear and distinct of all predications. No linguistic predications are as clear and distinct as they are. Thus, Cantor and Hilbert map closely onto Frege and Russell. Gödel blurs things a little bit.

The least mathematical of all language, however, is Chinese. It is the language game of language games. It points, it mimes, it is so like a language game. It imitates. It is much more like a children's game than a game structured by formal rules, like chess. The more child-like, the more game-like. It is prior to the differentiation of script, poem, painting and song. Hence the focus on children's games in Walter Benjamin's essay on China's mimetic faculty. How is predication possible – even in the mathematical sense in which the predicates are the elements of a set – when the unit of meaning, as it is in pre-modern Chinese, is not the sentence but the word? In a language where in many instances there are no verbs, in which the same word is adjective, noun and adverb, male or female. Singular or plural is not clear or distinct. In which definitions are a very recent thing. Let us approach this from closer up.

— 7 —

AESTHETIC MULTIPLICITY: THE VIEW AND THE TEN THOUSAND THINGS

7.1 Fuzzy Singularities

7.1.1 Views

Orhan Pamuk's *My Name Is Red* is about murder and art. It is about a struggle between Middle Eastern and Islamic art from Istanbul and more widely the Ottoman, Persian and Mughal empires with Western art as encountered in Venice of the early seventeenth century. The protagonists are miniaturists who design and draw figures of men and women, horses and dogs for the shahs, sheikhs, sultans and khans of whoever was triumphant in the land stretching from Istanbul to today's Kyrgyzstan via Iran and Afghanistan. Some were Western-influenced, towards the individualism of the signature and the portrayal of singularity among humans. Others were tied to Islam. The 'Islamists' and 'Western-ists' blinded and killed one another over this cultural clash. But how did they understand Western versus Islamic art? Well, they understood it in terms of 'the view'. What sort of view? In the case of Allah and Islamic art, the view was Allah's view, a view from above. In the case of Venetian and Western art, it was what the Islamists saw as a 'dog's-eye view', a human Renaissance perspective view; that is, a view from below. Pamuk, however, identifies a third kind of spatiality of art, and this was from much further east down the Silk Road, from China, which the Islamist miniaturists saw as 'trapped' in an art of 'the infinite'.

What could this mean? In China, there is neither Allah nor God, but above there instead is heaven or *tian* (天). And *tian*, unlike the

Middle Eastern above and Western below, is neither a person nor a personal god nor even a god at all, but instead a place. Then what can Pamuk possibly mean by infinity? Heaven in *tiandi* (天地) is above earth and spherical in contrast to the 'square' geometry of earth. But it is not necessarily seen as infinite. It is just big enough to overlap and thus enclose earth. Where can we, then, find infinity or something like the infinite in Chinese thought and art? Is infinite something like eternal, in German, *Unendlichkeit*? The infinite set is about number and thus more time than space. The Abrahamic and modern Western views from above and below are somehow spatial in a way that the Chinese infinite may not be. It is not a spatial category as are the views from above and below in Islam and the West. It is instead temporal. And there is something profoundly temporal in Chinese art, the slide into shade and light, from *yin* to *yang* that François Jullien describes in *The Great Image Has No Form: On the Non-Object*. We might say that Chinese thought and art is a process of the temporalization of space, while Western thought and art tend to – as Deleuze with Bergson has observed – spatialize time.

This refers also to the never-endingness of the Dao, of the flow, the flux that Confucius saw as a river, and in such we can begin to understand the Chinese notion of time as *shi* (时), and not of container time. This is time not as a medium as in Kant in which objects appear, but more a medium of disappearance, in which no-things appear, in which, much like the Buddha or the Bodhisattva, there is a 'thusness' or a 'suchness' in which time is a coming and a going. This is not even a past, present and future like in phenomenology, but a coming and a going and as such a void. There is something of an art and architecture of the void that is temporal.

The view is also necessarily a question of experience: of also aesthetic experience. But who or even what is doing the experiencing? In the Islamic case, it is Allah. Who is doing the experiencing in the Western case? It is 'the eye', the human eye. Now the eye is not the subject, and what is going on is not a question of subject–object experience. And the origins of modern experience, of the modern in thought and culture, are also, in the Renaissance, aesthetic. You have the view which itself is already material. But you have also the aesthetic material, which itself is lifted out from its background, already in Rome, as Alois Riegl noted. This first and foremost definitely is a question not of the 'I' but of the eye.

If we segue to China what have we? In the West, the 'eye', the humanist eye, is creating art and producing space. In China, it is not the eye nor God, but *tian* which is already a space/place. Chinese space was not of, course, the empty Westernized container space or *kongjian* but *tiandi* and *yuzhou* (宇宙), and overhanging of earth, of place that is the *di* of *tiandi* by *tian*, by the roof over the eaves. Yet perhaps the answer regarding who is doing the experiencing in Chinese space/art may be that no one at all is doing the experiencing. Wang Hui, referring to the New Culture Movement – from the positivist Hu Shih to the critical thinkers Liang Shuming and Zhang Taiyan – has written extensively of the juxtaposition of the universal principle (*gongli*) and the heavenly principle (*tianli*). For Wang, *tianli* is associated with empire and *gongli* with nation-state (Wang 2014). *Tianli* works on a principle of the past and *gongli* on the future. Hence in the Axial Age, Confucius looked back to the harmony of *xia*, *shang*, *zhou*, while Judaism and the prophets (not the priests but Isaiah, Ezekiel, Jeremiah) looked forward to the future of redemption and paradise regained. What we have seen is that *tianli* and *gongli* are spatial. In the one the sphere is dominant over the square. In the other, in *gongli* and the West, the square dominates the sphere (*tianyuan difang*); in the West, the view is from below, instead of the views from the infinite (who is no one). But *tianli* and *gongli* are not just temporal but also spatial. And Western *gongli* or *dili* (地理) makes earth and nature the dominant thematic.

Gongli is becoming pervasive in China: the word *shi* of ancient Chinese was prior to *shijian* for time in modern Chinese. And *yuzhou* and *tiandi* come before *kongjian* for space. A *jian* is a room and its space, but also a between, an among, a border. *Kong* means air but also, with *xu*, *xukong* means void. *Kongjian* for space means empty space, whose units are separated by this border. Container space almost. *Shijian* is the moments of time separated by these betweens, these sections, these borders. How does this stack up with Newtonian time whose *shi* (时) are connected by causes, but is it *shi* or objects? And what about the *shi* of the sort of time of the radical empiricism of Hume, James and Deleuze, where moments are connected by the conjunctions, facts connected by and … and … and …?

But *gongli* has, may have, changed. *Gongli* was broadly based on Newtonian classical mechanics as a notion of nature: on mechanical Newtonian matter. With Einstein, matter becomes energy; we have now vital matter. And the point of view descends from the universal subject of Kant, Descartes and Newton to Einstein's situated subject, now less a universal than a singular and situated in the system itself. Mind is now in matter. This deconstruction of subject–object thinking in *gongli* itself is seen in Zhang Taiyan's Husserl and Liang Shuming's Bergson, which is already giving in part a basis for a Chinese critical theory, which deconstructs subject and object while juxtaposing *tianli* and *gongli*. *Tianli*'s spatiality is the heavenly sphere and heaven's mandate over the spatial hierarchy of the emperor and his bureaucrats. This hierarchical verticality is displaced by the thought of Zhang Taiyan and Liang Shuming, which is against bureaucratic hierarchy and the exams, and instead is a *wei shi*, consciousness-only Buddhism (Alitto 1986; Wang 2008).

In conscious-only Buddhism the temporality in the flow of the river is displaced onto consciousness. But it is a flow, a flow of not just time but also life. It is the flow of the eighth level of Yogacara, *wei shi*, Buddhism, in which the seventh level is a grasping possessive individualism, an analytic individualism, and the eighth level is a flow, not a foreground but a background of forms of life. This dominance of the background in Chinese art has always opposed the foreground in Western art – first with Renaissance perspective and then even when perspective is foreshortened. But we see the hegemony of background in the architectural thematic in contemporary Chinese art of Liu Wei. We see it in the nature videos of Yang Fudong. In the use of *hanzi* as a calligraphy background in Xu Bing and Gong Jian. It is a question of the background. Also, Wittgenstein's forms of life change the apodictic predications of his *Tractatus* into the performatives, the language games of *Philosophical Investigations*, in which the language games, the forms of life, are a background.

What about the object in art? In the West, we now have object ontology without an observer: an aesthetics of non-experience. Very much the opposite of Tuan Yifu, *Space and Place: The Perspective of Experience* (1977). But Einstein (Barad 2007) never said we do not experience. He said we experience from no longer outside, but now inside the assemblage, the *agencement*. In place of Western object ontology, we have Zhang Taiyan's Ten Thousand Things, the *wan wu*, the Daoist *wan wu* and Zhang Taiyan's and Zhuangzi's 'equalization of things'. But these things are not objects. They are a multiplicity of *wu*. They are also not exactly beings and none of them is *Dasein*. Objects by definition are actuals; they are not potentials, and the *wan wu* are potentials or are somehow between potentials and actuals. To get to the *wan wu*, we must break with object thinking. The *wan wu* for Zhang Taiyan, drawing on Zhuangzi's 'equalization of things', means also no concept, no word and no name. Each of the *wan wu* is different to every other. In this sense, they are singularities: that is, neither particulars nor universals. In the West, we reject the common name with Walter Benjamin to arrive at the proper name, which is a singularity. For Zhang Taiyan, we take away also the proper name.

Western singularities are clear and distinct from one another. The *wan wu* are unclear and indistinct. They often form a collective, a collective that comes before the singularity. They merge with one another in *renyi*; they feel for one another. So in the *wan wu*, in which the one is already a two in *ren* (仁), we have a very special regime of singularities: of fuzzy singularities. Gödel gave us fuzzy logic. Chinese critical theory, Zhang Taiyan, and possibly Chinese art, give us fuzzy singularities.

7.1.2 Art and Singularities

Aesthetic experience in general is about singularities. Cognitive experience is about universals and particulars. It is not about singularities. The mould for cognitive experience set by Kant's *Critique of Pure Reason* was very much based on the paradigm of Newtonian mechanics. This was a 'mechanical materialism'. Such a mechanical materialism stands in contrast to both dialectical materialism and today's 'new' vibrant or vital materialism. The contrast of cognitive and aesthetic experience partly recapitulates the methods debates that Weber was well aware of in regard to nomothetic and ideographic knowledge in the human sciences, especially in Germany. History and the ideographic sciences, also *Literaturwissenschaft,* were ideographic and studied singularities, while sociology was to follow the Kantian nomothetic paradigm; that is, positivism based on an epistemology drawn from Newtonian physics. In ideographic knowledge, there are singularities, characterized by their uniqueness; every one is different from every other. In nomothetic knowledge, particulars are subsumed by universals. As subsumed by universals these particulars are identical to one another. We see this in classical sociological studies using aggregate data. But also in Kant's Second Critique there is subsumption of particulars by a universal. Particular cases are meant to come under the aegis of the moral law, the categorical imperative. The First Critique is clearly about nature in the sense of natural science. But Kantian ethics as well can be seen as coming under such a natural paradigm (of universals and particulars). Again, nature is on the lines of Newtonian physics. But Kant's Third, aesthetic, Critique is different. Here the 'subject' that is doing the experiencing becomes itself singular, each different from every other. What is experienced is also singular, each different from every other.

The Third Critique became the basis for Romanticism and German idealism, in Fichte, Schelling, Hegel and Hölderlin. Fichte's famous 'ich' that then posits the world is not a universal 'ich' but a singular

'I'. Descartes' 'I' was a universal. Schelling deals with singularities in his juxtaposition of Second-Critique 'freedom' or *Endzweck* and Third-Critique finalities without end (*Zweckmäßigkeit*). Here the subject of cognitive experience is displaced by the singular subjectivity of aesthetic experience, at the same time as the object is displaced by the singularity of the work of art. In the *Phenomenology of Spirit*, Hegel (1977) starts not from the subject but instead from consciousness, which is itself Third-Critique singular subjectivity. In the Preface to the *Phenomenology*, Hegel at least implicitly breaks with the Romantic past that he shared with Schelling and with the Romantic comprehensive sensibility (as in Spinoza and Leibniz) of singularities. If Kant's First Critique subjects encountered objects, now consciousness encountered not objects but appearances (*Erscheinungen*). This move from subject–object positivism to consciousness–appearance thinking was in an important way the founding of phenomenology. So far Hegel's idealism did not disagree with Schelling's and was thus not yet dialectical. The dialectic would embrace also Kantian–Newtonian mechanism, but only as derivative from the singularity of finite spirit or mind as consciousness. Hegel's dialectic, revisited endlessly in the *Phenomenology*, is a move from the singular–singular relation of consciousness–appearance to the universal–particular relation of subject–object.

This is the motor of the dialectic. This ends up with very much the triumph of the universal in the 'march of reason'. And this is why Kierkegaard had such disdain for Hegel. For Kierkegaard, God was singular and so was Abraham. God may have been ruthless, even more than cruel in commanding the death of Abraham's progeny. But this was not the cruelty or the subsumption of the particular by the universal. God indeed *chose* Abraham: chose and enabled him to become a father in his nineties. Hegel and Kierkegaard's contemporaneous Lutheran Church religion was based on universal norms. In contrast, 'faith' for Kierkegaard and St Paul – as we can see in the commentaries by Taubes and Agamben – is a question of such singularities. This is the distinction of faith, on the one hand, and law, on the other. If the New Testament Matthew, Mark and Luke are a question of law, then John and Paul's epistles are about faith. Law is about universal and particular. Thus, salvation – as in Max Weber's *Protestant Ethic* – can be normatively regulated, more a question of law as the contrary of Kierkegaard's religious experience as faith. In Weber's *Protestant Ethic*, there is a quasi-utilitarian calculation of salvation, whereas in Kierkegaard the focus is much less on the salvation than on the fear and trembling, the dread that accompanies our having been cut loose from our certainties, including the certainties of universal–particular subsumption. In this context, at stake in Chinese art are indeed singularities. But singularities in a context in which *renyi* (仁义), or righteousness, as the character indicates, is already communication between the two. It is not righteousness in the Western or Christian sense of the individual. Chinese singularities are in their process of individuation and de-individuation. They are in this sense also as mountains become mist, and as communicating with one another as not fully distinct from one another, they are *fuzzy* singularities.

7.2 The Gaze as Multiplicity

Let us track back to Pamuk's enigmatic statement and ask, if Western art is the view from below, from man's eye, from Alberti's vanishing point and its critique, then what does it mean to be trapped in an infinity? What can it mean? It depends what is meant by infinity. If infinity is a question of numbers, like the sets of natural numbers or square numbers, or square roots in Galileo, or in Cantor, then this could not relate to any Chinese notion of aesthetic experience. William of Ockham spoke of infinity in terms of continua, yet of continua with parts. Any infinity of the Dao, or a Chinese infinity, cannot be an infinity of numbers, or of parts. But an infinity of the boundless, because the Dao is certainly boundless, is a rather different matter. Infinity would here be more Anaximander's boundless as the origins of everything. Trapped in this infinity that is the Middle Kingdom, to have bounds or boundaries is in some sense to have form. Not just in landscapes but in language, especially in ancient Chinese, the mountain is never with the definite article, or even indefinite article, never a mountain or the mountain, it is just *shan* or mountain. It is only mountain. Ancient Chinese did not distinguish between nouns and adjectives; it had no definite or indefinite articles. It is incredibly uninflected. Modern Chinese is far more synthetic than the fully analytic ancient language. Almost all words are two characters, two morphemes. Ancient Chinese words are one character. Chinese, and especially ancient Chinese, is an analytic and not synthetic language. A very low rate of morphemes per word. The more morphemes per word, the greater synthesis through which a language can attain precision. In this sense for Marx, German was the ultimate language for philosophizing. Chinese, in its very imprecision, is more poetic.

166

7.2.1 Beauty: China against Metaphysics

What is aesthetic experience in China? To what extent is the notion of experience itself altogether Western? Aesthetics in Mandarin is *meixue* (美学), literally the study of beauty. And art schools are *meishu xueyuan*, where *shu* is skill or technique. Technology is *jishu* and an artist is also a *yishujia* (艺术家), where *yi* is also skill. Aesthetics in the West, which develops with modernity and Baumgarten, Hutcheson and others, is very much the study of beauty. But the word beauty, as François Jullien (2016) notes, almost never appears in the writings of the great Chinese painters until the mid-eighteenth century, when Western influence arrives. Beauty, as Jullien argues, is metaphysical. It is where experience does not happen. Chinese art is much more experiential, though it does not feature the experience of the viewer. Jullien's argument is stronger than this. It is that Western metaphysics needed beauty and the beautiful in order to exist at all. Western metaphysics needed to (1) isolate the valorization of the perceived object. In Homer, he notes, we look at a beautiful body, there is a functionality, it is an adjective. Only with the metaphysics in Plato does it become substantialized (as a substantive and noun in 'the beautiful'). To substantialize it is to essentialize it, as what is apart from all objects becomes now a 'pure and detached pleasure'. All this was also made possible by the Greek language. Chinese does not distinguish between substantive and adjective. An adjective is a *xingrongci* (形容词): a form-containing word.

Beauty is metaphysical: beauty itself is not experienced. Beautiful things are experienced, often on something along the lines of the erotic: this is so for both Plato and Plotinus. In the *Hippias Major*, Socrates triumphs in dialectic over his Sophist counterpart Hippias. This is an early work of Plato in his early thirties, which is about the nature of beauty. This comes from Hippias's lecturing tour in Sparta, in which instead of lecturing on mathematics, the Spartans wanted to hear about beautiful pursuits in the foundations of cities in ancient times. In response, Socrates suggests they inquire into the nature of beauty. Hippias starts by *pointing* to beautiful things. He starts with a beautiful girl, with gold epitomizing beauty. But Socrates is not interested in pointing. He is interested in what makes beautiful things beautiful. Socrates runs through his own itinerary, moving away from pointing and into definitional language, giving a definition in which the beautiful is, too, mixed with the good to be suitable, before finally settling on the not fully satisfactory 'what gives pleasure to the eyes and ears'. Let us note in this context that Chinese art (Chinese language) does not define as much as point. The move from Wittgenstein I to Wittgenstein II is very much from a language of proposition and definition to a pointing language. An art of form is like a definitional language. To define is to analyse; it is to set boundaries. It is, says Jullien, a question of form. And in the *Dao De Jing*, it is stated in the title of another of Jullien's (2009) books, 'the great image has no form'. The great square has no corners. It is literally *informe*, formless. It takes form, it undergoes formation as vapours and indeed ink stroke concretized into mountains. But then it deforms; it 'decants' back really into 'spirit'. Chinese landscapes are always in a process of formation and deformation. Of dissolution and decanting, of becoming matter and becoming spirit. But there is never the separation of spirit and matter, of beauty as spirit as fully separated from matter.

When Marx said that German was the best language to philosophize in – as opposed to English and French – he was saying it was highly or at last optimally inflected, with genitives and datives, applying also to nouns and adjectives. English is a very uninflected language. Russian, for example, has six cases including locative. English historically became progressively more and more uninflected, starting from the very inflected Proto-Indo European spoken millennia ago on East European steppes. We did away with all of our cases. But Chinese did not start out as a phonetic language, but iconographic. English makes up for the absence of definition with indefinite and definite articles, with singulars and plurals, none of which Chinese has. English has clitics, not Chinese.[1] Chinese comes closer with modern Chinese to precise meanings, by the doubling of characters in words. Simplified Chinese has fewer than 3,000 characters but considerably more words. In a sense, the more synthetic (normally inflected) a language is, the more definitional it is. *Wissenschaft* is, for example, more synthetic and precise and definitional than is 'science'. Words made up of many morphemes are more definitional than only single-morpheme words, which work much more through pointing. English Latinate words are thus more synthetic and definitional than our Germanic words. Chinese makes sense through the use of many many words, through idioms, through context. Chinese is a pointing language; it is as close as you get to pure Wittgenstein II. It is about backgrounds, about forms of life. It works more than elsewhere through Michael Polanyi's tacit knowledge. It makes sense that Chinese art can work through background.

---

[1] I am inspired in this context by conversations with Li Shiqiao.

This is what Socrates was getting at. As he was criticizing Hippias in dialectic (not rhetoric), he was moving from pointing to the definitional. He was disembedding beauty from the maiden and the gold. As beauty became definitional, it became metaphysical, it became form. Chinese landscapes are the highest form of Chinese art (a genre that is wide-angle and thus largely about background); in the West it is a rather lowly form, historically, compared to portrait and historical painting. But landscape is not meant to depict – much like Western landscape made its apogee with the Romantics and especially Turner, as the non-definitional. Landscape is then much less definitional. Indeed, the romantics celebrated the indefinability of beauty. It became *informe*. Landscapes come not from the professionals but from the literati who were from Mi Fu to Shitao, from Tang through Ming, painters, poets and calligraphers all three, for whom painting was one of three (four if you count music, and they played music) types of intellectual expression. They paint out of their imaginations.

For Jullien, the beautiful is at the basis of *all* Western metaphysics. Just as Socrates versus Hippias moves from designation to definition, now, as Jullien observes, 'thought will cease to travel from one occurrence to another … [but] from now on, it will construct itself in its own terms, above all by definition' (Jullien 2016: 173). We are on the way to Kant's impeccable definition in terms of disinterested pleasure, of any kind, of any of the senses, yet always involving (see Chapter 5) the *sensus communis*. The *sensus communis* had an implicit reference to Hutcheson's moral sense. Only while Hutcheson's moral sense – like Smith's moral sentiments – was empirical, Kant's *sensus communis* was transcendental. Yet there is still delight, there is still pleasure/displeasure, there is still desire in Kant's Third Critique. For the Greeks, this too was true. There is always eros in beauty as we see so explicitly in the *Phaedrus*, yet the point is not in the modality of the beloved, but to the extent that the beloved incorporates the form, the idea of beauty. Even in Aristotle's *Metaphysics*, there is an in-itself and for-itself of the beautiful, a quiddity of the beautiful although inseparable from sensible experience. Jullien (2016: 16) further invokes Augustine's *De Pulchro* in terms of 'what is acknowledged by itself', by the 'conformity of an object with what it should be, what it is acknowledged to be'. Again, a certain quiddity, a quiddity of form.

But what about in China without a notion of the beautiful? This is for Confucians (Jullien 2016: 23) 'simply a question of ritual performance or musical emotion', each of which balances the other: not about form but about 'spiritual rambling', 'freed from correctness and favourable to the release of authentic talent', like in Song dynasty landscape artists. Jullien notes that none of the 64 hexagrams of the *I Ching* explicitly deals with beauty, only hexagram 22 with 'adornment embellishment', connected with vegetation, a budding, a spring blossoming. This embellishment also points to the absence of distinction between decoration and art in Chinese 'aesthetics', of the absence of distinction between background and foreground. In many ways landscapes themselves are backgrounds, but in the Chinese painters from Tang to Qing, they are just as much foregrounds. Language as foreground is also definitional; as background it is context, it is language games, forms of life. To speak of beauty is to move to the idea and also to the concept. It is to move away from perception. And Chinese reason stays closer to experience, stays closer to perception; for Jullien (2016: 33), Chinese reason does not so much conceptualize as 'schematize'. Embellishment's somehow strong connection to what is embellished is also such a schematization. Reason as distinct from perception embraces concepts and the pure ideas of reason, of the true, good, beautiful and just, but also the understanding and concepts – for Kant quantity, quality, mode and relation; for Aristotle, the qualifying categories – are metaphysical and they are quoted from experience into the realm of reason. Kant tried to connect reason and perception – the sensible and supersensible – with the schemata. Yet the schemata (of the imagination) are closer to perception and the material (sensible) than they are to the supersensible. In Chinese, *xing* (形) is form. In modern Chinese it is often *xingshi* (形式). *Xing* here is closest to form in Western metaphysics, *shi* is more like pattern and shape. *Xingshi* in this sense connects form and schema, the metaphysical and physical. The question for Western thought and Western notions of beauty is, how do we connect form and schema?

There is something geometrical about Plato on beauty, Jullien notices. Mathematics is abstract in the sense that the sciences are not. Physics, biology and chemistry are about nature. There is something Pythagorean and mathematical about Plato's notion of the Good. For Pythagoras, all things are numbers and the cosmos is based on numerical principles, thus there is a physical world of becoming and a mathematical world of being. Chinese thinking through schematism, Chinese ideographic language working through schematisms, for Jullien (2016: 35), keep us 'close to the dynamism', that 'never ceases animating the world'. Shitao: you walk up the hill and you see concrete plurality, you get to the top and there is a moment of unitary abstraction. There are 'generated couplings', harmony under tension. The idea that is also the space of the Neoplatonist Plotinus'

170

(204–70 AD) asceticism. Plotinus follows Anaxagoras on *nous*, on mind. Mind presumes a breaking with all particulars. It is unconditioned. It is excluded from every condition. This connects to a sort of negative theology in which God is neither god nor vengeful nor wise, but is excluded from any qualification in the sense that even a qualification would be a condition (Jullien 2016). In this sense, God as kind or, say, vengeful is already conditioned. In negative theology, God is without quality, without condition. This pure principle of anti-experience tells us about the pure idea of beauty, fully excluding any dividing up or coupling that is the hallmark of Chinese art and Chinese thought. In the *Symposium*, beauty is eternal, unproduced, not in relation to anything, 'determination is neutralized'.

But what about the Dao? Chinese landscapes are not so much beautiful as spiritual, as animated by spirit, as we see in the writings of landscape masters such as Guo Xi and Shitao. They are driven by energy (*qi*, 气), as regulated or channelled into arteries as forming veins through deformation by *li* (理), which is reason. The Dao as the boundless, the *wu wei*, the void, energized by *qi* and regulated by *li* to generate the forms and *informes*, the mountains and vapours of landscape. *Qi* and *li* work in forming and deforming. Deforming is a decanting into spirit, and forming a condensation into the mountains. Indeed, *shan* and *shui* are also the vertical and the horizontal (*shui* – water, stream) about the solidity, the *yang*-likeness of mountains, and the movements, the fluidity, of the stream. Is the Dao in some sense an a priori? The Dao is empty; it may not be conditioned, but it is not a condition for anything else. *Qi* and *li* co-construct, as it were, individuations and thus solidity out of the emptiness of the Dao. The Dao as an emptiness is not being and the mountains in landscapes are not physical beings.

An unconditional beauty does not relate to anything. It is self-referential. For Jullien, the transcendence of the Idea itself is conceived in the model of Beauty in the *Phaedrus*, starting from the eros of the lover to the beloved. The point here is that beauty is the only idea (not the just, the good, the true) that has a 'luminosity'. Alone of the Ideas, beauty is incarnated in the sensible world. We can infer to the theology of incarnation. Beauty is the 'bolt' holding together philosophical dualism. In this context Jullien invokes the Neoplatonist, Plotinus, who was Greek-speaking, not a Christian but an inspiration to Christianity. Plotinus had a distrust of materiality with an idea of the One that is at the same time the Good and Beautiful, a distrust that saw no Being in the materiality of phenomena. For Plato and Plotinus beauty is thus a question of not life but 'existence'. Chinese landscape in contrast is about life, but also life not as the pure material, but instead a coupling and intercommunication of spirit and the sensible.

Plotinus' 'aesthetic' is purified in Kant's doctrine of disinterest. Yet Kant was faced with the same problem of a beautiful that also linked the sensible to the supersensible (*übersinnlich*). Kant needs to connect First Critique nature with Second Critique freedom. He is faced with a different problem than the Greeks (Plato, Plotinus), who before the Augustinian watershed of the free will were working with a metaphysics based not in a morality of the free will, but in an episteme of a pure axiomatic of geometry. So Kant, a modern (working in the register not of analytic but of synthetic judgments), is faced with a radically different problem. And he has a vastly different solution. The Greek supersensible was the clear and distinct axiomatic of geometry. Kant's supersensible is freedom and the free will. Both are acknowledged metaphysics, but very different kinds of metaphysics: one is pure form and the second of the subject.

Kant's solution – a basis, if not *the* basis, of modern aesthetic experience – is through conceiving art – and aesthetic experience – in regard to nature as freedom, or conversely freedom as nature. In the First Critique, we have nature as instrumentality, as a means to an end, hence necessity. In the Second, we have pure freedom, which Jullien perceptively renders as 'freedom as a finality'. In the Third, we have, instead, nature as a finality. Nature as free from being a means to an end. We have the *sinnlich* as freedom: nature as its own end. Thus, for Schiller, by beauty man is led to form and thought. Kant reconstructs the Greek mediation by the beautiful of the sensible and supersensible through the theory of the faculties (Jullien 2016: 54–5). This is important in a book like ours that is inquiring into experience as a foundation for the human sciences. The Greeks did not have human sciences. They did not have the problem of synthetic a priori judgments as synthesizing with the matter, the social nature.

Kant's main break with metaphysics in *The Critique of Pure Reason* is in the move from analytic to synthetic judgments. Kant's solution in *Critique of Judgment* is that you should not encounter nature objectively in terms of synthetic judgments, but you should engage nature subjectively in judgments of the beautiful. In this the beautiful is in the feeling of pleasure from such disinterested subjective judgments. But for it to be disinterested – unlike Hutcheson's agreeable – you need a *sensus communis*, for Kant not an empirical but a transcendental *sensus communis*. If the First Critique is foundational for the (positivist) social sciences, then the Third Critique is the foundational

172

text for not the social but the human sciences, *Geisteswissenschaften*. It is through the faculties that the free will is presupposed. But the other critiques did not focus on the faculties as much as did the third. The other two critiques are not critiques of a faculty. They are not in the same way mainly about a faculty – *Urteilskraft*, the faculty of judgment. They are instead critiques of reason. The first concerns pure reason. It says knowledge is not a question of pure reason or metaphysics, but presumes synthesis with nature, in other words presumes experience. The second is about pure freedom. It is a critique of practical reason, which it locates in, for example, the moral sense theorists. For Kant, moral sense theory locates morality in the sensible or empirical. The sensible or empirical is the realm of necessity. Kant, very much on the paradigm of Augustine's free will, relocates morality transcendentally in the sphere of freedom. The Third Critique is a critique not of reason, but of judgment. Again, it is partly aimed at empiricist thinkers (we remember it is the empiricist Hume who awakened Kant from his metaphysical slumber). But empiricism is never enough. It is the basis of Kant's critique of metaphysics, but it loses the free will of the Augustinian revolution (Chapter 5 above), which is itself the basis of the subject in modern thought, most forcefully formulated in Descartes (Blumenberg 1985). So, the First Critique restores the metaphysics of the free will in the transcendental unity of apperception, which unites the categories; the Second Critique leaves experience behind in the pure freedom of the moral imperative, whose aim is not primarily morality but the free will itself, the a priori basis of the First Critique's unity of apperception and the possibility of knowledge.

The Third Critique also has major reference to Hutcheson and British empiricism. Hutcheson wrote on beauty, and Edmund Burke on the sublime and the beautiful. But for them judgment was a question of taste. Judgments were judgments of taste, and as such were, not transcendental but empirical. Bourdieu nails it in his book *Distinction*, which has as subtitle 'A Social Critique of the Judgment of Taste'. Taste here is empirical in early British aesthetics and Bourdieu's sociology. Kant's critique is to relocate judgment, aesthetic judgment, in the transcendental, in restoring to it the dimension of freedom. In this he means the freedom of both the judge and the judged. In this, both judge and judged are neither transcendental nor empirical, but transcendental–empirical couples: the judger as the *sensus communis* – which takes empirical sense in combination with the transcendental *communis* – and the judged is empirical in as much as it is nature, and transcendental in as much as it is its own end and thus free. The paradigm is thus not mechanical but instead organic nature. Without this restoration of a dimension of metaphysics, Kant would be a materialist, not an idealist. Idealism entails experience and synthetic judgments, unlike the analytic judgments of Descartes' rationalism. Rationalists deal, like Euclid, in a priori analytic judgments, while the more fully modern idealists – from Kant through Fichte to Shelling – give us experience, give us judgments that synthesize with matter, under of course the star of the transcendental.

Back to Jullien and Greece versus China. Beauty entails the centrality of substance. Substances have qualities, subjects (like Kant's subject) have faculties. For Jullien, the formations – and not forms – of Chinese landscapes also have, if not faculties, then capacities; they are operators in processes of individuation and disin-dividuation. They have not the qualities of beings but the capacities of becomings and, as it were, unbecomings. Here there is a massive individuation of landscapes (Jullien 2016: 56), as the 'actualization of energy which at times becomes denser, hardens, is made opaque, and at times dilutes, diffuses, becomes evasive'.

What kind of experience, though, are we talking about in Jullien's Chinese landscapes? We have had three types of experience in this book. The first is Kant's straightforward *Erfahrung*. It is objective experience like in physics with the observer. It presumes a subject. Indeed, it is constitutive of the subject as the transcendental unity of apperception. In this sense, experience is quintessentially modern. It works through a priori synthetic judgments of this objective subject. This kind of experience then generalizes through the social sciences as positivism. It works through especially economics, again through a priori synthetic judgments, the a priori here being *homo economicus* of neoclassical economics' utilitarian assumptions. This same subject characterized most of neoliberalism. It is an in-your-face dominant ideology today. So dominant that it is not even noticed: on markets that are so ubiquitous that they are not even seen as institutions. That is the brilliance of Polanyi's insistence that markets are just one of many institutions. It is seen as the real world that we have to face. It is, but only as institutionally constituted. This is Polanyi's critique of positivism. All of Foucault's discourses, his discourses of the human sciences in the *Order of Things* and sciences from *Birth of the Clinic*, etc., are comprised of such a priori synthetic judgments. In this sense, Foucault is a sociologist of modernity. Foucault's modern episteme is that of a priori synthetic judgments.

Our second kind of experience is the truly radical empiricism of Hume. This is the fullest rejection of metaphysics. Hume, and Deleuze's

Hume, takes cause away. Hume's understanding is fully empirical and a posteriori. In this sense, it is largely an extension of the imagination. This is a radical empiricism of sensation and sense data, or sense data that are recorded as facts. They are the facts of perception. They, unlike Durkheim's positivist social facts, are facts without a symbolic.

The third kind of experience comes in this book through William James. For James, experience comes prior to the division into subject and object. Many have argued that this itself reinstates experience as a metaphysical, as an a priori. Dilthey thus understood James's experience as *Erlebnis*, lived and subjective experience. Dilthey also saw this in Husserl's phenomenology. *Erlebnis* is phenomenological experience. This is traceable via Romanticism and Hegel's *Phenomenology* to Kant's Third Critique. It is a basis of interpretive sociology, where in place of James's psychology and Husserl's ego, there are instead – in Wittgenstein's sense – social forms of life.

But what can these three Western types of modern experience say to Jullien's classical and Chinese aesthetics? First, we need to ask, how can experience be thought in Greek antiquity? The answer is nothing that we moderns could easily recognize. Plato's rejection of experience is largely based in his acceptance of the a priori analytic judgments of Pythagorean number and geometry. All three modern notions of experience presume the free will of Augustine's subject. In antiquity, man is a substance like any other substance. Man, too, is subject to efficient, material, final and formal causes. Man, more than other substances, is driven by teleological, hence final, cause. This, however, is not the free will. In Greece, as Arendt notes, freedom is a question of the 'can', in the sense that citizens have more of this 'can' than do women and slaves in the *oikos*. In modernity it is defined, in contrast, by the 'will', with a basis in original sin. In antiquity, man, like nature, follows the cyclical time of the seasons. In modernity, he follows the rectilinear time of redemption, salvation and end times. Hence Carl Schmitt is not wrong to understand modern politics in terms of the *katechon* – the space of the indefinite delay of the end times. In this he does not differ from Blumenberg. The difference is that, for Schmitt, this is illegitimate and yields a political theology. For Blumenberg, modernity instead is legitimate. This rectilinear time is also, we recall, the time of Aristotle's chrematistics and hence the time of capital (Alliez 1991). But it is difficult to speak of experience in antiquity, with the predominance of substance. Jullien is conscious that substance entails the primacy of qualities, which are qualities of beings (and being). If ancient substance is determined by qualities, then the modern subject is in part specified by its faculties. For Jullien

175

and classic Chinese theory of painting, not the subjects, but more or less the objects – the mountains and mists and clouds of landscapes – are endowed with not qualities but faculties. The actuals (and being) of the qualities are displaced by the potentia and becoming of faculties in Chinese landscape art.

7.2.2 Mountains That Breathe (and Perceive)

What about China in which substance, subject and form are modern borrowed words? What kind of experience is possible with neither subject nor substance? Without even form, but instead continual formation and deformation. Where is the view from? With Alberti, we Europeans get the view. The Greeks are more concerned with form than with the view. *Qi* (matter-energy) and *li* (reason as order) are constitutive of landscape through the imagination of the literati. The literatus is very different from, say, Michelangelo and Leonardo. The literatus is not consumed with the clear and distinct of geometry. He does not speak the inflected language of many morphemes. He speaks and writes in less a propositional than a poetic language. His experience is not that of objectivity, nor is it of subjectivity. This is not Alberti's view from below, nor is it Islam's and Zoroaster's view from above. It is a view from the emptiness, the *wu wei* of the Dao that is at the same time a way, a stream. In Daoism we have the Dao, then the *yin* and *yang*, in the *Dao De Jing* and then the ten thousand things. We will just below return to the ten thousand things.

Guo Xi (1020–90), born in Wen county, Henan, was perhaps the most famous of all Northern Song landscape painters. His most famous painting is *Early Spring* (see Figure 1). The painting was on scrolls, either hand scrolls or hang scrolls. Guo Xi, like the other painters, had a calligrapher's brush strokes, not always colour or form or oils but brushes and ink wash. The question was always to get balance between *shan* and *shui*, between mountains and stream. *Early Spring* was commissioned by the emperor. All works were commissioned by some sort of patron. *Early Spring* was a monumental painting, aimed not just at the emperor but to be shown to a public. You see some tiny human specks towards the bottom; the paintings were never pure *shan* and *shui* but always were busy, had people in, to give some idea of the monumentality, indeed the sublimity of the mountain (Harrist 1998). The eye is meant to follow the paths up the slope of the mountain, but as you do the mist bites in and begins to dissolve the mountain. You are meant to follow the serpentine shape in the structure of the mountain, in a sort of 'dragon vein', through which the mountain takes on organismic shape; the mountain breathes. Here nature is not mechanism, but like the Third-Critique organism. There is energy in the veins, in the brush strokes that paint the veins: in the sort of transition from form to nothingness, from mountain to mist. Guo Xi wrote a famous essay on landscape painting that was recorded by his son Guo Si (Cahill 1980).

Figure 1: Guo Xi, *Early Spring*, c. late 11th century. National Palace Museum, Taipei.

Guo Xi was a court artist at a very calm and stable time in the eminently open and liberal Northern Song. He painted the Huang Shan, the Yellow Mountain from the southern tip of Anhui province. The idea was to replace roaming in the mountains for the busy court literati and to bring to the city forests and streams, mists and vapour, to dazzle your eyes and capture your heart. The importance here was of the wide-angle shot, the distance, for both Shandong (northeast) and Shanxi schools of landscape painting. Seasons had to do also with moods. Winter mountains had strong clouds, and depressed mood. But this was early spring and things were vaporizing, decanting again; the water coursing in *Early Spring* is in the 'arteries' of the mountain, the mist and the clouds, the mountain's breathing, as in the neo-Confucian and Daoist idea of the world as a great organism. There were poems on the themes of the paintings and the paintings were meant to express poetic content. You travelled to see Huang Shan. You stored the memories in your mind. And when you were back in Henan or Shandong, you sat and relaxed and painted naturally like the landscape itself. Guo Xi was a court painter, the imperial patron the Emperor Shenzong (1068–85), and destined for a public, architectural context. The painting was in three parts as we move upwards, masses of stone at the bottom, towards a temple on the top of the mountain.

Old Trees, Level Distance was a much less monumental hand scroll, again of brush and ink. This is not the form and colour of Western art and landscape (Jullien 2016), but the brush and ink of the East: not form but energy (*qi*) and spirit is at the heart of this. It animated the brush strokes, which in turn animated the landscape. *Old Trees, Level Distance* was ink and light colour on silk, the hand scroll meant to be unravelled on a table and read from right to left, in a narrative way. On the right, we see two fishing boats in the chilly autumn river with layers of graduated ink wash. This is very different from the 'daybreak' of the early spring. It is a bleaker landscape. The mountains in this are low-lying and again at a distance. We see the foliage, the brushwood on the river bank (Foong 2000). What is being depicted, and often is, is 'atmosphere', in this case an atmospheric depiction of early autumn. It is only the foliage that allows us to see the difference between land and water, mountains and mist. They blend into one another, the solid and the ephemeral, all this till we come to what is the 'foreground', the large old withered trees, which are forcefully presented and outlined in black ink. There is not just *shan* and *shui* but so much else going on in these landscapes. There are fisher boys on the right of the landscape. As we read

178

towards the far left past the trees, we see some old probably literati men and servant boys walking up the hill over the bridge crossing the river to a pavilion for probably a leisurely lunch with lute playing. The trees, the 'old trees', sway in front of the smaller and squatter mountains in a sort of 'level distance', as if in conversation with one another. Again, organic and communicative themes dominate, with a not at all mechanical nature as in most Western landscapes. Space, and thus point of view, are in a sense plural, in diagonals and not 'from a unified ground' (Foong 2000: 90). In *Early Spring*, too, there is tightly controlled ink gradation 'building the plasticity' of the rock formations (Foong 2000: 92). Also, the base of the rock disappears into the water; *shan* dissolves into *shui*. These are 'baseless mountains, weightless rock'. Again, line is used in transitions from 'layered ink wash into substantial rock'.

Let us fast-forward to the most articulate of theorists, the early Qing landscape artist Shitao (*c.*1642–1707) – Shitao, the resolutely individualist painter. Both Shitao and Guo Xi were perceived as highly original, but Shitao was a conscious and eccentric individualist whose paintings were as irreverent as his poetry (Hay 2001). Shitao was born in far south and central Guangxi province, as a héritier of the imperial Ming lineage. His family was massacred by the Qing Manchus, his uncle committing suicide in Guanxi's historic city, Guilin, when a traitorous general attacked his lineage. Shitao was smuggled away to a Buddhist monastery. He travelled incessantly, to Anhui, and settled later in Jiangsu, in Nanjing and then Yangzhou. He was, like all of the landscape painters, a literatus – painting, calligraphy, poetry, music. He had taken and passed the civil service exams. He was a Buddhist and later, as Buddhism became corrupt and in league with the Manchu Qing, he turned to Daoism and lived in Yangzhou. He never, like many Ming loyalist literati, accepted office under the Qing, yet was highly social with literati and monk friends. Again, we have the organism of the mountain; his *Qin Huai* seems to depict a mountain in the process of bowing. He was a great theorist, the author of *Treatise on the Philosophy of Painting* (*Hua yu lu*, 画语录). Coleman (1971) reads it fully in the context of the *Dao De Jing*, of the 'image of the image-less, the form of the formless'. He understands Shitao's method as the method of no-method, challenging Western thought of 'form as existence'. Influenced also by Zen and Japanese thought, Coleman sees formlessness as the Dao, as the infinite that itself expresses form. His Zen reading, and Shitao was at first Buddhist and then Daoist and a Confucian, was also Zen's refusal of forms, whether physical (schema) or mental form proper.

This is an 'austere sublimity' devoid of the sensuous, a 'deep reserve of subtle profundity'. Here the Dao – though nothing like a personal god or even the Geek geometrical form of forms – is the One, but the One as formless. The Dao as the One is the 'unity of multiplicity'. Thus, as in Chapter 39 of the *Dao De Jing*, 'obtaining the One, all things lived and grew' (Coleman 1971: 5).

Shitao focused on a method without method, on the oneness of brush strokes. A oneness that carried within it a multiplicity, a oneness of stroke (*yi-hua*, 一画) that 'embraces all strokes before differentiation'. From this oneness, the 'myriad of brush strokes and ink wash all differentiate'. Coleman insists that Shitao was talking about *strokes* and neither lines nor marks. *Hua* is noun and verb and adjective all together, a '*hua jia*' a painter, a *hua* is a painting, to *hua* is to paint, it is to 'brush stroke'. The one stroke (the *yi-hua*), the stroke as one, is, for Shitao, the standard of excellence, the 'measure of excellence in painting'. This is again nature as organismic, not mechanism, in which measure itself is organismic. Jacques Lacan was famously influenced by Shitao. Is this measure, this organic measure, a bit like Lacanian topology? Is Shitao the painter also the mediator, the measure? Above we discussed mediation and measure, in Barad's portrayal of Bohr's quantum mechanics: is this also a mediation between ourselves and the multiplicity of the material world? For Barad, as we discussed, the measure, the device, was a mediation between meaning and matter. For Shitao, the work is to proceed from the one to the multiplicity like 'water flowing naturally downward and flame burning upward', the painting an 'outpouring of spirit'. In Chapter 8 of the *Dao De Jing*, Coleman notes this same sort of move from oneness of the Dao to the ten thousand things, from the ten thousand things as a oneness. Thus for Shitao 'the oneness of strokes is the origin of all beings, the root of myriad forms (形)'. Painting is here a microcosm in the macrocosm of the universe, a measured microcosm that mediates between painter, proto-modern painter (?) and the universe in the landscape. Thus, the brushstrokes are formless as the One, though they yield the myriad of things (forms). The One or the formless expresses itself in the many, in the forms. Still 'the great image has no form', but it gives rise to the myriad of images (forms). Shitao wrote most of this in his *Treatise*, some of it in colophons, in inscriptions, that can also be emblems in his scrolls, his hanging or hand scrolls. In such a colophon we see that painting is 'liberated from methods'. There follow a number of Shitao's principles of painting. The first is the *meng yang*, where *meng* (蒙) is cover and *yang* (样) shape. Cover here is the one, the non-differentiated, but the One as concealed – the concealment is 'supreme simplicity of non-differentiation' prior to 'dispersion'. For Shitao, 'before putting ink wash on paper, you must contemplate upon the state of non-differentiation and focus on its concealment'. Thus, in Chapter 5 of his *Treatise*, the 'ink wash cannot be spiritual unless one has achieved a state of non-differentiated concealment'. Then, as you awake from non-differentiation, painting becomes a 'complete potentiality' (Coleman 1971: 15). The ink wash itself conceals here by its misty vagueness. This is the Dao itself; 'the blurred or amorphous atmosphere projects the "form of the formless"'. It is atmosphere, not '*qi*', but '*kongqi*', '*qifen*', '*fengqi*' (空气, 气氛, 风气). *Qi* with very little help from *li*, gives rise to *kongqi*. Another principle is *yin* (絪) and *yun* (蕴) (Chapter 7 of the *Treatise*), translated by Coleman as 'harmonious atmosphere'. This refers to the 'generative forces of heaven and earth', from the *I Ching*, 'When heaven and earth unify into a harmonious atmosphere, 10,000 things will be transformed and purified' (Coleman 1971: 10). This, for Shitao, is 'a union of brush strokes and ink washes'. From Chapter 7 of the *Treatise*:

> when brush strokes and ink wash are unified, it is called *yinyun*. You apply it to painting a mountain, the mountain is spiritualized. Apply it to painting a stream, the stream moves. Apply it to human figures, and they are free from mundane defilements. To transform oneness into this harmonious atmosphere, this is the highest achievement of art in the world.

In this the harmony of the heavens and earth is expressed in the mist. The *yinyun* is a mistiness of a spiritualization (Coleman 1971: 11). Thus, in Chapter 13 of Shitao's *Treatise*, the discussion of sublimity and commonplace in that 'the mountain is the sea, the sea is the mountain'.

Moreover, the juxtaposing of emptiness and solidity, the *xu* (虚)-*shi* (实), in Chapter 9 of the *Treatise*: 'the brush strokes are the proper measure between the *xu* (emptiness, need) and the *shi* (solidity, affirmation), when the brush strokes are full of life's rhythms' (Coleman 1971: 19). Thus, to draw trees and rocks with solid strokes, clouds and mists with vacant strokes, 'through that which is vacant the solid is moved and that which is solid becomes vacant, the entire picture will be full of the life rhythm'. And 'for those who can control movement of their brushwork to inwardly real (solid, 实) and outwardly transparent (empty, 虚)'. In sum, as Coleman, paraphrasing Shitao, notes, 'the potentialities of mountains and rivers reside in the painting; the evasive concealment of the painting lies in the ink; the vitality of the ink depends on catching the absolute moment'. So the principle of *sheng* (生) *huo* (活), of living spirit, comes from the *meng yang*. The *meng yang* (concealed shape) is the passive, dark, formative side of life. The *sheng huo* is dynamic and active.

Finally, the liberation from method, the *liaofa* (了法). This is freeing the real self from all obstacles (Coleman 1971: 21), including both method and lack of method, this itself being the perfect method. This is, notes Coleman, the space of the *wu wei*, of which Shitao's *wufa* (无法) is derivative, the *wu wei* itself being a sort of middle way between complete inactivity and artificial striving. All this circles back to the unity of multiplicity, and indeed the unity of opposites, in which every 'particular retains the potentialities of universality'. In the unity of opposites, man identifies with other beings. Here *meng*

Figure 2: Shitao, *Waterfall on Mount Lu*, *c.*1700.
Sen-Oku Hakkokan, Sumitomo Collection. Photograph courtesy of Vassar College Slide Library.

182

yang as concealed potential differentiation is the quiescence of the uncarved block, put later into action and life spirit (*shenghuo*).

So to finally once again come back to Orhan Pamuk and *My Name is Red*, Chinese experience is trapped in the infinity, in the boundlessness of the Dao. The view is coming from the boundlessness of the Dao, in which the culture is more or less 'trapped'. But the Dao also gives rise to the ten thousand things, which for Shitao are ten thousand forms. All of these forms are quite different from one another, though in their indistinction from one another, they communicate in Benjamin's sense of *mitteilen*, of sharing with, of a sharing with of this boundless infinity of the Way. The mountains themselves in their formation and deformation breathe; they are organic. The ten thousand things from the *Dao De Jing* are, as Shitao said, potentialities. Unlike qualities, potentialities and capacities are like faculties. And it is Kant's faculties that are doing the experiencing. So, experience, and the view, in China do come from the infinity of the Dao, from which there is no getting out. Is Islam trapped in the view from above? Is the West trapped in some variant of Alberti's view from below? Then the view from the infinity of the Dao is also the view from the capacities, the potentialities of the mountains that breathe. It is the view from the ten thousand things. In China, experience is perhaps less of the unified subject than of this multiplicity.

— 8 —

CONCLUSIONS

8.1 Technology

You might wonder why a book subtitled *New Foundations in the Human Sciences* should end with an excursus on eleventh- and seventeenth-century Chinese landscape, or even more so, begin with one on Aristotle. But Chapter 2 is on Aristotle's *Nicomachean Ethics*, not as in, say, Arendt or MacIntyre and communitarianism as ethics, but instead as technics. And Chapter 7 on art is also about the experience of matter, of mountains and the ten thousand things, which brings it together with the 'new materialism' of technological experience (Chapter 6), with its underlying theme of how forms of life have become, now, as much mathematical as linguistic. Thus, Chinese art – like post-Cantor mathematics – is also treated as an infinity, the infinity of the boundless Dao, as opposed to the focus on the person, whether the person is the God of Islamic art or the human person of Alberti's Western art and its critique. We recall that Foucault's critique of the episteme (the knowledge/power) complex of modernity's discourses ends also in a technics, a technics of the self. As such, it contests the epistemic self of cognitive reason and positivism that is still, and perhaps ever more, pervasive in the social sciences. I have argued that this epistemic self of cognitive reason and positivism is above all the driver of economics, whose utilitarian *homo economicus* is so pervasive, so dominant, perhaps less as ideology than as atmosphere, that we do not even notice it. Today, this formalism is paralleled by a bad substantivist national populism that could make Polanyi turn in his grave; that – if she were still alive – Hannah Arendt could with Angela Merkel worry about a future second coming. After some 65 years of '*Nie wieder*',

Arendt's spirit and Europe worries – and Arendt was a European – about '*wieder*'.

So this book has thematized technics and technological experience and has, if often obliquely, addressed these new foundations. And we must not underestimate the extent of how technologized our societies are. There was a phase of finance capitalism, in which the major banks, investment banks and hedge funds dominated economic life, from the 1990s, surely from Alan Greenspan's reign as Chair of the Federal Reserve. But since the 2008 crisis, though bankers are still exorbitantly paid, it is the tech companies that have carried the day: what the French call GAFA (Google, Apple, Facebook, Amazon) and what Anglo-American commentators call the FAANGtastic Five', adding Netflix into the mix. The bankers may have the income, but it is Jeff Bezos and Mark Zuckerberg that have the wealth. It is signal that in the first months of Trump, traditional stocks, expecting lower taxes and infrastructure investment, took off – they have since calmed – and the tech stocks, having little to do with Trump, and being opposed to his withdrawing the US from the 2015 Paris climate agreement, have continued to thrive and increase vastly in value: some 20 per cent in 2017. Look, in autumn 2017, at the biggest companies by market capitalization. Apple, Alphabet (Google), Microsoft and Amazon make up the top four, with Facebook eighth, while JPMorgan Chase and Wells Fargo are down at ninth and tenth. Silicon Valley triumphs over Wall Street. Or better, Silicon Valley in Wall Street. Look at the World's rich list. Bill Gates still at number one, Jeff Bezos weighs in at number four, Mark Zuckerberg at five and Larry Ellison (Oracle) at number seven, with only Michael Bloomberg from the financial sector at number 10. Maurizio Lazzarato has observed that both banks and technology work not through language, but through number, through valuations and algorithms. This is already implicit in Deleuze and Guattari's notion of control. For Lazzarato and the Antonio Negri and Mario Tronti idea of the social factory, this control moves out of just the manufacturing factory or the enclosure, to all areas of social life. Thus Lazzarato, in *Governing through Debt*, sees debt as pursuing indebted man, outside of all enclosures, wherever he goes. This is also the thesis of the 'multiplication of labour' (that is, not Durkheim's or Adam Smith's division of labour), again escaping the confines of enclosures for labour taking over all areas of social life (Mezzadra and Neilson 2013). This thesis has merit but forgets the extent to which the tech companies generate new enclosures – that is, platforms – from which others are, through intellectual property rights and also technologically, excluded.

These are the new tech monopolies. At least the old monopolies paid their taxes where they made their profits. The new ones are more evil (Fuller and Goffey 2012). The tech companies – e.g., Facebook – who deny they are media companies have taken over much of the media, in an age where most under-35s get their news from social media. The tech companies – Netflix and Amazon have moved into content creation, Apple into content distribution and more – think they are absolved of fourth-estate responsibilities, of especially fact checking, violent and racist and brutally sexist content, because they are primarily tech companies. They, along with nationalist populisms, challenge our rule of law. The tech companies have taken over retail, hotels (Airbnb), driving (Uber, Tesla). They operate not in a juridical order but in the space of Carl Schmitt's state of exception, leading to legitimation crises, in which, for example, Merkel in Germany and Macron in France support the rule of law and challenge the legitimacy of the neoliberal states of exception (Ong 2006). For Europe, legitimacy is very much a question of legality. For today's national populisms it is more a question of states of exception to the rule of law, whether for migration or offshore tax havens (Urry 2014). The tech firms have targeted finance with bitcoin and fintech, with Alibaba and Tencent in China, and Apple in the West. We live in a truly algorithmic capitalism (Rossiter 2016).

8.2 Institutions

In winter–spring 2017, I was teaching the course on PhD thesis development in a major Chinese university, and found myself teaching back-to-back Giddens's *New Rules of Sociological Method* and Max Weber's 'Objectivity in Social Sciences and Social Policy'. I couldn't help thinking how the title of this book, *Experience: New Foundations in the Human Sciences*, sounds so similar to *New Rules of Sociological Method* published 42 years before. Rereading *New Rules* four decades later, I expected it to be an interpretive sociological critique of positivism in Durkheim's original *Rules of Sociological Method*. I was surprised to see it was instead a critique of interpretive sociology. It was a non-positivist critique of interpretivism, one that brought in the importance of structure. The book also nodded towards a macrosociology and, implicitly, the importance of institutions. Probably 25 years later, I remember quarrelling with the late Ulrich Beck about the importance of institutions, which he argued for and I argued against as sites of domination. I was wrong. Institutions are not just modes of domination. In two very important ways, both of which relate to the modes of experience this book has tried to address.

Institutions are at the heart of the rule of law. These are formal institutions. They are what can protect us from – though they may not stand up to – nationalist populisms. Our Chapter 5 on Arendt, above, had as one of its focuses the importance of institutions. For Arendt, it was because of these formal institutions that the Romans, and not the Greeks, were the political people par excellence. This starts with (formal) Roman Law as a builder, but above all, a preserver of political and public worlds. This was the *Pax Romana* which established an institutional peace of formal rights. Now we see the *Pax Americana* threatened by the US president's refusal to explicitly endorse NATO's Article 5; his hostility to democratic and rule-of-law Europe, while cosying up to dictators around the world. This rule-of-law formal rationality of institutions has for its foundation Kant's *Erfahrung*, objective experience of indeed the subject's equal-rights formalism incorporated in *Rechtsstaate*, in legal orders that protect our democracies.

Weber's objectivity intervention touched on institutional formalism, as well as substantivism. Weber's essay touched on the balance between positivist objectivity and interpretivist subjectivity. Weber's reading of objectivity was based on J.S. Mill's positivism, featuring utilitarian assumptions of *homo economicus*, which Weber also echoed in the *Methodenstreit*, supporting Carl Menger's neoclassicism. This was economics formalism as Menger's substantivist opponent from the Historical School, Werner Sombart, was aware. Thus, a formally rational law-state (a *Rechtsstaat*) would guarantee the formal rationality (*Zweckrationalität*) of economic action, of the just mentioned *homo economicus*. It also thought its checks and balances can guarantee human rights. Weber was a friend of Hugo Preuss, the author of the Weimar Republic's constitution. Weber endorsed but was critical of Preuss to the extent that the Constitution was a *Sozialrechtsstaat*; that is, it was given substantive content in supporting institutions, conducive to social welfare and non-market rights of workers and the poor. Preuss's influence in this was Otto von Gierke's *Deutsche Genossenschaftsrecht*. A *Genosse* is a comrade and von Gierke also harks back to the price-setting powers of guilds in earlier German cities. Now, it is also Preuss who wrote the emergency powers in Article 48 of the Constitution, which became paradigmatic for Carl Schmitt's state of exception. In both workers' rights (associated with a 'status group') and the emergency powers,

Preuss and the Constitution departed from the formal rationality of the law. Weber, critical of plebiscitary democracy, was on the side of formal rationality – and hence experience as *Erfahrung*, objective experience – in both senses.

But Weber endorsed also a *verstehende* sociology – that is, also the interpretive dimension of sociology – in which subjective experience was at stake. For Weber, good sociology would capture both objective and subjective experience. And this substantivism was closer to another side of institutions, another side of experience. This is subjective experience, and the kind of institutions at stake are the drivers of Karl Polanyi's substantivism. Polanyi saw more clearly than perhaps anyone that markets were just one institution among many. That price setting historically was a matter of different institutions – guilds, families, cities – and later, but unfortunately decreasingly now, trade unions, and say the state's capping energy prices. As we also know, institutions, like monopoly firms, set prices. Foucault's neoliberalism had prime focus on ordoliberalism, based not on state but legal guarantees of market pricing. This is echoed partly by the Chicago School's R.H. Coase (1937). Coase's focus was more the firm than markets. His 'The Problem of Social Cost' (1960) outsourced the costs of social and ecological externalities from the state onto laws guaranteeing the firm's responsibilities in this. Further, Coase, unlike the ordoliberals, did not support the legal prohibition of monopoly pricing. For him, if firms in comparison to markets could save on transaction costs, then this could justify monopoly pricing. Coase, along with Oliver Williamson (1983), is the founder of the new institutional economics. Both are very aware that firms and markets are 'economic institutions of capitalism'. But both, in comparison with the very substantivism of first-wave institutional economics of Veblen and Commons, are resolutely formalist and neoclassicist. In comparison with Coase, the ordoliberals wanted the state to withdraw from legal regulation of non-monopoly, hence competitive, labour markets. Hence, they are anti-union in terms of price setting and against any industrial policy that favours some firms or sectors over others. They also support strong state spending, setting up a social safety net, which they see as necessary for the market setting of the price of labour. Ordoliberalism's, hence anti-Keynesian, social-market economy was influential under Christian Democratic rule in the 1950s and early 1960s and again since Gerhard Schroeder's labour market flexibilization. Schmitt was a fierce critic of ordoliberalism, seeing it as an economization of the state.

Polanyi's institutions were a counter to formalism, and especially to the formalism of neoclassical economics. A number of institutions are substantivist as well as formal. The family, though perhaps increasingly informal – with pre-nups, dating services and the like – is a substantivist institution, in particular the many-generation lineage family in, for example, China. Substantivist institutions are much more about identity, about forms of life. About not just objective experience and formal law, but about subjectivity. The state itself is on the one side formalist – a political space for the accumulation of capital and, indeed, for human rights, both as human rights and accumulation space, which Schmitt saw as a political theology – but on the other side, the state is also substantivist and a matter of identity. When the French identify with the state, it is part of their identity. You (as in Benedict Anderson on nation) had to be willing to die for the polis. Indeed, all three of Aristotle's proto-institutions, his forms of association – household, tribe and polis – were substantive. Ulrich Beck was thinking of institutions, and institutional reflexivity, in terms of risk and individualization. This was as much substantivist as formalist. Risk as the insurance principle is formal and relates to *homo economicus*. Risk as uncertainty, in terms of what cannot be insured – that is, as one-offs – which comprises most of life risks, are substantive: a question of not possessive but a substantive individualism and thus subjective and not objective experience.

But substantivism is not just for us 'good guys' of Karl Polanyi and the commons. It is also the basis of national populisms, today's illiberal, plebiscitary democracy. Carl Schmitt's integral state, his *nomos* of the earth, a *nomos* of not just *Boden* but also *Blut*, is clearly a substantivism: one that rejects formal political institutions as theological and illegitimate. Schmitt is aware of the *katechon*-constituted nature of the world we live in. Partly because of this, his state of exception must also be law. The question then is the balance of law and exception. This is the (vast) difference between Schmitt, on the one hand, and Arendt and Hans Blumenberg, on the other. For the latter, even though we live in the context of, no longer the Greek polis but an Augustinian – that is, Christian and Roman – political theology, featuring the free will, these legal and political institutions bequeathed to us are legitimate. They are the basis of possible 'new beginnings' and constitute a civilizational space irreducible to just social contract and a respite from Hobbesian friend-versus-enemy politics as war. Arendt and Blumenberg endorse this formal institutionalism. Agamben, of course, in *States of Exception* supports Benjamin and justice versus Schmitt and law. Agamben supporting the messianism of Benjamin's pure violence is also him critically acknowledging with Blumenberg the legitimacy of political theology and modernity. Agamben sees Foucauldian governmentality on the one hand and biopolitics on the other as opposite to one another. Governmentality is juridical order and biopolitics is a state of exception. It is sovereignty as state of exception (which has become Schmittian law) that creates and expels *homo sacer* to the bare life that can be killed and not sacrificed, that creates the camps – both Auschwitz and today's border-defining Muslim internment camps, and Guantánamo. This reading of state of exception, then, has been subsequently extended by Aihwa Ong (2006) to a full account of neoliberalism. If previous liberalism had been a juridical order, then it is neoliberalism that is the biopolitical state of exception: in tax havens and special economic zones as states of exception, from Shenzhen to offshore Britain, with zero-hour contracts in the UK and Filipino maids in Hong Kong, confined to six-meter-square windowless rooms in upper-class new builds. All this in violation of the juridical order, the rule of law, the *Rechtsstaat* of liberalism and social democracy. Other analysts such as Bruno Latour are more wholehearted in their, not critique but embrace of Schmitt. For Latour, ecological politics must move from the juridical order – that is, the order of the neutral arbiter of the now outmoded Holocene – to the Schmittian *nomos*-of-the-earth ethos of the Anthropocene. Donna Haraway in *Staying with the Trouble* has argued subtly against Latour's Anthropocene. For her the *Erde*, the earth, is not a question of pure war of friend and enemy in nature, but a complex multiplicity, of dyings and indeed Arendtian new beginnings. This is a very different, more biological forms-of-life notion of earth, that we must 'stay with' in our ecological politics. Latour says the mega-polluters among industry act as if there is no arbiter. But that the Paris Accords of 2015 are such a neutral arbiter it seems has not inconsiderable value.

Many others today would associate normativity with Carl Schmitt's *nomos* of the earth. Latour, in his important and influential Gifford Lectures, offered support for a Schmittian *nomos* of the earth; that is, an Anthropocene *nomos* of the earth for climatologists and environ-mentalists. Latour has gone on to argue that critical theory itself is no longer relevant. This Anthropocene earth *nomos* would be against the Holocene ethos of 'Science' as a neutral arbiter, and against the notion of the neutral arbiter more generally. Here the *nomos* of the earth is juxtaposed to '*nomos* of the sky', to a more transcendental or universal normativity, which for Schmitt is part and parcel of political theology. In this book, we argue for an a posteriori human sciences, reasoning from the particular in thought, politics and technics. Yet one which – in the light of Brexit and Trump – reminds us of the importance of less earthbound instances of norms, such as human rights, rule of law and cosmopolitan values (Beck 2006). Though this chapter and the previous support reasoning from the particular, in both technics and politics, this does not mean that there is no place for the formal and the universal. That is, in the context of today's plebiscitary authoritarianisms, we cannot reduce *nomos* to Schmitt's *Nomos der Erde*.

8.3 Metaphysics or Empirical Multiplicity

In Chapter 4, above, on the economy, all three notions of experience are at stake. In this the early debates about experience around the *Geisteswissenschaften* and Dilthey were about *Erfahrung* and *Erlebnis*. *Erfahrung*, the basis also of neo-Kantian positivism, was the objective experience of Kant's First Critique. It is, to repeat, also the forerunner of neoclassical (and most neoliberal) economics. In this sense, Chapter 4 deals most directly with positivism. *Erlebnis* is lived experience, the basis of interpretive sociology, is subjective experience. The opponents of neo-Kantian formalism in the German Historical School understood such substantive and subjective experience as Hegelian. This makes sense for two reasons. The first is that Hegelian dialectic (very different from Socrates) is a sort of dialogue in antagonism of form and substance. Every time there is a formalism of, say, the categories or the moral imperative, the next move is to ground it in the substance of, for example, *Sittlichkeit* or convention. Hegel announces this at the beginning of the *Phenomenology*, where he says he will depart from the heavy substantivism of his Romantic colleagues like the Spinoza- (substance)-oriented Schelling, to move always also to form, to categories. It is a dialectic of *Erlebnis* and *Erfahrung*. Starting with the *Erlebnis* of consciousness, which is not a subject but prior to the subject–object split, and ending at the very end with synthesis of subject–object, i.e. substance–form (or *Erlebnis–Erfahrung*), but under the banner of substance; that is, the substantial state and substantive reason. The basis for this is – as for all of idealism and the Romantics – Kant's Third Critique, i.e. the subjective experience of judgment. *Erlebnis* is phenomenology, and also more sociological forms-of-life phenomenology, in which social relations replace Husserl's consciousness. The *leben* in *Erlebnis* means that these are also forms of *life*; we recall the biological or organic paradigm of Kantian judgment, to be reiterated in intellectual history from Nietzsche to Simmel.

191

But Chapter 4 ends with a third kind of experience – that is neither *Erfahrung* nor *Erlebnis* – which is a radical empiricism that undercuts both *Erfahrung* and *Erlebnis*, and which is perhaps best called sensory experience. Only this sensory experience is consistently anti-metaphysical. Whereas both objective and subjective experience synthesize the admittedly (by Kant) metaphysical subject, this third and actually original modern notion of experience is a full rejection of metaphysics. This, of course, is empiricism proper from David Hume. Sensory experience is neither objective nor subjective: it resides in perception, in sensation, even – if we are to think of Georg Simmel's notion of money – in desire. Sensory experience is consistently anti-metaphysical. First-Critique Kant accepts David Hume's rejection of metaphysics, except for its rejection of causation. This is causation as in Newtonian mechanics. Kant acknowledges that causation is metaphysical, and yet needs to reinstate it. His idea of knowledge is, though synthetic, much more apodictic, much more a notion of certain knowledge than Hume's. It is a bit of a contrast between correlation (Hume), indeed temporal correlation, hence the conjunction, the and, on the one hand, and causation, on the other. Key texts in methodology like Campbell and Stanley (1963) have argued that causation must be imputed by the social scientist. It is not out there in, as it were, social nature. In Hume and his truly radical empiricism, there is knowledge, but it is precarious, it is uncertain. There is a human understanding as in *An Enquiry Concerning Human Understanding*, but it too has its basis in sense impressions. 'Hume's Fork' breaks down human reason or enquiry into, on the one hand, relations of ideas and, on the other, matters of fact. Ideas here are a priori and universal; facts are to do with the experience of the observer. They are hence a posteriori. Hume is not arguing for induction as against deduction. His critique of causation is mainly a critique of inductive reasoning: that two events regularly happened in succession in the past does not mean that they will do so in the future. Proponents of inductive reasoning attribute causation. For Hume, we rely on habit or custom to fill in the gaps. For Hume, we are judging animals by instinct, by nature and not transcendental principle. Kant's self or subject as the transcendental unity of apperception is (before unification through the transcendental) instead the self as a bundle of sense impressions, a bundle of experiences. A Humean would thus see (modern) subjectivity not as the transcendental unity of apperception, but instead as the empirical multiplicity of perceptions. This is radical, empiricism that does away with both objective and subjective experience for such sensory experience. We have judgment;

our nature is to have imagination and an understanding; that is, to reason. Aristotle makes the distinction between the healer who relies on just past experience for medication and the doctor, who, trained in science, reasons inferentially and provides reasons through reflection on the nature of the medication, on the nature of the disease. Animal nature will have perception and imagination – a dog remembers the past and anticipates the future – but does not naturally reason inferentially, does not even fill in the gaps with habit and customs: a dog does not in this sense have an understanding, does not judge. For this, the dog would need to think in symbols; dog societies would have to have a symbolic, would have to have, in Durkheim's sense, elementary forms of religious life. Adam Smith, for his part, in the *Moral Sentiments*, takes this problematique of sensory experience further into the realm of ethics. For Smith, there is no categorical imperative of pure reason. We perceive our own feelings: but can only imagine the feelings of another. Moral sentiments are thus an extension of moral sense, of a sensory-based morality. They are a posteriori, experience-based. Indeed, Foucault's contrast of liberalism with the beginnings of neoliberal governmentality praises Smith. Smithian empiricism – Foucault's Smith and Deleuze's Hume – work a posteriori, while the a priori of utility maximization and *homo economicus* sets in with J.S. Mill – foreshadowed by Bentham's Panopticon – and continued into neoclassical and neoliberal economics and economies (Gane 2014).

Some have likened Hume's self as a multiplicity of the senses to Buddhism and Eastern thought. In chapter 7, we spoke of Shitao's *Treatise on Painting*, from the formlessness of one to the 10,000 forms to the ten thousand things, which also came into use in Buddhism as the uncountable number of forms in which life-force or Buddha-nature exists. If the Humean self is a multiplicity so is the Dao in its expression in the ten thousand things. The Dao is in a sense at the same time the ten thousand things, the ten thousand forms, which themselves take on powers of breathing, communicating, or as François Jullien (2016) says, 'coupling'. We have been talking about mostly human experience or machine-mediated experience, but we need to ask with Shitao how can objects, themselves, experience? China's 1930s New Culture Movement proponent and writer on the commons, Liang Shuming, was influenced by Bergson and consciousness-only Buddhism. Liang read Bergson in the broadest sense as a phenomenologist. Consciousness-only Buddhism, the main Chinese variant, John Makeham (2014) observes, is phenomenological in contrast to the more ontological frame of Theravada Buddhism. In Bergson, matter has memory; it works through image-remembrance. In Deleuze's

Bergson, matter experiences matter, through matter's imagination. We note that, for Alfred North Whitehead, all matter works through experience, for Gabriel Tarde through communication. In the future, experience will, it seems, inevitably undergo processes of further informationalization, on the one hand, and more or less easternization, on the other. Eastern thought, and grammar, are about place, about time, much less about subjects, verbs and objects than the location, the infrastructure in which we live our lives. The One Belt, One Road Initiative is about infrastructure-building as distinct from a US foreign policy, a geopolitics of drones. Drones are about subjects, verbs and objects; infrastructure is adverbial, about background, about time and space. Drones are about foreground; infrastructure roads are background: hard power versus soft power. The subject, like causation, is metaphysical. Indeed, causation only makes sense for Kant as an operational mode of the transcendental unity of apperception. For Hume, to deconstruct cause is also to deconstruct the subject. Hume replaces the subject as a unity of concepts with the self as a multiplicity of percepts. The multiplicity of percepts echoes the multiplicity of points of view in Chinese landscape, the multiplicity of experiences of the ten thousand things. Deleuze and Guattari (1972) moved on from the experience of Hume's self as multiplicity of percepts and his (and William James's) replacement caused by conjunction to the connectivity in the anti-Oedipus of desiring machines. The information society is, as the MIT Media Lab has had it, about 'things that think', about thinking machines. How things think is also a question of how things perceive. Data is, for Hume, about observation and recording as facts. Big data (or 'big facts') is about machine observation (and recording). In big data, machines do not just think, they experience. Their active memory does work on what is taken in through such machine experience. The future may be not just about how machines, how objects, experience, but about how, or if, they communicate. Here communication is also power that has become control; and control works decreasingly through language, and increasingly through algorithms and mathematical symbols: in which there is a shift from what Deleuze, echoing Nietzsche, understood as from 'qualitative extensity' to 'quantitative intensity'. We may have a choice, as Donna Haraway implies, whether to live in a hierarchical war-like world of control, (only strategic) communication, command and intelligence, on the one hand, or a 'flat' earth, of coupling and communication, on the other. To live in a world of friend versus enemy or to live in Walter Benjamin's world of communication as *mitteilen*, as sharing. Experience may be undergoing vast changes. But let us not forget experience.

REFERENCES

Agamben, G. (1998) *Homo Sacer: Sovereign Power and Bare Life*. Stanford, CA: Stanford University Press.
Agamben, G. (2005) *States of Exception*. Chicago, IL: University of Chicago Press.
Agamben, G. (2011) *The Kingdom and the Glory: For a Theological Genealogy of Economy and Government*. Stanford, CA: Stanford University Press.
Agamben, G. (2013a) *The Highest Poverty: Monastic Rules and Forms of Life*. Stanford, CA: Stanford University Press.
Agamben, G. (2013b) *Opus Dei: An Archaeology of Duty*. Stanford, CA: Stanford University Press.
Alitto, G. (1986) *The Last Confucian: Liang Shuming and the Chinese Dilemma of Modernity*. Berkeley, CA: University of California Press.
Alliez, E. (1991) *Les temps capitaux*. Paris: Cerf.
Arendt, H. (1958) *The Human Condition*. Chicago, IL: University of Chicago Press.
Arendt, H. (1982) *Lectures on Kant's Political Philosophy*. Chicago, IL: University of Chicago Press.
Arendt, H. (2006) *Between Past and Future*. London: Penguin.
Aristotle (2002) *Nicomachean Ethics*. Oxford: Oxford University Press.
Arrighi, G. (1994) *The Long Twentieth Century*. London: Verso.
Arrighi, G. (2007) *Adam Smith in Beijing*. London: Verso.
Badiou, A. (2003) *Saint Paul: The Foundation of Universalism*. Stanford, CA: Stanford University Press.
Badiou, A. (2013) *Being and Event*. London: Bloomsbury Academic.
Baehr, J. (2006) 'A Priori and a Posteriori', *Internet Encyclopaedia of Philosophy*. http://www.iep.utm.edu/apriori/
Barad, K. (2007) *Meeting the Universe Halfway: Quantum Physics and the Entanglement of Matter and Meaning*. Durham, NC: Duke University Press.
Barton Perry, R. (2003). Introduction to W. James, *Essays in Radical Empiricism*. Mineola, NY: Dover.
Beck, U. (1986) *Risikogesellschaft*. Frankfurt: Suhrkamp.
Beck, U. (2006) *Cosmopolitan Vision*. Cambridge: Polity.
Benhabib, S. (1992) *Situating the Self: Gender, Community, and Postmodernism in Contemporary Ethics*. New York: Routledge.

195

Benjamin, W. (1977a) 'Über Sprache überhaupt und über die Sprache des Menschen', in W. Benjamin, *Aufsätze, Essays, Vorträge: Gesammelte Schriften, II-1*. Frankfurt: Suhrkamp, pp. 140–57.

Benjamin, W. (1977b) 'Zur Kritik der Gewalt', in W. Benjamin, *Aufsätze, Essays, Vorträge: Gesammelte Schriften, II-1*. Frankfurt: Suhrkamp, pp. 179–203.

Benjamin, W. (1979) 'On Language as Such and On the Language of Man', in W. Benjamin *One-Way Street*. London: Verso, pp. 107–23.

Bennett, J. (2009) *Vibrant Matter: A Political Ecology of Things*. Durham, NC: Duke University Press.

Bergson, H. (2011a) *The Two Sources of Morality and Religion*. London: Lightning Source.

Bergson, H. (2011b) *Matter and Memory*. London: Martino.

Berthoud, A. (2002) *Essais de philosophie économique: Platon, Aristote, Hobbes, A. Smith, Marx*. Paris: Presses Universitaires de Septentrion.

Blumenberg, H. (1985) *The Legitimacy of the Modern Age*. Cambridge, MA: MIT Press.

Braudel, F. (1992) *The Perspective of the World. V. 3. (Civilization and Capitalism 15th-18th Century)*. Berkeley, CA: University of California Press.

Broadie, A. (2001) *The Scottish Enlightenment*. Edinburgh: Birlinn Books.

Broadie, S. (2002a) 'Philosophical Introduction' to Aristotle, *Nicomachean Ethics*. Oxford: Oxford University Press, pp. 9–91.

Broadie, S. (2002b) 'Commentary' to Aristotle, *Nicomachean Ethics*. Oxford: Oxford University Press, pp. 261–452.

Cahill, J. (1980) *An Index of Early Chinese Painters and Painting*. Berkeley, CA: University of California Press.

Campbell, D.T. and Stanley J.C. (1963) *Experimental and Quasi-Experimental Designs for Research*. New York: Rand McNally.

Caygill, H. (1997) *Walter Benjamin: The Colour of Experience*. London: Routledge.

Chun, W. (2013) *Programmed Visions*, Cambridge, MA: MIT Press.

Coase, R.H. (1937) 'The Nature of the Firm', *Economica*, 4(16), 386–405

Coase, R.H. (1960) 'The Problem of Social Cost', *Journal of Law and Economics*, 3(1), 1–44.

Cobb, S. (2013) *Speaking of Violence*. Oxford: Oxford University Press.

Cohen, G.A. (1978) *Karl Marx's Theory of History: A Defence*. Oxford: Clarendon.

Coleman, E.J. (1971) 'Philosophy of Painting by Shih-T'ao: Translation and Exposition of his Hua-p'u (Treatise on the Philosophy of Painting)'. PhD dissertation, University of Hawaii.

Cui, Z. (2012) 'Making Sense of the Chinese "Socialist Market Economy"', *Modern China*, 38, 665–76.

Deleuze, G. (1991) *Empiricism and Subjectivity: An Essay on David Hume's Theory of Human Nature*. New York: Columbia University Press.

Deleuze, G. (2005) *Francis Bacon: The Logic of Sensation*. London: Continuum.

Deleuze, G. (2006a) *The Fold*. London: Continuum.

Deleuze, G. (2006b) *Nietzsche and Philosophy*. London: Continuum.

Deleuze, G. and Guattari, F. (1972) *L'Anti-Oedipe*. Paris: Les Éditions de Minuit.

Derrida, J. (1994) *Force de loi*. Paris: Galilée.

Derrida, J. (2001) *Writing and Difference*. London: Routledge.

Dewey, J. (2012) *The Public and Its Problems*. University Park, PA: Penn State University Press.

REFERENCES

Dilthey, W. (1883) *Einleitung in die Geisteswissenschaften*. Leipzig: Duncker & Humblot.
Durkheim, E. (1961 [1912]) *The Elementary Forms of the Religious Life*. London: Collier.
Esposito, R. (2011) *Immunitas*. Cambridge: Polity.
Fairclough, N. (1995) *Critical Discourse Analysis*. Boston, MA: Addison Wesley.
Foong, P. (2000) 'Guo Xi's Intimate Landscapes and the Case of *Old Trees, Level Distance*'. *Metropolitan Museum Journal*, 35, 87–115.
Foucault, M. (1966) *Les mots et les choses*. Paris: Gallimard.
Foucault, M. (1988) *The Care of the Self: The History of Sexuality, 3*. New York: Vintage.
Foucault, M. (2008) *The Birth of Biopolitics*. Basingstoke: Palgrave Macmillan.
Fuller, M. and Goffey, A. (2012) *Evil Media*. Cambridge, MA: MIT Press.
Gane, N. (2012) *Max Weber and Contemporary Capitalism*. Basingstoke: Palgrave Macmillan.
Gane, N. (2014) 'The Emergence of Neoliberalism: Thinking Through and Beyond Michel Foucault's Lectures on Biopolitics', *Theory, Culture & Society*, 31(4), 3–27.
Gasché, R. (2003) *The Idea of Form: Rethinking Kant's Aesthetics*. Stanford, CA: Stanford University Press.
Giddens, A. (1984) *The Constitution of Society*. Cambridge: Polity.
Graeber, D. (2014) *Debt: The First 5,000 Years*. New York: Melville.
Gunder Frank, A. (1998) *ReORIENT*. Berkeley: University of California Press.
Habermas, J. (1986 [1981]) *The Theory of Communicative Action, vol. 1*. Cambridge: Polity.
Habermas, J. (1989 [1962]) *The Structural Transformation of the Public Sphere*. Cambridge: Polity.
Hall, S. (1973) 'Encoding and Decoding in the Television Discourse'. Council of Europe Colloquium on Training in the Critical Reading of Televisual Language, Leicester University, September.
Haraway, D. (1991) *Simians, Cyborgs and Women*. London: Free Association Books.
Haraway, D. (2016) *Staying with the Trouble: Making Kin in the Chthulucene*. Durham, NC: Duke University Press.
Hardt, M. and Negri, A. (2001) *Empire*. Cambridge, MA: Harvard University Press.
Hardt, M. and Negri, A. (2009) *Commonwealth*. Cambridge, MA: Belknap Press of Harvard University.
Harman, G. (2002) *Tool-Being. Heidegger and the Metaphysics of Objects*. Chicago, IL: Open Court.
Harrist, R. (1998) *Painting and Private Life in Eleventh-Century China*. Princeton, NJ: Princeton University Press.
Harvey, D. (2007) *A Brief History of Neoliberalism*. Oxford: Oxford University Press.
Hay, J. (2001) *Shitao: Painting and Modernity in Early Qing China*. Cambridge: Cambridge University Press.
Hayles, N.K. (1990) *Chaos Bound*. Ithaca, NY: Cornell University Press.
Hayles, N.K. (1999) *How We Became Posthuman*. Chicago, IL: University of Chicago Press.
Hegel, G.W.F. (1972) *Grundlinien der Philosophie des Rechts: Naturrecht und Staatswissenschaft*. Frankfurt am Main: Ullstein.

Hegel, G.W.F. (1977) *Phenomenology of Spirit*. Oxford: Oxford University Press.

Heidegger, M. (1954) 'Die Frage nach der Technik', in M. Heidegger, *Vorträge und Aufsätze*, Stuttgart: Verlag Günther Neske, pp. 9–40.

Heidegger, M. (1986) *Sein und Zeit*. Tübingen: Niemeyer.

Heidegger, M. (2010) *Being and Time*. Albany, NY: State University of New York Press.

Heidegger, M. (2012) *Basic Problems of Phenomenology*. London: Athlone.

Hennis, W. (1988) *Max Weber: Essays in Reconstruction*. London: Allen & Unwin.

Hirst, P.Q. (2013) *Durkheim, Bernard and Epistemology*. London: Routledge.

Hofstadter, D. (1979) *Gödel, Escher, Bach*. New York: Basic Books.

Hui, Y. (2016) *On the Existence of Digital Objects*. Minneapolis, MN: University of Minnesota Press.

Hutcheson, F. (2017 [1725]) *An Inquiry into the Original of Our Ideas of Beauty and Virtue*. Charleston, SC: CreateSpace Independent Publishing Platform

James, W. (1983 [1902]) *The Varieties of Religious Experience*. Harmondsworth: Penguin.

James, W. (2000 [1890]) *The Principles of Psychology, vol. 1*. Mineola, NY: Dover.

James, W. (2003) *Essays in Radical Empiricism*. Mineola, NY: Dover.

Jay, M. (2005) *Songs of Experience*. Berkeley, CA: University of California Press.

Jullien, F. (2009) *The Great Image Has No Form; Or, On the Nonobject through Painting*. Chicago, IL: University of Chicago Press.

Jullien, F. (2016) *The Strange Idea of the Beautiful*. London: Seagull Books.

Kampowski, S. (2008) *Arendt, Augustine, and the New Beginning*. Grand Rapids, MI: Eerdmans.

Kant, I. (1929 [1781]) *Critique of Pure Reason*. London: Macmillan.

Kant, I. (2009 [1790]) *Critique of Judgment*. Oxford: Oxford University Press.

Kant, I. (2017 [1788]) *Critique of Practical Reason*. Oxford: Oxford University Press.

Kierkegaard, S. (1985) *Fear and Trembling*. Harmondsworth: Penguin.

Kohn, J. (2006) 'Introduction', to H. Arendt, *Between Past and Future*. London: Penguin.

Koolhaas, R. (2001) *Mutations*. Barcelona: Actar.

Laplace, P.-S. (2017) *The Mechanics of Laplace*. London: Forgotten Books.

Lash, S. (2002) *Critique of Information*. London: Sage.

Lash, S. (2005) 'Lebenssoziologie: Georg Simmel in the Information Age', *Theory, Culture & Society*, 22, 1–23.

Lash, S. (2015) 'Performativity or Discourse: An Interview with John Searle', *Theory, Culture & Society*, 32(3), 135–47.

Lash, S. and Lury, C. (2007) *Global Culture Industry*. Cambridge: Polity.

Last, N. (2008) *Wittgenstein's House*. Bronx, NY: Fordham University Press.

Latour, B. (2014) 'Agency at the Time of the Anthropocene', *New Literary History*, 45, 1–18.

Lazzarato, M. (2015) *Governing by Debt*. New York: Semiotexte.

Leibniz, G.W. (2014) *Monadology*. Edinburgh: Edinburgh University Press.

Li, S. (2014) *Understanding the Chinese City*. London: Sage.

Lin, T. and Wong, K. (2016) 'Nonparametric Identification of a Wiener System Using a Stochastic Excitation of Arbitrarily Known Spectrum', *Signal Processing*, 120, 422–37.

Luhmann, N. (1989) *Gesellschaftsstruktur und Semantik: Studien zur Wissenssoziologie der modernen Gesellschaft 3*. Frankfurt am Main: Suhrkamp.

Lury, C. and Wakeford, N. (eds.) (2013) *Inventive Methods*. London: Routledge.

MacIntyre, A. (1981) *After Virtue*. London: Duckworth.

Mackenzie, A. (2006) *Cutting Code*. Bern: Peter Lang.

Mackenzie, A. (2010) *Wirelessness: Radical Empiricism in Network Cultures*. Cambridge, MA: MIT Press.

Makeham, J. (ed.) (2014) *Transforming Consciousness: Yogacara Thought in Modern China*. Oxford: Oxford University Press.

Malinowski, B. (2013 [1922]) *Argonauts of the Western Pacific: An Account of Native Enterprise and Adventure in the Archipelagoes of Melanesian New Guinea*. Long Grove, IL: Waveland Press.

Marres, N. (2012) *Material Participation: Technology, the Environment and Everyday Publics*. Basingstoke: Macmillan.

Marx, K. (1967) *Capital, Vol. 1*. New York: New World.

Marx, K. (1993) *Grundrisse*. London: Penguin.

Maturana, H. and F. Varela (1980) *Autopoiesis and Cognition*. Dordrecht: Springer.

Meillassoux, Q. (2008) *After Finitude*. London: Continuum.

Menand, L. (2011) *The Metaphysical Club*. New York: Flamingo.

Menger, C. (1883) *Untersuchungen über die Methoden der Sozialwissenschaften, und der Politischen Oekonomie*. Leipzig: Duncker & Humblot.

Mezzadra, S. and Neilson, B. (2013) *Border as Method; Or, the Multiplication of Labor*. Durham, NC: Duke University Press.

Milbank, J. and Pabst, A. (2016) *The Politics of Virtue: Post-Liberalism and the Human Future*. Lanham, MD: Rowman & Littlefield.

Mirowski, P. (1991) *More Heat than Light: Economics as Social Physics, Physics as Nature's Economics*. Cambridge: Cambridge University Press.

Mirowski, P. (2002) *Machine Dreams*. Cambridge: Cambridge University Press.

Ong, A. (2006) *Neoliberalism as Exception*. Durham, NC: Duke University Press.

Orléan, A. (2014) *The Empire of Value*. Cambridge, MA: MIT Press.

Ostrom, E. (1990) *Governing the Commons*. Cambridge: Cambridge University Press.

Parisi, L. (2004) *Abstract Sex*. London: Continuum.

Pickering, A. (2011) *The Cybernetic Brain*. Chicago, IL: University of Chicago Press.

Polanyi, K. (1957) *The Great Transformation*. Boston, MA: Beacon.

Prigogine, I. and Stengers, I. (1989) *Order out of Chaos*. New York: Bantam.

Rawls, J. (1971) *A Theory of Justice*. Cambridge, MA: Belknap Press of Harvard University Press.

Ricardo, D. (2004) *The Principles of Political Economy and Taxation*. Mineola, NY: Dover.

Roch, A. (2009) *Claude E. Shannon: Spielzeug, Leben und die geheime Geschichte seiner Theorie der Information*. Berlin: Gegenstalt Verlag.

Rossiter, N. (2016) *Software, Infrastructure, Labor: A Media Theory of Logistical Nightmares*. New York: Routledge.

Schmitt, C. (1985) *Political Theology*. Cambridge, MA: MIT Press.

Schmitt, C. (1996) *The Concept of the Political*. Chicago, IL: University of Chicago Press.

Schmitt, C. (2003) *The Nomos of the Earth*. New York: Telos Press.

Schumpeter, J.A. (1954) *History of Economic Analysis*. London: Allen & Unwin.

Searle, J. (1969) *Speech Acts: An Essay in the Philosophy of Language*. Cambridge: Cambridge University Press.

Sen, A. (2009) *The Idea of Justice*. Cambridge, MA: Harvard University Press.

Shannon, C. and Weaver, W. (1963) *The Mathematical Theory of Communication*. Champaign-Urbana, IL: University of Illinois Press.

Simmel, G. (2001) *The Philosophy of Money*. London: Routledge.

Simondon, G. (1958) *Du mode d'existence des objets techniques*. Paris: Aubier.

Simondon, G. (2007) *L'individuation psychique et collective: À la lumière des notions de forme, information et métastabilité*, Paris: Aubier.

Sloterdijk, P. (2004) *Sphären 3: Schäume*. Frankfurt am Main: Suhrkamp.

Smith, A. (2010) *The Theory of the Moral Sentiments*. Harmondsworth: Penguin.

Sombart, W. (1928) *Der moderne Kapitalismus*. Munich: Duncker & Humblot.

Stanford Encyclopedia of Philosophy (2010) 'Philosophy of Technology', in E.N. Zalta (ed.) *The Stanford Encyclopedia of Philosophy* (Spring 2010 Edition), http://plato.stanford.edu/archives/spr2010/entries/technology/

Stiegler, B. (1998) *Technics and Time, 1. The Fault of Epimetheus*. Stanford, CA: Stanford University Press.

Stiegler, B. (2004) *La misère symbolique*, vol. 1. Paris: Galilèe.

Stiegler, B. (2010) *Technics and Time 3. Cinematic Time and the Question of Malaise*. Stanford, CA: Stanford University Press.

Strauss, L. (1965) *Natural Right and History*. Chicago, IL: University of Chicago Press.

Strauss, L. (1978) *The City and Man*. Chicago, IL: University of Chicago Press.

Taylor, E. and Wozniak, R. (1996) 'Pure Experience, the Response to William James: An Introduction', *Classics in the History of Psychology*, http://psychclassics.yorku.ca/James/TaylorWoz.htm

Tribe, K. (2008) *Strategies of Economic Order*. Cambridge: Cambridge University Press.

Tuan, Y. (1977) *Space and Place: The Perspective of Experience*. Minneapolis, MN: University of Minnesota Press.

Urry, J. (2014) *Offshoring*. Cambridge: Polity.

Veblen, T. (1904) *The Theory of the Business Enterprise*. Livingston, NJ: Transaction Books.

Veblen, T. (1919 [1901]) 'Gustav Schmoller's Economics', in T. Veblen, *The Place of Science in Modern Civilisation and Other Essays*. New York: B.W. Huebsch, pp. 252–78.

Virno, P. (2015) *When the Word Becomes Flesh*. New York: Semiotexte.

Vogl, J.R. (2014) *The Specter of Capital*. Stanford, CA: Stanford University Press.

Von Neumann, J. and O. Morgenstern (1944). *Theory of Games and Economic Behavior*. Princeton, NJ: Princeton University Press.

Von Uexküll, J. (2010) *A Foray into the Worlds of Animals and Humans*. Minneapolis, MN: University of Minnesota Press.

Wallerstein, I. (1974) *The Modern World System*. New York: Academic Press.

Wang, H. (2008) 现代中国思想的兴起. *Xiandai zhongguo sixiang de xingqi*. Beijing: SDX Joint Publishing.

Wang, H. (2014) *From Empire to Nation State*. Cambridge, MA: Harvard University Press.

Weber, M. (1949) 'Objectivity in Social Science and Social Policy', in E. Shils (ed.) *Max Weber on the Methodology of the Social Sciences*. New York: Free Press.

REFERENCES

Weber, M. (1966) *The City*. New York: Free Press.
Weber, M. (1992) *Economy and Society*. Berkeley, CA: University of California Press.
Whimster, M.S. (2007) *Understanding Weber*. London: Routledge.
Williamson, O. (1983) *Markets and Hierarchies*. New York: Macmillan.
Wittgenstein, L. (2009) *Philosophische Untersuchungen/Philosophical Investigations*, 4th edn. Oxford: Wiley-Blackwell.

INDEX

202

and Romans 97–8, 102, 106, 107, 115, 187
and rule of law 115–16
and sense(s) 119–20
and the social 134
and sovereignty 99, 100, 109
and taste 118, 119
and theodicy 117
Aristotle 5, 6, 9, 17, 22, 50, 63, 73, 94, 96–8, 105, 107, 113, 116, 117, 147, 158, 189, 193
a posteriori technics 33–49
Categories 37, 43, 45
chrematistics 24, 33, 44, 75, 85
De Anima 46
and deliberative rhetoric 133
and form 11–13, 43–7, 133, 134
god as the unmoved mover 45–6
and the good 18, 34–6
and happiness 35, 36, 37, 41
and individuation 44, 45, 125
and justice 96, 98
Metaphysics 19, 43, 45, 136, 169
Nicomachean Ethics 1, 33–6, 37–42, 47, 54, 59, 98, 100
and oikos 26, 44, 74, 88, 105, 107
and perception 41–2
Physics 43, 45–6
Politics 33, 74–5, 87, 100
and substance 37, 43–7, 57, 97, 136
technics 25, 73
on theoretical and practical reason 38–40, 54
on trade 88
zoon politikon 94, 99, 100, 128
art 31, 32
Chinese 158, 160–1, 163, 166–84, 194
object in 163
and singularities 164–6
Western versus Islamic 160–1
artificial intelligence (AI) 144, 151
assemblages 15–16
association 56, 57
atom bomb 151
Augustine 6, 8, 45, 46–7, 94, 104
City of God 102, 104
Confessions 134
DePulchro 169
and free will 21, 22, 27, 97, 102–3, 107–12, 129, 175

influence on Arendt 100
Austrian School of Economics 15, 23, 75
automata 155
autopoietic systems 30, 125, 141, 150
axioms/axiomatization 148–9, 157

Bacon, Francis 31–2, 89
Badiou, Alain 16, 55
banks 185
Barad, Karen 28–9, 141–2, 152, 158, 180
Bataille, Georges 20, 49, 71, 92
beauty 92, 167–76
Beck, Ulrich 24, 122, 186–7, 189
Becker, Gary 93
Benjamin, Walter 8, 26, 100, 127, 135, 157
'Critique of Violence' 31, 131
and justice 96
'The Mimetic Faculty' 69
notion of divine violence 101
On Language' 8, 132, 135
Bennett, Jane 152
Bentham, Jeremy 13
Bergson, Henri 4, 52, 68–9, 157, 193–4
Berthoud, Arnaud 20
Betrieb 84–5
biopolitics 21, 73, 131, 190
Blumenberg, Hans 27, 46, 51, 175, 189
Legitimacy of the Modern Age 108, 175
Böhm von Bawerk, Eugen 75
Bohr, Nils 28, 142, 149, 180
Boltzmann, Ludwig 140, 143
Boolean algebra 154
Born, Max 148–9
Bourdieu, Pierre, *Distinction* 173
Broadie, Sarah 35
Buddhism 163, 193
Burke, Edmund 133, 173
business enterprise 78

cameralism 79, 89
Cantor, Georg 16, 148, 157
capitalism 7, 14, 72
finance 138, 185
origins and roots 23–4, 74–6
and Sombart 84–5

cybernetic 144
distinction between chrematistics
and 44
formalist 12, 73, 74, 75–86
institutional 22–3, 75, 76–7, 86, 188
neoclassical 3, 10, 12, 13, 14, 15,
20, 21, 22, 31, 100
and physics 86–90
substantivist 12, 73, 74, 75–86, 87
EDVAC (Electronic Discrete Variable
Automatic Computer) 148
Einstein, Albert 140, 149, 162, 163
embeddedness 21, 22
Emerson, Ralph Waldo 64
empiricism 13, 15, 18, 25, 86–7, 115
transcendental 68
see also radical empiricism
engineering 17, 28–9, 126–7, 145–7,
156, 157, 159
English language 168
Enlightenment 115; see also Scottish
Enlightenment
entropy 152, 153
thermodynamic 154–5
vs negentropy 139–45
episteme 5, 6, 17–18, 38, 40, 73,
99–100, 137, 147, 184
Erfahrung 2, 73, 81, 82, 132, 153,
174, 187, 188, 191
erklären 3, 15, 23
Erlebnis 2, 65, 73, 78, 81, 82, 153,
175, 191
Esposito, Roberto 128
Immunitas 128
ethics 83, 84
and Aristotle 33–6, 37–42, 47, 54,
59, 98, 100
Euclid 10
Elements 9
eudemonia 21, 39, 46–7, 98, 100,
107, 122
exchange value 13, 19, 37, 49, 88, 93
exclusion, and forms of life 128–31

Facebook 30, 185, 186
facts 14, 39, 52–5, 57–9, 70
affectional 60–1
and Hume 70
and James 60–1, 70
Fairclough, Norman, Critical
Discourse Analysis 29

family 189
feminist theory 152–3, 158
Fichte, Johann Gottlieb 78, 164–5
field theory 90
finance capital/capitalism 138, 185
financial crisis (2008) 25, 138, 185
Fisher, Irving 90
formal rationality 12, 20, 79, 187–8
formalism 21, 22, 23–6, 93, 191
formalist economics
distinction between substantivist
economics and 74
versus substantivist economics 73,
75–86
formless 20
form(s) 11–13, 43–9, 125
and Aristotle 11–13, 43–7, 133, 134
and Plato 43, 45, 133
and substance 11–13, 43–7, 134
forms of life 27–8, 128–59
communicational 137–9
entropy against negentropy 139–45
and exclusion 128–31
and language 132–7
technological 126–7, 137–56, 157
Foucault, Michel 10, 17, 68, 93, 98–9,
134, 174, 188
Birth of Biopolitics 21, 73
epistemic discourses 73, 184
History of Sexuality 99
and technologies of the self 18, 73
Franklin, Benjamin 85
free will 6, 8, 46, 51, 97, 122–3, 123,
189
Augustine's 21, 22, 27, 97, 102–3,
107–12, 129, 175
Freud, Sigmund 4, 52, 55, 126
Friedman, Milton 93

Gaia hypothesis 152
game theory 136, 138, 143, 144–5,
148, 151
gaze, as multiplicity 166–83
George, Henry 77
German economics 79
German Historical School see
Historical School
German language 168
Giddens, Anthony, New Rules of
Sociological Method 186
gift 138

James, William 4, 25, 50–71, 175
and activity 61–4
and consciousness 55–6, 59–60, 64, 67, 68, 70
and facts 60–1, 70
and positivism 52
and pragmatism 53, 54, 60, 61–5, 67, 68, 69
Principles of Psychology 52, 64
radical empiricism 25, 50, 51–61, 62, 64, 67, 69
Some Problems of Philosophy 54
and truth 67, 68
Varieties of Religious Experience 50, 52, 64, 65
'What Pragmatism Means' 53
Jevons, William Stanley 81
Joyce, James 4
judgment 113–14, 121
and Arendt 101, 109, 113–15
determinate 121–2
and Kant 114, 117–18, 119–20, 121–2, 124, 173–4
moral 121
reflective 101, 113–14, 121–2
teleological 101, 113–14, 116
Jullien, François 7, 32, 158, 161, 167, 168–71, 175–6, 193
justice 26, 39, 100–1
and Agamben 131
and Aristotle 96, 98
and Benjamin 96
and Derrida 96, 97, 101
and forms of life 128
and Sen 34, 109

Kant, Immanuel 9, 11–12, 19, 25, 52, 53, 91, 96–7, 106, 110, 113–24, 169, 170, 192, 194
and aesthetic experience 172
and beautiful 172–3
categorical imperative 94, 95
and cognition 115
and common sense 121
Critique of Judgment 6, 11, 31, 112–14, 117, 120, 164–5, 169, 172, 173, 191
Critique of Practical Reason 11
Critique of Pure Reason 1–2, 6, 11, 31, 51, 58, 94, 101, 113, 123, 124, 164, 165, 172–3, 191

'Idea for a Universal History' 116, 118
and institutions 114, 115–16
and judgment 114, 117–18, 119–20, 121–2, 124, 173–4
and morality 173
'Perpetual Peace' 118
and positivism 119–20
and rationalism 114
and rule of law 115–16
Second Critique 164, 172
'Strife of the Faculties' 116
and substance and form 48
and taste 118
and theodicy 117
and trans-empirical categories 57–8
'What is Enlightenment?' 116
katechon 27, 175
Kelsen, Hans 20–1, 129
Kierkegaard, S. 51, 96, 110, 165
kinetic theory 143
Knies, Karl 23, 76, 84
Knight, Frank 25
knowledge 56–8
Kohn, Jerome, *Between Past and Future* 102

labour, distinction between work and 93–4, 98, 99, 109
Lacan, Jacques 180
language 8, 27, 153
and Benjamin 132, 135
and forms of life 132–7
Saussurean 135
and Wittgenstein 134–6
language games 7, 71, 126–7, 132, 134, 135, 137, 138–9, 153, 159
Laplace, P.S. 90
Latour, Bruno 30, 158, 190
law
contract 26, 89, 104, 129
natural 5, 83
pure 129
Lazzarato, Maurizio 30, 185
Governing through Debt 185
Leibniz, Gottfried William 111–12
Lévi-Strauss, Claude 138
Levinas, Emmanuel 96
Liang Shuming 163, 193
liberalism 73

207

Pamuk, Orhan, *My Name Is Red* 7,
160–1, 166, 183
Parisi, Luciana, *Abstract Sex* 152
Parmenides 45, 116
Parsons, Talcott 141
Structure of Social Action 82
Paul, St 103, 104, 112
Pax Americana 187
Pax Romana 102–4, 107, 187
Peace of Westphalia 99
Peirce, Charles Sanders 65
Pelagius 102, 103, 104
perception 41–2
performativity/performatives 155, 156–7
Perry, Barton 54
phenomenology 4, 10, 19, 28–9, 51,
124–5, 165
technological 142
see also Hegel, G.W.F.
phronesis (practical reason) 5, 38–9,
42–3
physiocracy/physiocrats 79, 80, 87, 88
physics, and economics 86–90
Pirenne, Henri 23, 24, 74
Planck, Max 149
Plato 18, 36, 40, 125, 133, 167, 175
and beauty 170, 171–2
and eudemonia 21, 46
and forms 43, 45, 133
and the good 36
Hippias Major 167, 169
Laws 17, 21, 115, 130
Phaedrus 9, 17
Republic 11, 17, 18, 21, 100, 115
Timaeus 46
Plotinus 170–2
pluralism, and Aristotle 34–5
Polanyi, Karl 12, 21–4, 74, 128, 174,
188, 189
The Great Transformation 21
Polanyi, Michael 146, 156
polis 6, 18, 24, 26, 34, 43–4, 88, 89,
99, 100, 104, 105, 113, 114, 122,
129, 131
political, and the economic 93–5
political experience 5, 35, 36, 73, 94,
129
political expertise 42
political theology 18, 27, 130, 190
politics, as aesthetic judgment 112–24
positivism 2, 3–5, 10, 13, 15, 18, 19,
31, 48, 54, 71, 86–7, 100, 174,
191
and Durkheim 48, 52, 92, 124
and James 52
and Kant 119–20
vs interpretivism 3
practical reason 38–9
pragmatism 4–5, 60, 61–5
and activities 61–5
and Dewey 66–7
and Habermas 67
and James 53, 54, 60, 61–5, 67,
68, 69
and truth 60
praxis 5, 6, 11, 17, 36, 41, 73,
99–100, 132, 137, 147
Preuss, Hugo 187
probable reasoning 58
profane 20
and sacred 48–9, 70
Protestant Ethic 45
Proust, Marcel 4
public spheres 5, 6, 11, 18, 67, 98
pure law 129
Pythagoras 170

qualities, primary and secondary 56,
61, 92
quantum mechanics/physics 141–2,
148–50, 153, 180
Quesnay, François 79, 80, 89
Tableau économique 88

radical empiricism 10, 62
and Hume 174–5, 192–3
and James 25, 50, 51–61, 62, 64,
67, 69
radical experience 31–2
rationalism 114–15, 124, 174
rationality
formal 12, 20–1
substantive 20–1
Rawls, J. 5, 11
reason/reasoning
deliberative 33, 39
demonstrative 39, 58
distinction between theoretical and
practical 38–40
probable 58
reflective judgment 101, 113–14,
121–2

209